United Kingdom

United States of
America

Uruguay

Venezuela

Vietnam

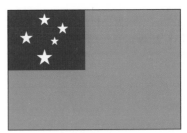

Western Samoa

Zimbabwe

Junior Worldmark Encyclopedia of the Nations

Junior Worldmark Encyclopedia of the Nations

Junior Worldmark Encyclopedia of the

Nations

Third Edition

GALE GROUP

THOMSON LEARNING

Detroit • New York • San Diego • San Francisco
Boston • New Haven, Conn. • Waterville, Maine
London • Munich

VOLUME

Uganda to Zimbabwe
CUMULATIVE INDEX

JUNIOR WORLDMARK ENCYCLOPEDIA OF THE NATIONS, THIRD EDITION

Timothy L. Gall and Susan Bevan Gall, *Editors*
Karen Hanson, Jennifer Jackson, Sarah Kunz, and Barbara Walker Dickinson, *Associate Editors*
Bram Lambrecht and Brian Rajewski, *Graphics and Layout*
Jennifer Wallace, *Editorial Assistant*
Janet Fenn and Matthew Markovich, *Proofreaders*
Maryland Cartographics, Inc., *Cartographers*

U•X•L Staff

Julie Carnagie, *U•X•L Senior Editor*
Carol DeKane Nagel, *U•X•L Managing Editor*
Thomas L. Romig, *U•X•L Publisher*
Evi Seoud, *Assistant Manager, Composition Purchasing and Electronic Prepress*
Rita Wimberley, *Senior Buyer*
Cynthia Baldwin, *Product Design Manager*
Barbara J. Yarrow, *Graphic Services Supervisor*
Mary Krzewinski, *Cover Designer*
Margaret Chamberlain, *Permissions Specialist (Pictures)*

Library of Congress Cataloging-in-Publication Data

Junior worldmark encyclopedia of the nations / [Timothy L. Gall and Susan Bevan Gall].
    p. cm.
    Includes bibliographical references.
    Contents: v. 1. Afghanistan to Brunei Darussalam -- v. 2. Bulgaria to Czech Republic
v. 3. Denmark to Guyana -- v. 4. Haiti to Kyrgyzstan -- v. 5. Laos to Myanmar -- v. 6.
Namibia to Portugal -- v. 7. Qatar to South Africa -- v. 8. Spain to Tuvalu -- v. 9. Uganda
to Zimbabwe.
    ISBN 0-7876-5366-7 (set : hardcover) -- ISBN 0-7876-5367-5 (v. 1) -- ISBN
0-7876-5368-3 (v. 2) -- ISBN 0-7876-5369-1 (v. 3) -- ISBN 0-7876-5370-5 (v. 4) --
ISBN 0-7876-5371-3 (v. 5) -- ISBN 0-7876-5372-1 (v. 6) -- ISBN 0-7876-5373-X (v. 7)
-- ISBN 0-7876-5374-8 (v. 8) -- ISBN 0-7876-5375-6 (v. 9)
    1. Geography--Encyclopedias, Juvenile. 2. History--Encyclopedias, Juvenile. 3.
Economics--Encyclopedias, Juvenile. 4. Political science--Encyclopedias, Juvenile. 5.
United Nations--Encyclopedias, Juvenile. [1. Geography--Encyclopedias.] I. Gall,
Timothy L. II. Gall, Susan B.

G63 .J86 2001
903--dc21
                           2001044239

CONTENTS

Guide to Country Articles

Every country profile in this encyclopedia includes the same 35 headings. Also included in every profile is a map (showing the country and its location in the world), the country's flag and seal, and a table of data on the country. The country articles are organized alphabetically in nine volumes. A glossary of terms is included in each of the nine volumes. This glossary defines many of the specialized terms used throughout the encyclopedia. A keyword index to all nine volumes appears at the end of Volume 9.

Flag color symbols

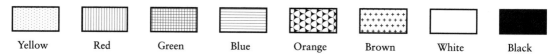

| Yellow | Red | Green | Blue | Orange | Brown | White | Black |

Alphabetical listing of sections

Agriculture	21	Income	18
Armed Forces	16	Industry	19
Bibliography	35	Judicial System	15
Climate	3	Labor	20
Domesticated Animals	22	Languages	9
Economy	17	Location and Size	1
Education	31	Media	32
Energy and Power	27	Migration	7
Environment	5	Mining	25
Ethnic Groups	8	Plants and Animals	4
Famous People	34	Political Parties	14
Fishing	23	Population	6
Foreign Trade	26	Religions	10
Forestry	24	Social Development	28
Government	13	Topography	2
Health	29	Tourism/Recreation	33
History	12	Transportation	11
Housing	30		

Sections listed numerically

1	Location and Size	19	Industry
2	Topography	20	Labor
3	Climate	21	Agriculture
4	Plants and Animals	22	Domesticated Animals
5	Environment	23	Fishing
6	Population	24	Forestry
7	Migration	25	Mining
8	Ethnic Groups	26	Foreign Trade
9	Languages	27	Energy and Power
10	Religions	28	Social Development
11	Transportation	29	Health
12	History	30	Housing
13	Government	31	Education
14	Political Parties	32	Media
15	Judicial System	33	Tourism/Recreation
16	Armed Forces	34	Famous People
17	Economy	35	Bibliography
18	Income		

Abbreviations and acronyms to know

GMT= Greenwich mean time. The prime, or Greenwich, meridian passes through Greenwich, England (near London), and marks the center of the initial time zone for the world. The standard time of all 24 time zones relate to Greenwich mean time. Every profile contains a map showing the country and its location in the world.

These abbreviations are used in references to famous people:
b.=born
d.=died
fl.=flourished (lived and worked)
r.=reigned (for kings, queens, and similar monarchs)

A dollar sign ($) stands for US$ unless otherwise indicated.

UGANDA

Republic of Uganda

CAPITAL: Kampala.

FLAG: The national flag consists of six equal horizontal stripes of black, yellow, red, black, yellow, and red (from top to bottom); at the center, within a white circle, is a crested crane, the national bird of Uganda.

ANTHEM: Begins "O Uganda! May God uphold thee."

MONETARY UNIT: The new Uganda shilling (NUSh) was introduced in May 1987 with a value equal to 100 old Uganda shillings. NUSh1 = $0.00065 (or $1 = NUSh1,525.80). There are coins of 1, 2, and 5 shillings, and notes of 10, 20, 50, 100, 200, 500, and 1,000 shillings.

WEIGHTS AND MEASURES: The metric system is now in use.

HOLIDAYS: New Year's Day, 1 January; Labor Day, 1 May; Martyrs' Day, 3 June; Independence Day, 9 October; Christmas Day, 25 December; Boxing Day, 26 December. Movable holidays include Good Friday, Easter Monday, 'Id al-Fitr, and 'Id al-'Adha'.

TIME: 3 PM = noon GMT.

1 LOCATION AND SIZE

A landlocked country in east-central Africa, situated north and northwest of Lake Victoria, Uganda has a total area of 236,040 square kilometers (91,136 square miles), slightly smaller than the state of Oregon. It has a total boundary length of 2,698 kilometers (1,676 miles).

2 TOPOGRAPHY

The greater part of Uganda consists of a plateau. Margherita Peak on the western border reaches a height of 5,109 meters (16,762 feet), while on the eastern frontier Mount Elgon rises to 4,321 meters (14,178 feet). By contrast, a valley runs through the western half of the country, known as the Western Rift Valley. Its elevation is only 621 meters (2,038 feet)

around Lake Albert. The Victoria Nile has its source in Lake Victoria.

3 CLIMATE

Although Uganda is on the equator, its climate is warm rather than hot, and temperatures vary little throughout the year. Most of the territory receives an annual rainfall of at least 100 centimeters (40 inches). On Lake Albert, the mean annual maximum is 29°C (84°F) and the mean annual minimum 22°C (72°F). At Kabale in the southwest, 1,250 meters (4,100 feet) higher, the mean annual maximum is 23°C (73°F), and the mean annual minimum 10°C (50°F).

4 PLANTS AND ANIMALS

Plant life in Uganda varies from region to region, and includes cultivated plots of plantain, long grass, forest, short grass,

Geographic Profile

Geographic Features

Size ranking: 77 of 192
Highest elevation: 5,109 meters (16,762 feet) at
  Margherita Peak (Mount Stanley)
Lowest elevation: 621 meters (2,038 feet) at Lake
  Albert

Land Use†

Arable land:	25%
Permanent crops:	9%
Permanent pastures:	9%
Forests:	28%
Other:	29%

Weather

Average annual precipitation: 125 centimeters (49.2
  inches). Annual rainfall ranges from just 69
  centimeters (27.2 inches) in the northeast to nearly
  200 centimeters (78.7 inches) near Lake Victoria.
Average temperature range in January (Kampala): 18–
  28°C (64–82°F)
Average temperature range in July (Kampala): 17–
  25°C (63–77°F)

†*Arable land:* Land used for temporary crops, like
meadows for mowing or pasture, gardens, and greenhouses. *Permanent crops:* Land cultivated with crops
that occupy its use for long periods, such as cocoa,
coffee, rubber, fruit and nut orchards, and vineyards.
Permanent pastures: Land used permanently for forage crops. *Forests:* Land containing stands of trees.
Other: Any land not specified, including built-on
areas, roads, and barren land.

and open woodland. At least 15 mammal species are found only in Uganda. Elephant, hippopotamus, buffalo, and many kinds of monkeys are plentiful. There are many species of birds but relatively few varieties of fish. Crocodiles are found in many areas.

5 ENVIRONMENT

Erosion is a major environmental problem due to overgrazing, primitive agricultural methods, and expansion of the desert. Attempts to control the reproduction of tsetse flies (flies that spread the disease called sleeping sickness) have resulted in the use of hazardous chemicals. The nation's water supply is threatened by toxic industrial pollutants; mercury from mining activity also is found in the water supply. Roughly 40% of the nation's city dwellers and 70% of the people living in rural areas do not have pure water. Uganda's three national parks total more than 6,300 square kilometers (2,400 square miles). In 1994, 8.1% of the land area was protected. That same year, 16 of the nation's mammal species and 12 of the nation's bird species were endangered, as well as 11 species of plants.

6 POPULATION

The most recent estimates in Uganda, in 2000, registered a population of nearly 23.4 million. The US Census Bureau projected a population of 27.2 million for 2005. Estimated population density in 1998 was 108 persons per square kilometer (280 per square mile) of land. In 2000, greater Kampala, the capital and largest city, had a population of 1.2 million.

7 MIGRATION

As of mid-1999, Uganda was sheltering 192,800 refugees. There were 175,000 from the Sudan, 8,000 from the Democratic Republic of the Congo (the former Zaire), 1,800 from Somalia, and 7,500 from Rwanda.

8 ETHNIC GROUPS

The Baganda, who populate the northern shore of Lake Victoria, constitute the largest single ethnic group in Uganda (about 17% of the total population). Other important tribal groups include the Iteso, Banyoro, Banyankole, Batoro, and Basoga. Perhaps 6% of the population (not counting refugees) is of Rwandan descent, either Tutsi or Hutu. In 1989 the Asian population was estimated at about 10,000.

9 LANGUAGES

English is the official language. Bantu and Nilotic languages, particularly Luganda (the language of the Baganda), are widespread, and Central Sudanic clusters exist in the northwest. Kiswahili and Arabic also are widely spoken.

10 RELIGIONS

About 66% of the population is Christian: 33% Roman Catholic, and 33% Protestant (mostly Anglican). About 16% is Muslim. The rest practice traditional African religions.

11 TRANSPORTATION

A landlocked country, Uganda depends on links with Tanzania and Kenya for access to the sea. There is a total of 1,241 kilometers (771 miles) of railroad track in Uganda. In 1999 there were 27,000 kilometers (16,778 miles) of roads. In 1995 there were 17,800 passenger cars and 25,300 commercial vehicles in Uganda. Three Ugandan ferries operate on Lake Victoria. Uganda's international airport is at Entebbe. In 1997, scheduled airline flights carried 100,000 passengers.

12 HISTORY

Cushitic speakers from eastern Africa probably penetrated the area that is now

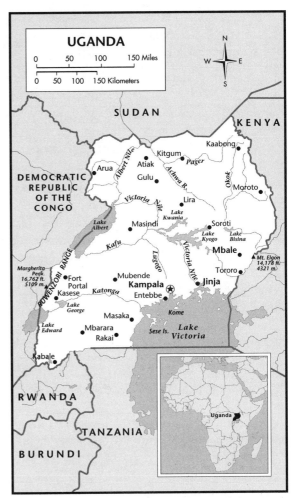

LOCATION: 4°7′N to 1°30′s; 29°33′ to 35°20′E.
BOUNDARY LENGTHS: Sudan, 435 kilometers (271 miles); Kenya, 933 kilometers (578 miles); Tanzania, 396 kilometers (247 miles); Rwanda, 169 kilometers (105 miles); Democratic Republic of the Congo (DROC), 765 kilometers (475 miles).

Uganda around 1000 BC. In the first millennium (thousand years) AD, they were followed by Bantu-speaking peoples of central and southern Africa and later by people of central and western Africa. Europeans began to arrive in the nineteenth century, beginning with the British explorers John Hanning Speke and J. A. Grant in 1862. Members of the Church Missionary Society of Great Britain, came to Buganda (present-day southeast Uganda) in 1877.

The missionaries were welcomed by the kabaka (ruler) of Buganda, Mutesa I. He hoped to gain their support in his effort to fight off the Egyptian attempts to expand. Later Mutesa became less cooperative, and his son, Mwanga, who succeeded to the throne in 1884, was even more hostile, fearing the influence of both missionaries and Arab traders. When Mwanga began to persecute the ethnic Bagandan adherents of both Christianity and Islam, the two groups joined forces to drive him from the country in 1888. He was restored to power early in 1890.

In 1894, the kingdom of Buganda became a British protectorate, which was extended in 1896 to cover most of what is now Uganda. In 1897, Mwanga led a revolt against the British, but he was quickly defeated and dethroned. Under the Uganda Agreement of 1900, Buganda was ruled indirectly by the British. Buganda's rejection of British policies following World War II marked the beginning of a conflict over independence for the territory. Kabaka Mutesa II was ousted in 1953 when he refused to force his chiefs to cooperate with the British, but was restored to power in 1955 under a compromise agreement.

At a 1961 constitutional conference in London, independence for a new state of Uganda, composed of Buganda and the kingdoms of Ankole, Bunyoro, and Toro,

was agreed to, effective 9 October 1962. In 1963, Sir Edward Mutesa (Kabaka Mutesa II of Buganda) became Uganda's first president. In February 1966, the 1962 constitution was suspended and the prime minister, Milton Obote, assumed all powers of government. Parliament formally repealed the 1962 constitution on 15 April 1966, and adopted a new one which created the post of president and commander-in-chief; Obote was elected to fill this position on the same day.

Amin Seizes Power

On 25 January 1971, while Obote was out of the country, Major General Idi Amin led a successful military coup, and the Second Republic of Uganda was proclaimed on 17 March 1971, with Amin as president. In September 1972, Ugandans who had followed Obote into exile in Tanzania staged an unsuccessful invasion. They were immediately overpowered, but tensions between Uganda and Tanzania remained high.

Under Amin, Uganda suffered a reign of terror that had claimed 50,000 to 300,000 lives by 1977. The expulsion of Asian noncitizens from Uganda in August 1972 took a heavy toll on the economy, especially on trade. Agricultural and industrial production also fell, and educational and health facilities suffered from the loss of skilled personnel. An Israeli commando raid on Entebbe Airport on 3–4 July 1976 freed 91 Israeli passengers and 12 crew members held captive by pro-Palestinian radicals in a hijacked aircraft. This raid was a severe blow to Amin's prestige. By January 1979, Tanzanian forces, supported by anti-Amin rebels, entered Ugandan territory. Kampala was taken on 11 April 1979, and all of Uganda was cleared of Amin's forces by the end of May. Amin fled to Libya and later to Sa'udi Arabia. A provisional (temporary) government was formed, and parliamentary elections were held on 10 December 1980. The elections were administered by Paulo Muwanga and other supporters of Obote, who returned from exile in Tanzania. The election results gave Obote's Ugandan People's Congress (UPC) a clear majority, and he was sworn in as president on 15 December 1980.

After Amin

Obote's second term in office was marked by continued fighting between the army and guerrilla factions, especially the National Resistance Army (NRA). On 27 July 1985, Obote was overthrown in a military coup and Lieutenant General Tito Okello, commander of the armed forces, was installed as president.

The NRA continued fighting, and on 26 January 1986 it occupied Kampala; by April it formed the National Resistance Movement (NRM) government, with Yoweri Museveni as president, and took control of most of the country. Armed rebels remained active in northern and northeastern Uganda, but by 1990 most were defeated. By 1992, work on a draft constitution had progressed. Parliament declared a ban on party politics, but opposition parties became more active. General elections were held at the end of 1994. The government has introduced constitutional changes allowing the Baganda to restore their monarchy (purely for ceremonial purposes). Ronald Mutebi, son of the former king, was installed as kabaka (ruler) on 31 July 1993.

During the 1990s, Uganda was plagued by a cult-like Christian rebel group known as the Lord's Resistance Army (LRA). The LRA is supported by the Islamist government of the Sudan. The group maintains bases in southern Sudan, from which it crosses the border into northern Uganda. The LRA makes sudden hit-and-run raids into northern Ugandan villages, abducting teenagers and torturing and killing villagers. The LRA also had planted landmines in random places. Half the Ugandan army had been stationed in the north to protect the people from LRA bandits.

In October 1995, a new constitution was written, replacing the National Resistance Council with a permanent parliament. However, political party activity was banned for five years. The first popular elections were held in May 1996, with Yoweri Museveni winning 74% of the vote.

13 GOVERNMENT

Under the 1995 constitution, a 279-member parliament replaced the 270-person National Resistance Council that had been established in 1986. The new parliament ensured representation for special interest groups (including 10 seats for the army, 8 for women, and 4 for youth). Parliamentary elections were first held on 27 June 1996, with the next elections scheduled for 2001. An appointed cabinet advises the president.

Photo credit: EPD/Office of the President.

Name:	Yoweri Kaguta Museveni
Position:	President of a republic
Took office:	29 January 1986
Birthplace:	Ntungamo, southwestern Uganda
Birth date:	1944
Education:	University College, Dar Es Salaam, Tanzania, bachelor of arts in economics and political science, 1970
Spouse:	Janet Kataaha
Children:	One son, three daughters
Of interest:	Museveni told the *Los Angeles Times* that when he leaves office, he would like to be remembered as "a freedom fighter, who helped to give the people of Uganda a key to their future, to give them democracy, get rid of dictatorship."

14 POLITICAL PARTIES

After the overthrow of Idi Amin, remaining parties included the Ugandan People's Congress (UPC); the Democratic Party (DP); the Uganda Patriotic Movement; and the Conservative Party. These parties, as well as Yoweri Museveni's National Resistance Movement and the Uganda Freedom Movement, were represented in the cabinet appointed in 1986. By 1991, party activity, although banned, began to increase. Despite the new constitution in 1995, President Museveni declared that political parties would not be allowed to participate in the parliamentary and presidential elections held in May and June 1996, respectively. However, 156 of the 279 members elected in 1996 were considered Museveni supporters.

15 JUDICIAL SYSTEM

At the lowest level are three classes of courts presided over by magistrates. Above these is the chief magistrate's court, which hears appeals from magistrates. The High Court hears appeals and has full criminal and civil jurisdiction. The three-member Court of Appeal hears appeals from the High Court.

16 ARMED FORCES

The Ugandan People's Defense Force was estimated at 30,000–40,000 in 2000 and defense expenditures were estimated at $95 million for 1998/99.

17 ECONOMY

Uganda's economy is based on agriculture, which engages about 80% of the population and represents 90% of the export economy. An economic reform process begun in 1986 has resulted in progress; the economic growth rate averaged 6% during 1986–94 and 8% during 1995–97. Even though the size of its economy has doubled during the past ten years, Uganda

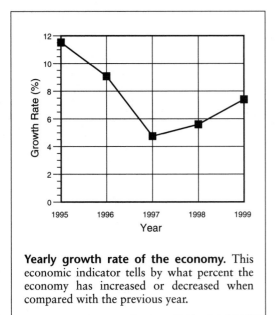

Yearly growth rate of the economy. This economic indicator tells by what percent the economy has increased or decreased when compared with the previous year.

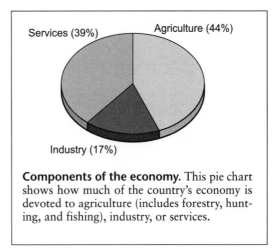

Components of the economy. This pie chart shows how much of the country's economy is devoted to agriculture (includes forestry, hunting, and fishing), industry, or services.

is still one of the poorest countries in the world and is highly dependent on foreign aid.

18 INCOME

In 1998 Uganda's gross domestic product (GDP) was $22.7 billion, or about $1,000 per person. In 1999, the average inflation rate was 2.6%, resulting in an annual growth rate in GDP of about 7.5%.

19 INDUSTRY

By 1997, industrial production was triple that of 1989. Industries include cotton, coffee, tea, sugar, tobacco, edible oils, dairy products, grain milling, brewing, vehicle assembly, textiles, and steel. Batteries, canned foods, medicines, and salt are other products being produced by Uganda's industrial sector.

20 LABOR

The vast majority of economically active Ugandans work outside the monetary economy. Agriculture engaged more than 80% of the total population of 16.7 million in 1991, manufacturing accounting for 2%. It has since dropped to about 80%. Working conditions, hours of work, and paid holidays are negotiated with the unions.

21 AGRICULTURE

About 44% of Uganda's GDP comes from agriculture, 80% of the population employed, and about 90% of export earnings. In 1998, food production estimates included plantains, 9.3 million tons; cassava, 2.3 million tons; sweet potatoes, 1.9 million tons; bananas, 585,000 tons; millet, 580,000 tons; corn, 750,000 tons; sorghum, 350,000 tons; beans, 220,000 tons; and potatoes, 3.6 million tons. Estimated production of major cash crops in 1998 included coffee, 180,000 tons; cotton (lint), 14,000 tons; tea, 26,000 tons; and raw sugar, 99,000 tons.

22 DOMESTICATED ANIMALS

Uganda had an estimated 5.4 million head of cattle, 3.6 million goats, 2 million sheep, 950,000 hogs, and about 23 million chickens in 1998. An estimated 591,000 cattle, 1.3 million goats, and 686,000 sheep were slaughtered in 1998; meat production was an estimated 220,000 tons.

23 FISHING

Lake Victoria and Lake Kyogo are the major commercial fishing areas. In 1997, the total catch was estimated at 218,236 tons.

24 FORESTRY

Forests cover approximately 28% of the total land area. In the same year, production of roundwood was estimated at 16.8 million cubic meters, of which about 88% was used for fuel.

25 MINING

Small quantities of tin, tungsten, and phosphates are mined. Limestone is quarried for use in cement, and salt is obtained by evaporation of lakes and brine wells.

26 FOREIGN TRADE

In recent years, coffee has been by far the most important export (83% of total exports in 1996) and the principal earner of income from abroad. The main exports include coffee, cotton, and tobacco. In 1998, Uganda's leading export partner was Spain, followed by France and Ger-

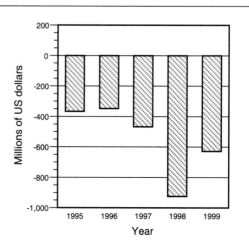

Yearly balance of trade measured in millions of US dollars. The balance of trade is the difference between what a country sells to other countries (its exports) and what it buys (its imports). If a country imports more than it exports, it has a negative balance of trade (a trade deficit). If exports exceed imports there is a positive balance of trade (a trade surplus).

many. Imports came primarily from Kenya, the United Kingdom, and India.

27 ENERGY AND POWER

In the early 1990s, hydroelectric potential was estimated at nearly 200,000 kilowatts. A total of 787 million kilowatts (almost all hydroelectric) was generated. However, fuel wood and charcoal supply 95% of required energy.

28 SOCIAL DEVELOPMENT

Responsibility for social welfare rests primarily with the Ministry of Culture and Community Development, but voluntary agencies play a supplementary role. In 1991, it was estimated that 1.2 million

---

Selected Social Indicators

The statistics below are estimates for the period 1996 to 2000. For comparison purposes, data for the United States and averages for low-income countries and high-income countries are also given.

Indicator	Uganda	Low-income countries	High-income countries	United States
Per capita gross national product (GNP)†	**$1,160**	$1,870	$25,690	$31,910
Population growth rate	**2.6%**	2.1%	0.7%	1.1%
People per square kilometer of land	**108**	73	29	30
Life expectancy in years	**42**	59	78	77
Number of physicians per 1,000 people	**<1**	1.0	2.5	2.5
Number of pupils per teacher (primary school)	**32**	41	17	14
Illiteracy rate (15 years and older)	**32%**	34%	<5%	3%
Television sets per 1,000 people	**28**	85	693	844
Energy consumed per capita (kg of oil equivalent)	**22**	550	5,366	7,937

† The GNP is the total dollar value of all goods and services produced by a country in a year. The per capita GNP is calculated by dividing a country's GNP by its population and adjusting for relative purchasing power. About 15% of the world's 6.1 billion people live in high-income countries, while 40% live in low-income countries.

n.a. = data not available   > = greater than   < = less than

Sources: World Bank. *World Development Indicators*. Washington, D.C.: The World Bank, 2001; Central Intelligence Agency. *The World Factbook*. Washington, D.C.: Government Printing Office, 2000.

Ugandan children were orphans, as a result of the AIDS epidemic and the past civil war.

29 HEALTH

AIDS (acquired immune deficiency syndrome) became a severe problem in the 1980s. As of 1995, 1.5 million Ugandans were infected with HIV, the virus that causes AIDS. Containment of other serious diseases, such as cholera, dysentery, tuberculosis, and malaria, is made difficult by poor sanitation and unclean water. Life expectancy in 2000 was only 42 years.

30 HOUSING

Most of the inhabitants live in thatched huts with mud and wattle (interwoven branches and reeds) walls. Even in rural areas, however, corrugated iron is used extensively as a roofing material.

31 EDUCATION

In 1995, there were 10,000 primary schools, with 2.9 million pupils and 82,745 teachers. At the secondary level there were 256,258 pupils and 14,447 teachers that year. Makerere College became Makerere University in 1970. It offers degrees in the arts, sciences, and agriculture. In 1997 there were 34,773 pupils and 2,606 teachers in all higher level institutions. In 2000, the adult illiteracy rate was 32%.

tion figures), are *Bukedde* (6,000), and *Ngabo* (15,000). Weekly newspapers in Kampala include the *Etop*, *Orumuri*, and *Uganda Confidential*.

33 TOURISM AND RECREATION

Tourism facilities are adequate in Kampala but limited in other areas. In 1996, 205,000 tourists visited Uganda, and tourism receipts totaled $117 million. Wildlife is the major tourist attraction.

34 FAMOUS UGANDANS

Sir Apollo Kagwa (1890–1926), chief minister to Kabaka Mwanga, was one of the dominant figures in Uganda's history. Mukama Kabarega of Bunyoro (r.1896–99) led his people against British and Buganda forces until captured and exiled in 1899. Major General Idi Amin Dada (b.1925) overthrew Milton Obote in 1971 and led a military government until ousted in 1979. Yoweri Museveni (b.1944), leader of the National Resistance Movement, became president in 1986 and was reelected in 1996.

35 BIBLIOGRAPHY

Barlas, Robert. *Uganda*. New York: Marshall Cavendish, 2000.

Blauer, Ettagale. *Uganda*. New York: Children's Press, 1997.

Byrnes, Rita M., ed. *Uganda: A Country Study*. 2d ed. Washington, D.C.: Library of Congress, 1992.

Caputo, Robert. "Uganda—Land Beyond Sorrow." *National Geographic,* April 1988, 468–492.

Creed, Alexander. *Uganda*. Philadelphia: Chelsea House, 1999.

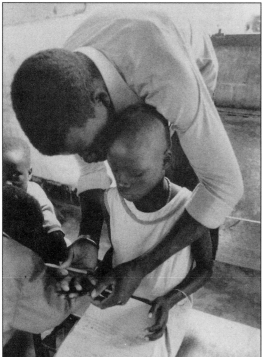

Photo credit: AP/Wide World Photos.

A young pupil under instruction in a third grade class at a Moroto primary school. Education is available, but many families do not make use of the system as their children are needed for agricultural work.

32 MEDIA

Radio Uganda broadcasts daily in 22 languages, including English, French, and Swahili; television programs are in English, Swahili, and Luganda. In 1997 there were 123 radios and 28 television sets per 1,000 population, and 50,000 telephones. The government-operated *New Vision* had a 1999 circulation of 37,000. Other dailies (with 1995 circula-

UKRAINE

Ukraina

CAPITAL: Kiev (Kyyiv).

FLAG: Equal horizontal bands of azure blue (top) and yellow.

ANTHEM: *The National Anthem of Ukraine.*

MONETARY UNIT: The official currency, introduced in early 1993, is the hryvnia (HRN), which consists of 100 shahy. $1 = HRN5.59.

WEIGHTS AND MEASURES: The metric system is used.

HOLIDAYS: New Year's Day, 1–2 January; Christmas, 7 January; Women's Day, 8 March; Spring and Labor Day, 1–2 May; Victory Day, 9 May; Ukrainian Independence Day, 24 August.

TIME: 2 PM = noon GMT.

1 LOCATION AND SIZE

Ukraine, the second-largest country in Europe, is located in eastern Europe, bordering the Black Sea, between Poland and Russia. Comparatively, Ukraine is slightly smaller than the state of Texas with a total area of 603,700 square kilometers (233,090 square miles). Its boundary length totals 4,558 kilometers (2,834 miles). Ukraine's capital city, Kiev, is located in the north central part of the country.

2 TOPOGRAPHY

The topography of Ukraine consists mainly of fertile plains (steppes) and plateaus. Mountains (the Carpathians) are found only in the west and in the Crimean Peninsula in the extreme south. The most important river in Ukraine is the Dnipro (Dnieper), the third longest river in Europe.

3 CLIMATE

Precipitation is highest in the west and north, least in the east and southeast. Winters vary from cool along the Black Sea to cold farther inland. Summers are warm across the greater part of the country, but hot in the south. The mean temperature is 10°C (66°F) in July and –6°C (21°F) in January. Northern and western Ukraine average 69 centimeters (27 inches) of rainfall a year.

4 PLANTS AND ANIMALS

Ukraine is famed for its rich agricultural soil. European bison, fox, and rabbits can be found living on the vast steppes of the country.

5 ENVIRONMENT

Three and one-half million hectares (8.6 million acres) of agricultural land and 1.5 million hectares (3.7 million acres) of

Geographic Profile

Geographic Features

Size ranking: 43 of 192
Highest elevation: 2,061 meters (6,762 feet) at Mount
  Hoverla
Lowest elevation: Sea level at the Black Sea

Land Use†

Arable land:	58%
Permanent crops:	2%
Permanent pastures:	13%
Forests:	18%
Other:	9%

Weather††

Average annual precipitation: 69 centimeters (27
  inches)
Average temperature in January: –6°C (21°F)
Average temperature in July: 10°C (66°F)

†*Arable land:* Land used for temporary crops, like
meadows for mowing or pasture, gardens, and greenhouses. *Permanent crops:* Land cultivated with crops
that occupy its use for long periods, such as cocoa,
coffee, rubber, fruit and nut orchards, and vineyards.
Permanent pastures: Land used permanently for forage crops. *Forests:* Land containing stands of trees.
Other: Any land not specified, including built-on
areas, roads, and barren land.

††The measurements for precipitation and average
temperature were taken at weather stations closest to
the country's largest city. Precipitation and average
temperature can vary significantly within a country,
due to factors such as latitude, altitude, coastal proximity, and wind patterns.

forest were contaminated by radiation
from the Chernobyl nuclear accident in
1986. Pollution from other sources also
poses a threat to the environment. The
water supply in some areas of the country
contains toxic industrial chemicals up to
10 times the concentration considered to
be within safety limits.

Air pollution also is a significant environmental problem. The nation's industries produced 611.3 million metric tons
of carbon dioxide in 1992, the world's
seventh highest.

6 POPULATION

The population of Ukraine was estimated
at 49.5 million in 2000, and a projected
population of 48.3 million for 2005. The
estimated population density in 2000 was
86 persons per square kilometer (223 per
square mile). Kiev, the capital, had a population estimated at 2.9 million in 2000.

According to United Nations estimates,
in 1998, Ukraine's population had the
world's lowest ratio of males to females:
there were only 87 men for every 100
women.

7 MIGRATION

Since the breakup of the Soviet Union in
1991, tens of thousands of ethnic Ukrainians have returned to the Ukraine. Between
1989 and 1995, 25,000 returned from
Azerbaijan and 39,000 returned from Kyrgyzstan. During 1991–95, 15,000
returned from Belarus, 82,000 from
Kazakstan, and 30,000 from Tajikistan.
By early 1996, 250,000 Tatars had
returned from Central Asia. During the
reign of Josef Stalin, 500,000 Tatars were
forced to move from their homes in the
Crimean peninsula.

Ukraine still has about 150,000 people
who cannot return to their homes due to
the 1986 Chernobyl nuclear accident.

There are an additional four million
ethnic Ukrainians living in the United
States, Canada, Australia, Western and
Central Europe, and South America.

LOCATION: 49°0'N; 32°0'E. **BOUNDARY LENGTHS:** Total boundary lengths, 4,558 kilometers (2,834 miles); Belarus, 891 kilometers (554 miles); Hungary, 103 kilometers (64 miles); Moldova, 939 kilometers (584 miles); Poland, 428 kilometers (266 miles); Romania (southeast), 169 kilometers (105 miles); Romania (west), 362 kilometers (225 miles); Russia 1,576 kilometers (980 miles); Slovakia, 90 kilometers (56 miles).

8 ETHNIC GROUPS

The population was 73% Ukrainian according to the latest estimates. Russians totaled 22%, mainly in eastern Ukraine. The population of the Crimean Peninsula is about 70% Russian. Crimean Tatars formed about 10% of the population of the Crimean Peninsula in 1992.

9 LANGUAGES

Like Russian and Belarusan, Ukrainian is an eastern Slavic language. Ukrainian began to emerge as a separate language from Russian in the late twelfth century.

10 RELIGIONS

The population is 85% Orthodox, based on 1998 estimates, but church life has been marked by disputes between the Ukrainian Orthodox Church and the Autocephalous (independent) Ukrainian Orthodox Church. In 1992, the two were united as the Kievan Patriarchy. Byzantine-rite Catholics account for some 15% of the population, and in 1990 there were 375,000 Jews.

11 TRANSPORTATION

As of 1996, there were 23,350 kilometers (14,508 miles) of railway. Highways in 1996 totaled 172,565 kilometers (107,232 miles).

The main marine ports are Berdyans'k, Illichivs'k, Kerch, Mariupol', Odesa, and Sevastopol'. The merchant marine fleet includes 181 ships (1,000 gross registered tons or more) for a total capacity of 1.02 million gross registered tons. The Dnipro (Dnieper) River is the primary inland waterway. The largest airports are in Kiev, Kharkiv, Donetsk, Odesa, and Simferopol.

Photo credit: Susan D. Rock.

Ukrainian girls pose for a photo in a park in Yalta.

12 HISTORY

Ukrainians, Russians, and Belarussians are eastern Slavs who trace their origins to the medieval Russian kingdom founded in Kiev in the ninth century AD. Internal strife in the twelfth century and the Mongol invasion in the thirteenth led to the destruction of this kingdom as a major power.

Ukrainian Cossacks (frontier people) were able to establish an independent state in the sixteenth and seventeenth centuries, but war between Russia and Poland resulted in the partition of Ukraine. Most of Ukraine's territory was absorbed by the Russian Empire.

A Ukrainian national movement arose in the nineteenth century. The fall of the tsar in 1917 amid the chaos of the Russian revolution allowed Ukraine to assert its independence. In 1917, the National Ukrainian Assembly proclaimed the creation of the Ukrainian People's Republic. An independent Republic of Western Ukraine was declared on 1 November 1918 after the disintegration of the Austro-Hungarian Empire. On 22 January 1919, the two republics united and established an independent Ukrainian state, recognized by more than 40 other nations.

By 1920, however, eastern Ukraine fell to the Bolsheviks (communists) and became the Ukrainian Soviet Socialist Republic while Poland occupied most of western Ukraine. Small areas of the west went to Romania, Hungary, and Czechoslovakia. Early policy in the Soviet Union allowed for cultural autonomy and local administration by Ukrainian communists. But Josef Stalin changed this liberal policy in the 1930s and began the persecution of Ukrainian nationalists.

The 1939 Nazi-Soviet pact assigned Poland's Ukrainian territory to the Soviet sphere of influence. After Germany invaded the Soviet Union in 1941, a resistance movement led by nationalists fought both the Soviet and German armies. During World War II (1939–45), Ukraine lost six million people through death or deportation and a total of 18,000 villages were destroyed.

The Ukrainian resistance movement continued to fight in Soviet Ukraine, and it was not until the 1950s that they were completely defeated by the better-equipped Soviet Red (communist) Army.

On 24 August 1991, following the failed coup in Moscow, the parliament proclaimed the independence of Ukraine and declared that only the constitution and laws of Ukraine were valid on its territory. On 1 December 1991, 90.3% of Ukraine's citizens voted in favor of independence and elected Leonid Kravchuk as their first president.

Ukraine joined Russia, Belarus, and other nations of the former Soviet Union in creating the Commonwealth of Independent States (CIS) in December 1991. However, Ukrainian-Russian differences have arisen in several areas, including the command and control of nuclear weapons, the formation of a unified military command, and the character and pace of economic reform.

Since its independence, Ukraine has experienced unrest in some of its mostly Russian areas, notably the Crimean Peninsula (Crimea), which declared independence on 6 May 1992. Demands for secession in Crimea have continued to complicate Ukrainian-Russian relations.

Ukraine adopted a new constitution in June 1996, and the Supreme Council adopted a new civil code in June 1997.

13 GOVERNMENT

The constitution of 1996 provides an elected parliament and president. The Ukrainian parliament consists of a single chamber with 450 seats called the Rada (Supreme Council). The prime minister and cabinet are nominated by the president and confirmed by the parliament. In Ukraine's first post-independence presidential elections, held in 1994, the incumbent Leonid Kravchuk was defeated by his former prime minister, Leonid Kuchma. In the presidential election of 1999, Kuchma was reelected with 56% of the vote.

Ukraine is divided into 24 administrative regions (oblasts) plus the autonomous Republic of Crimea.

Photo credit: EPD/Office of the President.

Name: Leonid Danylovich Kuchma
Position: President of a republic
Took office: 19 July 1994
Birthplace: Chaikine, Ukraine
Birth date: 8 August 1938
Education: Dniepropetrivsk University, 1960
Children: One daughter, one grandson
Of interest: Kuchma once worked as manager at Baikonur, the Soviet space facility in Kazakstan.

14 POLITICAL PARTIES

There are some 30 political parties active in Ukraine. They fall roughly into four different categories: radical nationalist; democratic nationalist (including the influential Rukh Party, which gained 20 parliamentary seats in 1994); liberal-centrist; and communist-socialist. The most important party in the last group is the Communist Party of Ukraine, which won 116 seats in the 1998 elections.

Aside from the communists and Rukh, all other parties won 12 seats or less. Independents hold most of the seats in the Rada.

15 JUDICIAL SYSTEM

The court system has not significantly changed since the former Soviet regime. The three levels of courts are *rayon* (also known as regional or people's courts), provincial or regional (*oblast*) courts, and the Supreme Court. All three levels provide first hearings for cases, the choice of court depending on the severity of the crime. They also hear appeals. In 1997, there were 742 rayon courts, 27 regional courts, 26 military courts, and an interregional court.

16 ARMED FORCES

Ukraine was able to quickly organize an impressive national army, in part because it had always been an important contributor to the Soviet armed forces. The armed forces numbered 311,400 in 2000. The army of 154,900 is organized into three commands and more than 30 specialized brigades and regiments. The air force numbers 100,000 with 521 aircraft and the navy has 13,000 personnel. The defense budget for 1999 was estimated at $414 million.

17 ECONOMY

The rich agricultural land of Ukraine (commonly called the "breadbasket" of the former Soviet Union) provided 46% of Soviet agricultural output in the 1980s. Ukraine's economic base is currently dominated by industry (accounting for more

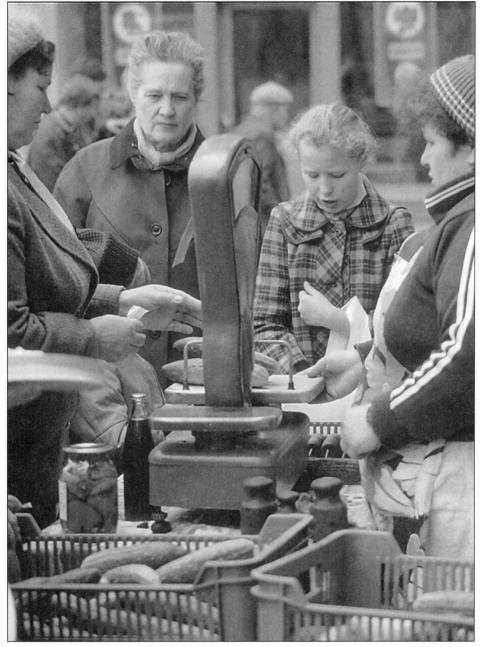

Photo credit: Susan D. Rock.

Streetside produce vendor in Yalta.

than 26% of GDP), but agriculture continues to play a major role in the economy (12%).

The 1991 dissolution of the Soviet Union led to shortages of supplies for business and industry, and of consumer goods as well. The gross domestic product (GDP) fell each year during 1990–95, and inflation reached 400% in 1994. In 1995, the government started reforms to slow inflation, and it also introduced a new currency and began privatizing industries.

In 1999, the GDP fell an estimated 1.7%. Inflation in that same year was 20%. In 1998, the International Monetary Fund announced a possible $2.2 billion loan to Ukraine, if the country carries out economic reforms, budget cuts, and faces its problems with corruption.

18 INCOME

In 1998, the gross domestic product (GDP) was $108.5 billion, or about $2,200 per person. In 1999, the average inflation rate was 20%, while the average annual decline of the GDP was just below zero.

19 INDUSTRY

Ukraine is a major producer of heavy machinery and industrial equipment for industries including mining, steelmaking, and chemicals. Ukraine also is an important supplier of products—including automobiles, clothing, foodstuffs, timber, and paper—to other former Soviet republics.

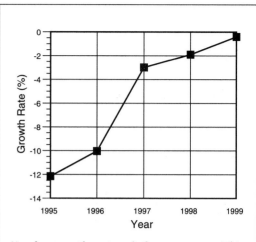

Yearly growth rate of the economy. This economic indicator tells by what percent the economy has increased or decreased when compared with the previous year.

20 LABOR

As of 1998, there were some 25.9 million in the labor force: 18.2% in manufacturing, mining, and utilities, 5.6% in construction, and 7.2% in transportation, storage, and communications. About 11.3% were officially reported as unemployed in that same year. In 1992, a minimum wage was established, but it is well below the cost of living.

21 AGRICULTURE

About 57% of the total land area is used for growing crops. Ukraine's steppe (plains) region in the south is possibly the most fertile region in the world. However, it is estimated that nearly 60,000 hectares (148,250 acres) of fertile land in the Chernobyl vicinity are now unavailable for cultivation. However, about half the crop land is depleted, a third is too acidic, and erosion is a problem for a third of the crop land.

Production amounts in 1998 included (in thousands of tons): sugar beets, 16,000; potatoes, 17,500; wheat, 14,937; dry peas, 1,085; fruit, 2,511; sunflower seeds, 2,260; cabbage, 980; grapes, 380; wine, 76; soybeans, 20; and tobacco, 3.

22 DOMESTICATED ANIMALS

About 13% of Ukraine's total land area is composed of permanent pastureland. As of 1998, there were 12.7 million head of cattle (including 7 million dairy cows), 9.5 million pigs, 2.3 million sheep and goats, and 116 million poultry. Horses, turkeys, ducks, and rabbits also are bred and raised. In 1998, meat production included: beef, 865,000 tons; pork, 690,000 tons; and poultry, 180,000 tons. Milk and egg production in 1998 amounted to 12.5 million tons and 491,000 tons, respectively. In 1997, exports of meat products totaled $261 million, and dairy and egg exports amounted to $59 million.

23 FISHING

In 1997, the total catch came to 403,336 tons, only one-third as large as the 1990 catch. Fishing occurs mainly on the Black Sea.

24 FORESTRY

About 18% of the total area was forest and woodland in 2000. Forestry production in 1997 included: roundwood, 10 million cubic meters; sawn timber, 275,000 cubic meters; wood pulp, 35,000 tons; and paper, 261,000 tons.

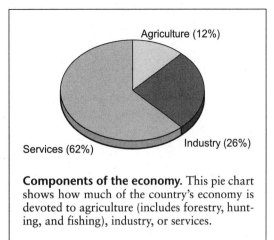

Agriculture (12%)

Services (62%)

Industry (26%)

Components of the economy. This pie chart shows how much of the country's economy is devoted to agriculture (includes forestry, hunting, and fishing), industry, or services.

25 MINING

Mineral production in Ukraine includes alumina, aluminum, antimony, coal, ferroalloys, graphite, iron ore, magnesium, manganese, mercury, nickel, potash, salt, soda ash, sulfur, talc, titanium, and uranium.

26 FOREIGN TRADE

Ukraine's main exports are iron metals and metal products, transport and mechanical equipment, food products, and fuel and petroleum products. Leading imports are transportation equipment, chemicals, machinery and parts, and energy. Relying heavily on trade, the Ukraine exports products to 140 countries in the world. In 1999, total exports amounted to $11.6 billion, while imports amounted to $11.8 billion. Russia, Germany, China, Turkey, and Italy were the leading export markets in 1998, while Russia, Germany, United States, and

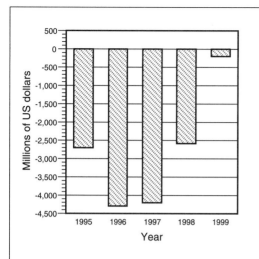

Yearly balance of trade measured in millions of US dollars. The balance of trade is the difference between what a country sells to other countries (its exports) and what it buys (its imports). If a country imports more than it exports, it has a negative balance of trade (a trade deficit). If exports exceed imports, there is a positive balance of trade (a trade surplus).

Poland were the leading sources of imports that year.

27 ENERGY AND POWER

Most electricity is generated by coal, natural gas, or oil, but nuclear power plants generated more than 40% of Ukraine's electricity in 1998. Power generation in 1998 was 157,915 million kilowatt hours. In 1992, the undamaged Reactor 1 at the Chernobyl nuclear power plant was restarted to provide much-needed electricity. Ukraine had 16 operating nuclear reactors at five facilities in 1996.

Oil production totaled about 74,000 barrels per day in 1998. Natural gas pro-

duction was 17.9 billion cubic meters (632 billion cubic feet) in 1998.

28 SOCIAL DEVELOPMENT

Ukraine's current welfare system was developed in 1992. It provides all employees with old age, disability, and survivor's pensions. There is a dual system of medical benefits. Cash benefits are paid to employed persons, while a universal medical care system exists for all residents. The law provides women with the same employment rights as men, but few women rise to high-level positions. Estimates suggest that women may account for as many as 90% of Ukraine's newly unemployed.

29 HEALTH

According to United Nations reports, approximately one million people were exposed to unsafe radiation levels following the Chernobyl nuclear accident by eating contaminated food. The government created special dispensaries and commissions to assess the amount of disease caused by the accident. As of 1994, 15,000 people were listed as affected.

In the mid-1990s there were five physicians per 1,000 persons, and a total of 700,000 hospital beds in Ukraine. Average life expectancy was 67 years in 2000. The leading causes of death were cardiovascular and respiratory diseases, cancer, traumas, and accidents.

30 HOUSING

At last estimate, average housing space per person totaled 18 square meters.

Selected Social Indicators

The statistics below are estimates for the period 1996 to 2000. For comparison purposes, data for the United States and averages for low-income countries and high-income countries are also given.

Indicator	Ukraine	Low-income countries	High-income countries	United States
Per capita gross national product (GNP)†	**$3,360**	$1,870	$25,690	$31,910
Population growth rate	**−0.4%**	2.1%	0.7%	1.1%
People per square kilometer of land	**86**	73	29	30
Life expectancy in years	**67**	59	78	77
Number of physicians per 1,000 people	**5**	1.0	2.5	2.5
Number of pupils per teacher (primary school)	**20**	41	17	14
Illiteracy rate (15 years and older)	**2%**	34%	<5%	3%
Television sets per 1,000 people	**413**	85	693	844
Energy consumed per capita (kg of oil equivalent)	**2,842**	550	5,366	7,937

† The GNP is the total dollar value of all goods and services produced by a country in a year. The per capita GNP is calculated by dividing a country's GNP by its population and adjusting for relative purchasing power. About 15% of the world's 6.1 billion people live in high-income countries, while 40% live in low-income countries.

n.a. = data not available   > = greater than   < = less than

Sources: World Bank. *World Development Indicators.* Washington, D.C.: The World Bank, 2001; Central Intelligence Agency. *The World Factbook.* Washington, D.C.: Government Printing Office, 2000.

31 EDUCATION

Ukraine has a 98% literacy rate, with nearly 15% of the adult population having completed higher education. There were 2.6 million students enrolled in the 21,720 general primary schools in 1994. The 156 institutions of higher learning had 1.5 million students in 1996.

32 MEDIA

Ukrainian TV and four radio networks broadcast from Kiev. In 1997 there were 872 radios and 413 television sets per 1,000 population. Ukraine had about 12.5 million telephone lines in 1998, as well as three Internet hosts per 1,000 population.

Among the leading daily newspapers (with 1999 circulation) are: *Holos Ukrainy* (768,000); *Pravda Ukrainy* (358,300); and *Demokratychna Ukraine* (311,000).

33 TOURISM AND RECREATION

Kiev, Ukraine's major cultural center, is known for its beautiful churches and golden-domed cathedrals, although much of its classic architecture was destroyed or obscured by communist planners in the 1930s. L'vin (formerly Lvov) offers architectural sights ranging from late-thirteenth-century Russian to sixteenth-century Gothic structures. Ukraine's tourism was affected by the aftereffects of the 1986 Chernobyl nuclear accident. In 1997

Photo credit: Susan D. Rock.

The Opera House in Odesa.

there were 7.3 million tourist arrivals, with tourism receipts at $3.7 billion.

34 FAMOUS UKRAINIANS

Leonid M. Kravchuk and Vitold P. Fokin were, respectively, the first president and prime minister of Ukraine. Leonid Brezhnev (1906–82) led the Soviet Union during 1966–82. Outstanding representatives of the culture and literature of Ukraine include poet Taras Shevchenko (1814–61) and Jewish writer Sholom Aleichem (Solomon Rabinowitz, 1859–1916).

35 BIBLIOGRAPHY

Bassis, Volodymyr. *Ukraine.* New York: Marshall Cavendish, 1997.

Clay, Rebecca. *Ukraine: New Independence.* New York: Benchmark Books, 1997.

Edwards, Mike. "Ukraine." *National Geographic,* May 1987, 595–631.

Kubijovyc, Volodymyr, and Danylo Husar Struk, ed. *Encyclopedia of Ukraine.* Toronto, Canada: University of Toronto Press, 1993.

Otfinoski, Steven. *Ukraine.* New York: Facts on File, 1999.

Ukraine. Minneapolis: Lerner Publications, 1993.

UNITED ARAB EMIRATES

United Arab Emirates
Al-Imarat al-'Arabiyah al-Muttahidah

CAPITAL: Abu Dhabi (Abu Zaby).

FLAG: The flag consists of a red vertical stripe at the hoist and three equal horizontal stripes of green, white, and black.

ANTHEM: The National Anthem is an instrumental piece without words.

MONETARY UNIT: The United Arab Emirates dirham (UD), introduced as the currency in May 1973, is divided into 100 fils. There are coins of 1, 5, 10, 25, and 50 fils and 1 and 5 dirham and notes of 5, 10, 50, 100, 200, 500, and 1,000 dirhams. UD1 = $0.27229 (or $1 = UD3.6725).

WEIGHTS AND MEASURES: The metric system and imperial and local measures are used.

HOLIDAYS: New Year's Day, 1 January; Accession of the Ruler of Abu Dhabi (Abu Dhabi only), 6 August; National Day, 2 December; Christmas, 25 December. Muslim religious holidays include Lailat al-Miraj, 'Id al-Fitr, 'Id al-'Adha', Hijra New Year, and Milad an-Nabi.

TIME: 4 PM = noon GMT.

1 LOCATION AND SIZE

Comprising a total area of approximately 75,581 square kilometers (29,182 square miles), the United Arab Emirates (UAE), is in the eastern Arabian Peninsula. It consists of seven states, or emirates: Abu Dhabi, Dubayy, Ash Shariqah, Ra's al-Khaymah, Al Fujayrah, Umm al-Qaywayn, and 'Ajman. Comparatively, the area occupied by the UAE is slightly smaller than the state of Maine. The UAE has a total boundary length of 2,185 kilometers (1,358 miles). The UAE's capital city, Abu Dhabi, is located on the Persian Gulf.

2 TOPOGRAPHY

The UAE consists mainly of sandy desert. It is bounded on the west by an immense *sebkha,* or salt flat; the eastern boundary runs northward over gravel plains and high dunes. The flat coastal strip that makes up most of the UAE has an extensive area of sebkha subject to flooding.

3 CLIMATE

The months between May and October are extremely hot, with average temperatures ranging between 28° and 41°C (82–106°F) and high humidity near the coast. Winter temperatures can fall as low as 2°C (36°F) but average between 14° and 28°C (57–82°F). Normal average annual rainfall is from 13 centimeters (5.1 inches).

4 PLANTS AND ANIMALS

Vegetation of the marshes and swamps includes the dwarf mangrove, and there is a wide range of desert plants.

Geographic Profile

Geographic Features

Size ranking: 113 of 192
Highest elevation: 1,527 meters (5,010 feet) at Mount Yibir
Lowest elevation: Sea level at the Persian Gulf

Land Use†

Arable land:	0%
Permanent crops:	0%
Permanent pastures:	2%
Forests:	0%
Other:	98%

Weather††

Average annual precipitation: 13 centimeters (5.1 inches)
Average temperature range in January: 14–28°C (57–82°F)
Average temperature range in July: 28–41°C (82–106°F)

†*Arable land:* Land used for temporary crops, like meadows for mowing or pasture, gardens, and greenhouses. *Permanent crops:* Land cultivated with crops that occupy its use for long periods, such as cocoa, coffee, rubber, fruit and nut orchards, and vineyards. *Permanent pastures:* Land used permanently for forage crops. *Forests:* Land containing stands of trees. *Other:* Any land not specified, including built-on areas, roads, and barren land.

††The measurements for precipitation and average temperature were taken at weather stations closest to the country's largest city. Precipitation and average temperature can vary significantly within a country, due to factors such as latitude, altitude, coastal proximity, and wind patterns.

Animal life includes jerboa (desert rat), gazelle, mongoose, hare, fox, wolf, jackal, wildcat, and lynx. There are 14 species of reptile, and four types of land snake. More than 250 species of small birds have been reported in the UAE, along with many of the larger birds—kites, buzzards, eagles, falcons, owls, and harriers. Sea birds include a variety of gulls, terns, ospreys, waders, and flamingos. Popular game birds include the houbara (ruffed bustard), as well as species of ducks and geese.

5 ENVIRONMENT

The clearing of natural vegetation, livestock overgrazing on rangelands, and loss of forest land have led to desertification, or expansion of the desert. The oil industry has contributed to air pollution.

The nation ranked among the highest in the world for carbon dioxide emissions in 1992. The Al-'Ayn zoological gardens (part of the government's effort to protect threatened species) contain some 280 species of wildlife, including the gazelle, which had been on the verge of extinction in the region. In 1994, four of the country's mammal species were endangered. Seven bird species were threatened with extinction.

6 POPULATION

The population was estimated at 2.4 million in 2000. The projected population for the year 2005 was 2.6 million.

The Abu Dhabi metropolitan area had a population of 928,000 in 2000.

According to United Nations estimates, in 1998 the UAE's population had the world's second highest (after Qatar) ratio of males to females: there were 175 men for every 100 women.

7 MIGRATION

About 80% of the UAE's population originates from outside its borders. In the early 1980s, the government tried to reduce the immigration rate by limiting the number of visas issued to foreign workers. In

1999, there were zero migrants per 1,000 population.

8 ETHNIC GROUPS

South Asians (Asian Indians, Pakistanis, Bangladeshis, and Sri Lankans) account for about 50% of the population, followed by Arabs (about 42%, 23% of whom are from outside the UAE). Westerners (Americans and Western Europeans) account for about 8%. Jordanians, Palestinians, Egyptians, Iraqis, and Bahrainis are employed throughout the government bureaucracy.

9 LANGUAGES

Arabic is the universal language. Farsi is spoken in Dubayy (Dubai), and English is widely used in business.

10 RELIGIONS

Almost all UAE citizens and many immigrants are Muslims. Most are Sunni Muslims, with the exception of a comparatively large Shi'ite Muslim community in Dubayy. The non-Muslims are principally Christians and Hindus.

11 TRANSPORTATION

In 1996 there were 4,835 kilometers (3,004 miles) of bituminized highways. In 1995 there were 313,000 registered passenger cars and 72,824 commercial vehicles.

Dubayy's Port Rashid is one of the largest artificial harbors in the Middle East. Other ports are the Jabal 'Ali complex and Abu Dhabi's Port Zayid. In 1998, the merchant fleet consisted of 74 ships with a

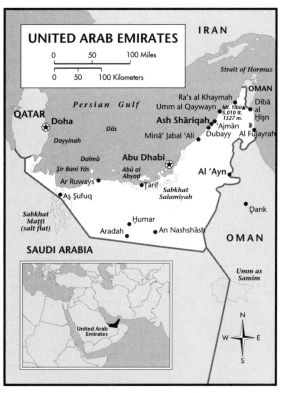

LOCATION: 51°3′ to 56°23′E; 22°30′ to 26°17′N.
BOUNDARY LENGTHS: Persian Gulf coastline, 1,318 kilometers (817 miles); Oman, 410 kilometers (256 miles); Sa'udi Arabia, 457 kilometers (285 miles). **TERRITORIAL SEA LIMIT:** 3 miles, except Ash Shariqah (12 miles).

capacity totaling 1.1 million gross registered tons.

A new international airport in Abu Dhabi opened in 1982. The other international airports in the UAE are in Dubayy, Ash Shariqah, and Ra's al-Khaymah. In 1997, 4.7 million passengers were carried on domestic and international flights.

12 HISTORY

Abu Dhabi island was settled by its present ruling family, Al-Nahyan, toward the end of the eighteenth century, and Dubayy was founded by an offshoot of the same family in 1833. The late eighteenth and nineteenth centuries brought the division of the area between the Nahyan and the Qawasim, who ruled Ra's al-Khaymah and neighboring territories.

Treaties signed in 1820 and 1835 established a formal relationship between the states of the southern Persian Gulf and Britain that was to last until 1971. In 1892, the United Kingdom promised to protect the coast from aggression by sea and land. In 1955, it intervened on the side of Abu Dhabi in its dispute with Sa'udi Arabia over the Al Buraymi oasis, near Al 'Ayn, control of which is now shared by Abu Dhabi and Oman.

When, in 1968, the United Kingdom announced the withdrawal of its forces from the area, an agreement was reached to establish a federation of Arab emirates—embracing the seven states of the present-day UAE, Bahrain, and Qatar. In 1971, six of the seven present-day UAE states agreed on the establishment of the United Arab Emirates. The UAE was officially proclaimed a sovereign, independent nation on 2 December 1971, with the seventh state, Ra's al-Khaymah, joining in early 1972.

UAE's independence created problems between the new state and its two powerful neighbors, Sa'udi Arabia and Iran. Sa'udi Arabia claimed a group of oases (fertile areas in deserts) in the south of the UAE, and Iran laid claim to its offshore islands. In 1974, a border agreement on the oases was signed with Sa'udi Arabia,

but has not been fully recognized by the rulers of either country.

The dispute with Iran over the islands became tense when Iranian forces tried to claim the UAE section of Abu Musa (a tiny island west of Ra's al Khaymah) in 1992. The Iranian government in Tehran backed down and relations between the two countries returned to a cautious normality.

The UAE became a founding member in 1981 of the Gulf Cooperation Council (GCC), a political and economic alliance that includes all the Persian Gulf countries (Bahrain, Kuwait, Oman, Qatar, Sa'udi Arabia, and the UAE) except Iran. During the Iran-Iraq War (1980–88), the UAE gave aid to Iraq but also maintained diplomatic relations with Iran and sought to mediate the conflict.

In the Persian Gulf War of 1990, forces from the UAE participated with allied troops against Iraq and the government gave some $4.5 billion to the coalition war effort. The UAE's generosity with foreign aid to Arab states (more than $15 billion through 1991) makes it a significant player in the affairs of the region.

In 1991, the international Bank of Commerce and Credit International (BCCI), which was based in the UAE and largely owned by the ruling family of Abu Dhabi, was accused of fraud and closed down, causing repercussions all around the world.

During civil unrest in Yugoslavia in the early 1990s, the UAE airlifted wounded Bosnian women and their families to Abu

Photo credit: EPD/Government of UAE.

Name:	Sheikh Zayid bin Sultan Al Nuhayyan
Position:	President of a federation
Took office:	2 December 1971
Birth date:	1918 (est.)
Education:	Self-taught
Of interest:	Zayid is able to converse in several languages.

Dhabi, where they were given free medical care, housing, and financial support for one year.

At the end of 1999, the UAE celebrated the 25th anniversary of its founding.

13 GOVERNMENT

The executive branch of government consists of the Supreme Council of Rulers, headed by the president, and the Council of Ministers. The Council of Rulers, composed of the hereditary rulers of the seven emirates, has responsibility for formulation and supervision of all UAE policies, ratification of federal laws, and oversight of the union's budget.

Sheikh Zayid bin Sultan Al Nuhayyan, emir of Abu Dhabi, was elected president upon independence and reelected to five-year terms from 1976 to 1996; he continues to hold the presidency in 2001. The president is assisted by the Council of Ministers, or cabinet, headed by the prime minister (Sheikh Maktum ibn Rashid al-Maktoum, ruler of Dubai). The Federal National Council can question cabinet ministers and make recommendations to the Supreme National Council.

Most of the individual emirates (states) are governed according to tribal traditions, including open meetings in which citizens express themselves directly to their rulers.

14 POLITICAL PARTIES

No political parties exist in the UAE.

15 JUDICIAL SYSTEM

Abu Dhabi, Dubayy (Dubai), and Ash Shariqah (Sharjah) have developed relatively sophisticated judicial systems based, as in other Persian Gulf states, on a combination of Shari'ah (Islamic) law and modern legal codes. The 1971 constitution established a Supreme Court and an unspecified number of lower courts. There are no jury trials.

16 ARMED FORCES

In 2000, the combined UAE forces totaled 64,500 men, all volunteers. One-third are Asian contract (hired) soldiers. The army

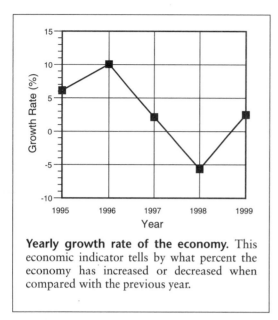

Yearly growth rate of the economy. This economic indicator tells by what percent the economy has increased or decreased when compared with the previous year.

had 59,000 men, organized into six brigades. The navy comprised 1,500 men and 19 patrol and coastal combatants. The air force had 4,000 men, 99 combat aircraft, and 49 armed helicopters.

17 ECONOMY

Traditionally, the economy of the UAE centered primarily on oil and oil-based industries. However, with its strategic location, modern communications and transportation facilities, and strong banking system, the UAE also has become the major trade center in the Gulf region.

In Abu Dhabi, by far the wealthiest of the seven emirates (states), oil revenues are supplemented by income from a huge investment fund. Dubayy's role as a center for trade plays a major role in its economy.

Although there are small industries in 'Ajman and Umm al-Qaywayn, these poorer areas depend on federal aid. Oil production in Ash Shariqah began in July 1974, and manufacturing and tourism there have been expanded. Ra's al-Khaymah has cement plants, a pharmaceutical factory, a lime kiln, and the gulf's first explosives plant. Al Fujayrah remains predominantly agricultural.

In 1998, petroleum and industry accounted for 52% of the gross domestic product (GDP); agriculture, 3%; and services, 45%.

18 INCOME

In 1998, United Arab Emirates' gross domestic product (GDP) was $40 billion, or about $17,400 per person. That year, the average decline in the rate of the GDP was about 6%, and average inflation, 2.4%.

19 INDUSTRY

In 1995, about 68% of the UAE's industrial establishments were located in Ash Shariqah (Sharjah) and Dubayy (Dubai). The industrial complex in Abu Dhabi includes an oil refinery with a processing capacity of 120,000 barrels per day; a fertilizer factory, with a production capacity of 1,000 tons of ammonia and 1,500 tons of urea per day; and a gas liquefaction installation. In 1995, the UAE produced 69.3 million barrels of refined petroleum products.

In Dubayy, the industrial port complex includes an aluminum smelter, which produced 239,900 tons of ingots in 1995. The

Photo credit: © Robert Azzi/Woodfin Camp & Assoc.

A view of the harbor at Dubayy (Dubai).

other developed industries produce construction-related materials such as cement, asphalt, and concrete blocks.

20 LABOR

In 1997, the total work force was estimated at one million, but only a minority were UAE citizens. The UAE leans heavily on foreigners for skilled labor and management ability. Non-UAE Arabs are employed at all economic levels, including the government bureaucracy and civil service. However, with declining oil revenues in the mid-1980s, well-paying, skilled jobs were becoming harder to find. A 1984 decree guarantees UAE nationals priority in hiring, in order to reduce dependence on foreign labor.

21 AGRICULTURE

About 24% of cultivated land is used to grow vegetables, 30% fruit, 10% feed crops, and 36% for other uses. The main crops are tomatoes, melons, and dates. In 1998, UAE agriculture produced 581,000 tons of vegetables and 297,000 tons of fruit.

22 DOMESTICATED ANIMALS

In 1999, the UAE had one million goats, 385,000 sheep, 170,000 camels, and 76,000 head of cattle. Local poultry and egg production satisfy 27% and 40% of domestic demand, respectively.

23 FISHING

Fishing is an important source of domestic food and animal feed. From 1988 to 1990, per person annual consumption of fish and shellfish in the UAE was 26.3 kilograms (58 pounds), more than any other country in the Middle East. Many varieties of fish are caught, including rock cod, tuna, mackerel, sardines, anchovies, jack, marlin, red mullet, bream, and snapper. The fish catch in 1997 was 114,358 tons, which supplied about 50% of local demand.

24 FORESTRY

Wooded areas covered only 60,000 hectares (148,000 acres), or about 0.7% of the total land area in 1995.

25 MINING

Apart from oil and natural gas, mining is limited to the production of construction materials, marble, and stone quarried in the northeast. In 1996, an estimated 56,000 tons of chromite ore were produced.

26 FOREIGN TRADE

In 1997, petroleum products accounted for around 45% of total exports. Consumer goods, especially food, accounted for about half of all imports, followed by business-related goods such as transportation equipment, oil-field equipment, and building materials.

Japan, India, South Korea, and Singapore are the leading purchasers of petroleum from the UAE. Japan, the United States, the United Kingdom, and Germany are the leading suppliers of imports.

27 ENERGY AND POWER

The UAE, with crude oil production of 2.34 million barrels per day in 1998, ranked as the third-largest oil producer in the Middle East that year (following Sa'udi Arabia and Iran). Total reserves of crude oil were estimated at 97.8 billion barrels in 1999. The UAE's proven natural gas reserves total about six trillion cubic meters (212 trillion cubic feet), and net production amounted to 37 billion cubic meters in 1998. All electricity is thermally generated from oil or natural gas. Electric power production was 20,110 million kilowatt hours in 1998.

28 SOCIAL DEVELOPMENT

There is no social security law in the UAE, but many welfare benefits are available to citizens, relief for any domestic catastrophe, provided from a disaster fund. If the father of a family is unable to work because of illness, disability, or old age, he receives help under the National Assistance Law; should he die or divorce his wife, the woman's future is secured.

Female employment is growing in government service and in occupations such as education and health. A married woman can work outside the home only with her husband's permission. Females

Selected Social Indicators

The statistics below are estimates for the period 1996 to 2000. For comparison purposes, data for the United States and averages for low-income countries and high-income countries are also given.

Indicator	United Arab Emirates	Low-income countries	High-income countries	United States
Per capita gross national product (GNP)†	$17,700	$1,870	$25,690	$31,910
Population growth rate	2%	2.1%	0.7%	1.1%
People per square kilometer of land	34	73	29	30
Life expectancy in years	75	59	78	77
Number of physicians per 1,000 people	n.a.	1.0	2.5	2.5
Number of pupils per teacher (primary school)	17	41	17	14
Illiteracy rate (15 years and older)	23%	34%	<5%	3%
Television sets per 1,000 people	252	85	693	844
Energy consumed per capita (kg of oil equivalent)	10,035	550	5,366	7,937

† The GNP is the total dollar value of all goods and services produced by a country in a year. The per capita GNP is calculated by dividing a country's GNP by its population and adjusting for relative purchasing power. About 15% of the world's 6.1 billion people live in high-income countries, while 40% live in low-income countries.

n.a. = data not available   > = greater than   < = less than

Sources: World Bank. World Development Indicators. Washington, D.C.: The World Bank, 2001; Central Intelligence Agency. The World Factbook. Washington, D.C.: Government Printing Office, 2000.

are not permitted to leave the country without the permission of a male relative.

29 HEALTH

Modern hospitals have been built in Abu Dhabi, Dubayy, and other towns. In 1990–97, there were 0.8 doctors per 1,000 population. Typhoid fever and tuberculosis are rare; malaria remains a problem, however. Average life expectancy was 75 years in 1999. In 1991–93, 95% of the population had access to health care services.

30 HOUSING

The federal government is attempting to make modern low-cost homes available to poorer families and supplying them with piped water, sewage systems, and electricity.

31 EDUCATION

Education is compulsory for six years at the primary level. At the secondary level, children go through six years of education in two stages. In 1997, there were 259,509 pupils and 16,148 teachers at the primary level and 180,764 pupils and about 11,000 teachers in secondary schools. Arabic is a compulsory subject, and classes are segregated by gender. United Arab Emirates University is at Al-'Ayn. In 1997, all higher level institutions had 16,213 students. For the year 2000, adult illiteracy rates were estimated at 23%.

32 MEDIA

In 1995, the UAE had 615,000 main telephone lines. A color television network connects Abu Dhabi with Dubayy and Ash Shariqah. UAE Radio has broadcasting stations in four emirates (states); the first commercial station was opened in Abu Dhabi in 1980. There were an estimated 354 radios and 252 television sets per 1,000 population in 2000.

Five Arabic-language dailies were published in 1999 in the UAE: *Al-Ittihad (Federation,* 1999 circulation 60,000), *Al-Fajr (The Dawn,* 20,700), and *Al-Wahdah (Unity,* 30,000 in 1995), in Abu Dhabi; *Al-Bayan* (32,650) in Dubayy; and *Al-Khalij* (85,000) in Ash Shariqah. There were three English-language dailies: the *Gulf News* (85,900) and *Khaleej Times* (48,000), published in Dubai; and the *Emirates News* (21,000), published in Abu Dhabi.

33 TOURISM AND RECREATION

Tourism is encouraged in all areas. The UAE's varied scenery includes mountains, beaches, deserts, and oases. Tourist activities include visits to Bedouin markets, museums, zoos, and aquariums. Many large world-class hotels have opened in recent years.

34 FAMOUS EMIRIANS

Sheikh Zayid bin Sultan Al Nuhayyan (b.1918) has been ruler of Abu Dhabi since 1966 and president of the UAE since 1971.

35 BIBLIOGRAPHY

Higgins, Kevin. *The Emirates: Abu Dhabi, Dubai, Sharjah, Ras Al Khaimah, Fujairah, Umm Al Qaiwain, Ajman.* Reading, Penn.: Garnet Publishing, 1995.

Johnson, Julia. *U.A.E.: United Arab Emirates.* Philadelphia: Chelsea House, 2000.

Vine, Peter. *United Arab Emirates: Profile of a Country's Heritage and Modern Development.* London: Immel, 1992.

UNITED KINGDOM

United Kingdom of Great Britain and Northern Ireland

CAPITAL: London.

FLAG: The Union Jack, adopted in 1800, is a combination of the banners of England (St. George's flag: a red cross with extended horizontals on a white field), Scotland (St. Andrew's flag: a white saltire cross on a blue field), and Ireland (St. Patrick's flag: a red saltire cross on a white field). The arms of the saltire crosses do not meet at the center.

ANTHEM: *God Save the Queen.*

MONETARY UNIT: The pound sterling (£) is a paper currency of 100 pence. Before decimal coinage was introduced on 15 February 1971, the pound had been divided into 20 shillings, each shilling representing 12 pennies (p) or pence; some old-style coins are still in circulation. Under the new system, there are coins of 1, 2, 5, 10, 20, and 50 pence and 1 and 2 pounds, and notes of 5, 10, 20, and 50 pounds. £1 = $1.64149 (or $1 = £0.6092).

WEIGHTS AND MEASURES: Although the traditional imperial system of weights and measures is still in use (sample units: of weight, the stone of 14 pounds equivalent to 6.35 kilograms; of length, the yard equivalent to 0.914 meter; of capacity, a bushel equivalent to 36.37 liters), a changeover to the metric system is in progress.

HOLIDAYS: New Year's Day, 1 January; Good Friday; Easter Monday (except Scotland); Late Summer Holiday, last Monday in August or 1st in September (except Scotland); Christmas, 25 December; and Boxing Day, 1st weekday after Christmas. Also observed in Scotland are bank holidays on 2 January and on the 1st Monday in August. Northern Ireland observes St. Patrick's Day, 17 March; and Orangeman's Day, 12 July, commemorating the Battle of the Boyne in 1690.

TIME: GMT.

1 LOCATION AND SIZE

The United Kingdom (UK) is situated off the northwest coast of Europe between the Atlantic Ocean and the North Sea. It is separated from the Continent by the Strait of Dover and the English Channel, and from the Irish Republic by the Irish Sea and St. George's Channel. Its total area of 244,820 square kilometers (94,526 square miles) consists of the island of Great Brit-ain—formed by England, Wales, and Scot-land—and Northern Ireland, on the island of Ireland. Comparatively, the area occupied by the United Kingdom is slightly smaller than the state of Oregon.

The United Kingdom also comprises several island groups and hundreds of small single islands. Its total boundary length is 12,789 kilometers (7,947 miles). The 0° meridian of longitude passes

33

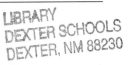

Geographic Profile

Geographic Features

Size ranking: 76 of 192
Highest elevation: 1,343 meters (4,406 feet) at Ben
  Nevis
Lowest elevation: −4 meters (−13 feet) at Fenland

Land Use

Arable land:	25%
Permanent crops:	0%
Permanent pastures:	46%
Forests:	10%
Other:	19%

Weather

Average annual precipitation: 78 centimeters (31
  inches)
Average temperature in January: 4.2°C (39.6°F)
Average temperature in July: 16°C (61°F)

through the old Royal Observatory, located at Greenwich. The United Kingdom's capital city, London, is located in the southeast part of Great Britain, in England.

2 TOPOGRAPHY

England is divided into the hill regions of the north, west, and southwest, and the rolling downs and low plains of the east and southeast. The Cheviot Hills run from east to west at the Scottish border. The Pennines mountain range runs from the Scottish border to central England. South of the Pennines lies a plains region. The highest point in England is in the northwest. The longest river is the Thames in the southeast.

Scotland has three distinct topographical regions: the Northwest Highlands, occupying almost the entire northern half of the country and containing the highest point in the British Isles, as well as Loch

Ness, site of the fabled "monster"; the area known as the Central Lowlands, containing Loch Lomond, Scotland's largest lake; and the Southern Uplands.

Wales is largely mountainous. The Cambrian Mountains occupy almost the entire area. There are narrow coastal plains in the south and west and small lowland areas in the north.

Northern Ireland consists mainly of low-lying plateaus and hills. At its center lies Lough Neagh, the largest lake in the United Kingdom.

3 CLIMATE

Despite its northern latitude, the United Kingdom generally has a temperate climate. Mean monthly temperatures range (north to south) from 3°C to 5°C (37°–41°F) in winter and from 12°C to 16°C (54°–61°F) in summer. Temperatures in summer rarely go higher than 32°C (90°F) or drop in winter below −10°C (14°F). Rainfall, averaging 78 centimeters (31 inches) throughout the United Kingdom, is heaviest on the western and northern heights (more than 380 centimeters/150 inches), and lowest along the eastern and southeastern coasts. Known for its mists and fogs, the United Kingdom has little sunshine—averaging from half an hour to two hours a day in winter and from five to eight hours in summer.

4 PLANTS AND ANIMALS

With its mild climate and varied soils, the United Kingdom has many types of plant life. Fairly large forests remain in east and north Scotland and in southeast

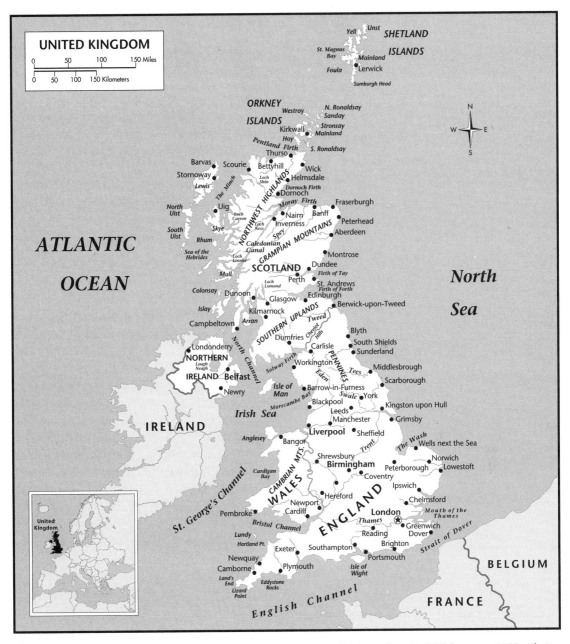

LOCATION: 49°56′ to 60°50′N; 1°45′E to 8°10′W. **BOUNDARY LENGTHS:** Total coastline, 12,429 kilometers (7,722 miles), of which Northern Ireland's comprises 375 kilometers (233 miles); Irish Republic, 360 kilometers (225 miles). **TERRITORIAL SEA LIMIT:** 3 miles.

England. Oak, elm, ash, and beech are the most common trees in England, and pine and birch in Scotland. Almost all the lowland outside the industrial centers is farmland, with a variety of cultivated grasses and flowering plants. Wild plants of the United Kingdom's woods, fens and marshes, cliffs, and mountain slopes include heather, grasses, gorse, and the bracken of the moorlands.

The animals are similar to that of northwestern continental Europe, although there are fewer species. Some of the larger mammals—wolf, bear, boar, and reindeer—are extinct, but red and roe deer are protected for sport. Common smaller mammals are foxes, hares, hedgehogs, rabbits, weasels, stoats, shrews, rats, and mice. Otters are found in many rivers, and seals frequently appear along the coast. Roughly 230 species of birds reside in the United Kingdom, and another 200 are migratory. Most numerous are the chaffinch, blackbird, sparrow, and starling. The rivers and lakes are full of salmon, trout, perch, pike, roach, dace, and grayling.

5 ENVIRONMENT

Air pollution is a serious problem for the United Kingdom. The country produces 564.2 million tons of particulate emissions and 2,277 tons of hydrocarbon emissions per year and contributes 2.4% of the world's total gas emissions; the nation had the world's 8th highest level of industrial carbon dioxide emissions in 1992. In addition, its sulfur adds to the acid rain problem in the surrounding countries of Western Europe. However, air quality has improved greatly in the United Kingdom as a result of the Control of Pollution Act of 1974 and other legislation. London is no longer densely smog-ridden, and winter sunlight has been increasing in various industrial cities.

Water pollution from farming also is a problem. About 3% of the nation's water is used for farming activity and 77% for industrial purposes. The United Kingdom's cities produce 22 million tons of solid waste and 2.4 million tons of toxic waste per year. A major recent environmental problem is the regulation of oil and gas development and of large-scale dumping at sea.

The National Trust (for Places of Historic Interest or Natural Beauty), an organization of more than 1.3 million members, has acquired some 750 kilometers (466 miles) of coastline in England, Northern Ireland, and Wales. By 1982, the United Kingdom had designated 10 national parks, covering 13,600 square kilometers (5,250 square miles), or 9% of the area of England and Wales. Scotland has 40 national scenic areas. Northern Ireland has eight designated areas of outstanding natural beauty, seven countryside parks, and one regional park. There also are seven forest parks in Great Britain and nine in Northern Ireland. In 1994, three of the nation's mammal species and 22 bird species were endangered, as were 24 types of birds.

6 POPULATION

The 2000 population estimate for the United Kingdom was 59.2 million. A population of 58.1 million was projected for 2005. During the 1990s, the United Kingdom's population grew by an annual average of 0.3%. The population of England was estimated at 48.4 million in 1992; Wales, 2.9 million; Scotland, 5.1 million; and Northern Ireland, 1.6 million.

Average population density in 2000 was 246 persons per square kilometer (637 per square mile). Major metropolitan areas in 2000 included Greater London, 7.6 million; Birmingham, 2.3 million; Manchester, 2.3 million; Leeds, 1.4 million; and Liverpool, 912,000. The major cities in Scotland are Glasgow, 654,000; and Edinburgh, 422,000. Belfast, the major city in Northern Ireland, had a 2000 population of 287,500; and Cardiff, in Wales, 277,000.

7 MIGRATION

Immigration is now on a quota basis. Between 1986 and 1991, 1.3 million persons left the United Kingdom to live abroad, and 1.5 million came from overseas to live in the United Kingdom, resulting in a net gain in population of 127,000. In 1991 there was a net gain of about 28,000. The total number of foreign residents in the United Kingdom was about 1.9 million in 1990. Of these, more than a third were Irish (638,000), Indians were second (155,000), and Americans third (102,000). In 1995, the United Kingdom had some 20,000 refugees.

8 ETHNIC GROUPS

The present-day English, Welsh, Scots, and Irish are descended from a long succession of early peoples: Iberians, Celts, Romans, Anglo-Saxons, Danes, and Normans, the last of whom invaded and conquered England in 1066–70. In 1998, about

Photo credit: Susan D. Rock.

Punk rocker bagpipe player in Edinburgh, Scotland.

97.2% of United Kingdom residents were native-born. The principal ethnic minorities are of West Indian or Guyanese descent (499,000) or of Indian (840,000), Pakistani (475,000), or Bengali (160,000) descent. There also are sizable numbers of Africans, Americans, Australians, Chinese, Greek and Turkish Cypriots, Italians, Spaniards, and Southeast Asians.

9 LANGUAGES

English is spoken throughout the United Kingdom. In northwestern Wales, Welsh (a form of Brythonic Celtic) is the first language of most inhabitants. According to the 2000 census, 26% of those living in Wales spoke Welsh (up from 19% in 1991). Some 80,000 or so persons in western Scotland speak the Scottish form of Gaelic. On the Isle of Man, the Manx variety of Celtic is used in official pronouncements.

10 RELIGIONS

The queen or king of England must be a member of the Church of England and, on taking the throne, promise to uphold the faith. In 1998, some 27 million people worldwide were members of the Church of England, whose membership also includes about 45% of the English population. In 1998, adult membership in the Church of Scotland was estimated at 800,000. The Roman Catholic Church in the United Kingdom had some 9 million members in 1998.

Other Protestant churches, with 1998 figures, include the Methodist Church (760,000 members); the Baptist Church (241,000); and the United Reformed Church. In 1991, the Presbyterian Church of Wales had some 58,000 members. The Salvation Army, founded in London in 1865, had 57,000 active members in the United Kingdom.

Many immigrants have established religious communities in the United Kingdom. Christian groups include Greek, Russian, Polish, Serbian Orthodox, Estonian and Latvian Orthodox, and the Armenian Church. Lutheran churches from various parts of Europe also are represented.

The Anglo-Jewish community, with an estimated 315,000 members in 1990, is the second-largest group of Jews in Western Europe. There also are sizable communities of Muslims (990,000 in 1991), Sikhs, Hindus, and Buddhists.

11 TRANSPORTATION

Under the 1968 Transport Act, national transport operations were reorganized, creating the National Freight Corporation, the Freight Integration Council, and the National Bus Company. In 1997, Great Britain had 372,000 kilometers (231,160 miles) of public highways. Licensed motor vehicles in Great Britain as of 1995 numbered 27.9 million, including 24.3 million passenger cars.

Eurotunnel, a British-French company, recently built two high-speed 50-kilometer (31-mile) rail tunnels beneath the seabed of the English Channel. The Channel Tunnel, referred to as the "Chunnel," links points near Dover, England, and Calais, France. The Channel Tunnel has the longest tunnel system (38 kilometers/24 miles) ever built under water.

There were 16,787 route kilometers (10,488 miles) of standard-gauge (1.435 meters) railway in Great Britain in 1996; included in this total are the underground railway systems that operate in London, Glasgow, and Liverpool. In early 1997, the government proposed privatizing London's subway system because of lacking funds needed to restore the aging network.

Great Britain has about 2,291 kilometers (1,424 miles) of navigable inland waterways. Great Britain has some 300

The mysterious stone monument at Stonehenge.

ports, including the Port of London, one of the largest in the world. Other major ports include Liverpool, Southampton, Kingston upon Hull, and the inland port of Manchester. The British merchant fleet of 155 ships totaled 2.5 million gross registered tons in 1998.

International flights operate from London's Heathrow Airport; Gatwick, London's second airport; Glasgow, in Scotland; Ringway, for Manchester; Aldergrove, for Belfast; and Elmdon, for Birmingham. The Concorde, a supersonic jetliner, was developed jointly in the 1960s by the United Kingdom and France. In 1997, the United Kingdom's airlines carried more than 62 million passengers.

12 HISTORY

Beginnings

The stone circles of Stonehenge in Wiltshire are the remains of Britain's earliest inhabitants, whose origin is unknown. Celtic tribes from the Continent invaded before the sixth century BC. In the first century AD, the Romans occupied most of the present-day area of England, staying until the fifth century. With the fall of the Roman Empire, the Celtic tribes fought among themselves. Early raids by Germanic tribes from the Continent—Angles, Saxons, and Jutes—soon turned into full-scale invasions. The leaders of the invasions established kingdoms in the conquered territory, while the native Celts retreated into the mountains of Wales and the southwest of England.

Among the new kingdoms of the invaders, that of the West Saxons (Wessex) became the overall ruling kingdom, chiefly through the leadership of Alfred the Great. However, the West Saxons were overthrown, first by the Danes in 1017, then by William, Duke of Normandy, in 1066. William invaded England and defeated Harold the Saxon in the Battle of Hastings, beginning the Norman Conquest, which lasted until 1070. He instituted a strong government, which continued through the reigns of his sons William II and Henry I. Henry II ascended the throne in 1154. Succeeding English kings expanded their holdings in France, beginning a long series of struggles between the two countries.

1215–1328

Long-standing conflict between the nobles and the kings reached a climax at Runnymede (on the bank of the Thames River, southwest of London) in 1215 when King John was forced to sign the Magna Carta—a document guaranteeing fundamental rights and privileges to the average citizen. Just half a century later, in 1265, Simon de Montfort, earl of Leicester, summoned the first Parliament, with representatives not only of the nobility but also of the boroughs and towns. In 1282, the last Welsh king, Llewellyn ap Gruffydd, was killed in battle, and Edward I completed the conquest of Wales.

By the end of the sixth century, four separate kingdoms had been established in Scotland. Most of the country was unified under Duncan I (r.1034–40). The Scottish king William the Lion (r.1165–1214) was captured by Henry II of England in 1174 and forced to accept the Treaty of Falaise, by which Scotland came under English control. Scotland later purchased its freedom from Richard I. In 1305, Edward I reestablished English rule, but after the decisive defeat of the English at Bannockburn (a town in central Scotland), Edward III signed a treaty once again giving Scotland its freedom in 1328.

1337–1588

Under Edward III, the Hundred Years War (1337–1453) with France was begun, which would eventually end with the English being driven out of France. The fourteenth and fifteenth centuries were a time of confusion and change for England. The plague, known as the Black Death, broke out in England in 1348, wiping out a third of the population. John Wycliffe led a religious reform movement and criticized many established doctrines and practices. Richard II ruled from 1377–99, then was overthrown and succeeded by Henry IV, the first king of the house of Lancaster. The Wars of the Roses (1455–85), in which the houses of Lancaster and York fought for the throne, ended with the accession of Henry VII, a member of the Tudor family, marking the beginning of the modern history of England.

Under the Tudors, business and trade were expanded, English sailors ranged far and wide, and conflicts with Spain grew worse. In 1531, Henry VIII separated the Anglican Church from Rome and proclaimed himself its head in order to divorce the first of his six wives. After his death (1547), the succession to the throne became a major issue during the reigns of Edward VI (1547–53), Mary I (1553–58), and Elizabeth I (1558–1603).

French influence in Scotland grew under James V (r.1513–42). His daughter, Mary, Queen of Scots, married the dauphin (prince) of France, where she lived and later ruled as queen. By the time Mary returned to Scotland (1561), a pro-English faction had the support of Queen Elizabeth I against the pro-French faction. Mary, who claimed the throne of England, was imprisoned and executed in 1587 by Elizabeth. Under Elizabeth, England acquired its first colony, Newfoundland, in 1583 and in 1588 defeated the Spanish Armada. It also experienced the beginning of a golden age of drama, literature, and music, which produced many great artists, including William Shakespeare.

1603–1707

Elizabeth was succeeded by Mary's son, James VI of Scotland, who became James I of England (r.1603–25), establishing the Stuart line. Under James and his son, Charles I (r.1625–49), the rising middle classes (mainly Puritan in religion) wanted to make Parliament superior to the king. The English Civil War broke out in 1642, and Charles I was tried and executed in 1649. Oliver Cromwell, as Protector, ruled the new Commonwealth until his death in 1658. In 1660, Charles II, eldest son of the executed king, regained the throne.

The following period, known as the Restoration, was marked by a reaction against Puritanism and by greater wealth. Charles II's younger brother, James II (r.1685–88), who tried unsuccessfully to restore Roman Catholicism, was overthrown in 1688. He was succeeded by his daughter, Mary II, and her Dutch husband, William III, who were invited to rule by Parliament. This transfer of power is known as the Glorious Revolution.

English colonial expansion developed further in the seventeenth and eighteenth centuries, and the English merchant marine became more successful than the Dutch. At home, the Act of Union of Scotland and England was approved by the two parliaments in 1707, thereby formally creating the kingdom of Great Britain under one crown and with a single Parliament composed of representatives of both countries.

1714–1900

George I of the House of Hanover took the throne in 1714 and established the modern cabinet system, with the king leaving much of the governing to his ministers. The eighteenth century was a time of rapid colonial expansion, internal stability, and literary and artistic achievement. Britain expanded its control of North America and India in the Seven Years' War (ended in 1763 by the Treaty of Paris). However, the American Revolution (1775–83) cost Britain its most important group of colonies. A few years later, Britain colonized Australia and New Zealand.

In 1800, with the Act of Union of Great Britain and Ireland, the United Kingdom formally came into being. Although the act established Irish representation in Parliament, the Irish question continued to cause trouble. There was a growing division between the 26 counties of southern Ireland and the six counties of the north, popularly called Ulster. While the north gradually became Protestant and industrial, the rest of Ireland remained Catholic and rural. Eventually, the northern Irish began a campaign that ended in the 1920 Government of Ireland Act, which established separate governments for the north and south, as well as continued representation in the United Kingdom Parliament. The six northern counties accepted the act and became Northern Ireland. The 26 southern counties, however, did not. In 1921, the Anglo-Irish Treaty was signed, by which these counties left the United Kingdom to become the Irish Free State (now the Irish Republic, or Éire), which was officially established in 1922.

The Industrial Revolution, beginning in the second half of the eighteenth century, provided the money needed for British colonial and military expansion throughout the 1800s. However, the growth of the factory system and cities also brought new social problems. The Reform Acts of 1832, 1867, and 1884 increased the rights and power of the new middle class and the working class. Factory acts, poor laws, and other humanitarian legislation did away with some of the worst abuses. The long reign of Queen Victoria (1837–1901) saw commercial and industrial growth like never before. Victoria was succeeded by her son, Edward VII (1841–1910). This was a period of great colonial expansion, especially in Africa, where at the end of the century Britain fought settlers of mostly Dutch origin in the South African (or Boer) War.

1900–1990s

The terrible economic and human losses of World War I (1914–18), in which nearly 800,000 Britons were killed, brought on serious disturbances in the United Kingdom as elsewhere. The economic depression of the 1930s resulted in the unemployment of millions of workers. During the late 1930s, the government of Prime Minister Neville Chamberlain hoped to avoid war by appeasing (making compromises with) Nazi Germany. But after Hitler invaded Poland, the United Kingdom declared war on Germany on 3 September 1939, marking the beginning of World War II (1939–45). Although it won the war, the United Kingdom suffered much destruction from German bombing, and the military and civilian death toll exceeded 900,000.

There was a succession of kings during this era. George V (1865–1936) succeeded his father, Edward VII as king in 1910; George V's son, Edward VIII (1894–1972), succeeded his father. However, Edward VIII abdicated (gave up the throne) before completing one year as king so that he could marry the American divorcee, Wallis Simpson. (It was unacceptable for a king or queen to marry a divorced person.) His brother, George VI (1895–1952), became king and ruled through World War II, serving as a role model to the British people by choosing to continue to live in Buckingham Palace, even though it was damaged by bombing. When he died, his daughter, Elizabeth II (b.1926) became queen. Her eldest son, Prince Charles (b.1948) was given the title, Prince of Wales, in 1958; he is heir to the throne.

The United Kingdom has remained firmly within the Atlantic alliance since World War II. A founding member of the North Atlantic Treaty Organization (NATO) and the European Free Trade Association (EFTA), the United Kingdom joined the European Community (EC) on 1 January 1973. The principal domestic problems in the 1970s were rapid inflation, labor disputes, and the continuing conflict in Northern Ireland. Civil rights protests in 1969 by Catholics drew a violent Protestant reaction. The Irish Republican Army (IRA), seeking the union of Ulster with the Irish Republic, began committing terrorist acts in both Northern Ireland and England. British troops were sent to Belfast and Londonderry in August 1969. In November 1985, the United Kingdom and the Irish Republic signed an agreement committing both governments to recognize Northern Ireland as part of the United Kingdom and to cooperate with each other.

In 1979, a Conservative government headed by Margaret Thatcher came to power with a program of income tax cuts and reduced government spending. Thatcher, who won reelection in 1983 and 1987, began a policy of "privatizing"—selling to private business—many of the United Kingdom's government-run businesses. The United Kingdom fought a brief but intense war (2 April–14 June 1982) after Argentina occupied the Falkland Islands off the south Atlantic coast of South America. British government was restored to the islands at the end of the war. In November 1990, Thatcher withdrew from power and was replaced by John Major. Major's government sought to redefine Conservative values with a renewed emphasis on law and order.

Labour Party leader Tony Blair was elected prime minister in May 1997, ending 18 years of Conservative Party rule. Blair pledged to create regional assemblies for Scotland and Wales as well as a municipal government for London. Blair also promised not to exceed Conservative Party spending limits, and pledged no new taxes for five years. Blair also promised a referendum on the status of Northern Ireland, which its voters approved in May 1998. Voters in the Irish Republic also approved the same referendum. Under the settlement, Northern Ireland remains a part of the United Kingdom, but there will be a new elected assembly, administrative links between the Irish Republic and Northern Ireland, and a council with representatives from the United Kingdom.

On 15 August 1998, a car bomb exploded in Omagh, Northern Ireland, killing 28 and wounding more than 200. The bombing appeared to be conducted by a Roman Catholic splinter group opposed to the referendum, and it raised doubts about the new peace agreement.

Photo credit: Susan D. Rock.

Big Ben and Houses of Parliament, London.

Tony Blair and his Labour Party won a second landslide victory in the June 2001 parliamentary election. The central issue dividing the nation was the UK's relationship with the European Union.

13 GOVERNMENT

The United Kingdom is a monarchy in form but a parliamentary democracy in substance. In British terms, the sovereign—Elizabeth II since 1952—reigns but does not rule. Although head of state, the sovereign is considered under the law rather than above it, ruling only by approval of Parliament and acting only on the advice of her ministers.

The United Kingdom is governed, in the name of the sovereign, by Her Majesty's Government—a body of ministers responsible to Parliament. Parliament itself, the supreme legislative authority in the realm, consists of the sovereign, the House of Lords, and the House of Commons. All four countries of the kingdom—England, Scotland, Wales, and Northern Ireland—are represented in the Parliament at Westminster, London. Northern Ireland had its own parliament (Stormont) as well; however, because of civil conflict in Ulster, the Stormont was suspended on 30 March 1972, and direct rule was imposed from Westminster.

The sovereign formally calls and dismisses Parliament. The House of Lords is comprised of about 1,200 peers, including hereditary peers, spiritual peers (archbishops and bishops of the Church of England), and life peers. Over the centuries, its powers have gradually been reduced. Today, its main function is to bring the wide experience of its members into the process of lawmaking. In 1997, the House of Commons, which is elected, had 659 members: England accounts for 80%; Scotland, 11%; Wales, 6%; and Northern Ireland, 3%. All British subjects 18 years old and over may vote in national elections.

Executive power rests with the prime minister, who, though formally appointed by the sovereign, is traditionally the leader of the majority party in Parliament. The prime minister is assisted by ministers chosen from the majority party—mostly from the House of Commons, which must approve general government policy and important specific measures. The ministers with the most seniority, about 20, compose the cabinet, which meets regularly to decide policy on major issues.

The United Kingdom is divided into 53 counties and 369 districts. Below the district level are some 10,000 parishes in England and about 1,000 communities in Wales. Scotland is divided into nine regions and three island areas: Orkney, Shetland, and the Hebrides. Northern Ireland has a system of 26 districts.

In May 1998, voters in Northern Ireland and the Irish Republic approved a referendum to settle the status of Northern Ireland. The settlement includes a new elected assembly, north-south administrative links between the Irish Republic and Northern Ireland, and a council with representatives from England, Ireland, Northern Ireland, Scotland, and Wales.

14 POLITICAL PARTIES

The main political parties represented in Parliament today are the Conservative Party, the Labour Party, and the Liberal Democrats (a coalition of the Liberal and Social Democratic parties, which voted in favor of a formal merger in 1988).

The Liberal Party was a major force during the late nineteenth century. Since World War I, the Labour Party has replaced the Liberal Party as the official opposition to a Conservative government. The Labour Party favors public ownership of manufacturing, improvement of the

Photo credit: EPD/British Information Services.

Name:	Tony Blair
Position:	Prime minister of a constitutional monarchy
Took office:	2 May 1997
Birthplace:	Edinburgh, Scotland
Birth date:	6 May 1953
Education:	Fetters College, Edinburgh; St. John's College, Oxford, studied law
Spouse:	Cherie Booth (lawyer)
Children:	Four children: Euan, Nicholas, Kathryn, Leo
Of interest:	During his college years, Blair performed as an actor and was a singer in a rock band. He also has worked in the basement of a department store. Some have stated that Blair's "intelligence, energy, charm, and discipline" helped him to rise through the political ranks quickly.

social and economic conditions of the people, defense of human rights, cooperation with labor and socialist organizations of other countries, and peaceful solutions to international disputes. In foreign affairs, there has been little difference between the Labour and Conservative Parties since World War II. They differ mainly on the degree of state control to be applied to industry and commerce. The Conservative Party supports free enterprise, individual initiative, and restraining the power of the unions.

After World War II, Labour has been in power during 1945–51, 1964–70, 1974–79, and since 1997; the Conservatives held office during 1951–64, 1970–74, and 1979–97. The general election of 9 April 1992 resulted in a continuation of Conservative government under prime minister John Major with 42% of the vote and 336 seats. Labour followed with 34% of the vote and 271 seats. The Liberal Democrats took almost 18% of the vote and 20 seats. Minor parties received 3% of the vote and 17 seats.

The Labour Party, under the leadership of Tony Blair, won a landslide victory in the general election of 1 May 1997. It was the first time in 18 years that Labour won the majority. Of 659 possible seats, the Labour Party won 418 seats (43.1%), gaining 146 seats. The Conservative Party won only 165 seats (30.6%), losing 178 seats. The Liberal Democrats won 46 seats (16.7%), the most held by that party since the 1920s.

15 JUDICIAL SYSTEM

The main civil courts in England and Wales are some 300 county courts for small cases and the High Court, which is divided into the chancery division, the family division, and the Queen's Bench division for the more important cases. Appeals from the county courts may also be heard in the High Court, though the more important ones come before the Court of Appeal. A few appeals are heard before the House of Lords.

In Scotland, civil cases are heard at the sheriff courts (corresponding roughly to the English county courts) and in the Outer House of the Court of Session, which is the supreme civil court in Scotland. Appeals are heard by the Inner House of the Court of Session.

Criminal courts in England and Wales include magistrates' courts, which try less serious offenses (some 98% of all criminal cases). These consist most often of three unpaid magistrates known as justices of the peace. There are about 90 centers of the Crown Court, presided over by a bench of justices or, in the most serious cases, by a High Court judge sitting alone.

In Scotland, minor criminal cases are tried without a jury in the sheriff courts and district courts, and more serious cases with a jury in the sheriff courts. The supreme criminal court is the High Court of Justiciary.

All criminal trials are held in open court. In England, Wales, and Northern Ireland, 12-citizen juries must unanimously decide the verdict unless (with no more than two jurors dissenting) the judge directs them to return a majority verdict.

16 ARMED FORCES

Total active army strength in 2000 was 212,400 (including 15,860 women), with

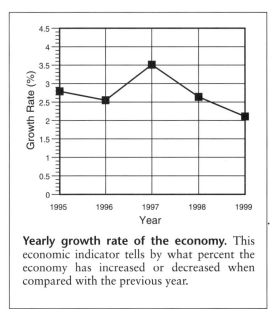

Yearly growth rate of the economy. This economic indicator tells by what percent the economy has increased or decreased when compared with the previous year.

4,367 enlisted outside the United Kingdom. As of 2000, 9,300 British troops were on active duty in Ulster, along with the 4,600 soldiers of the Royal Irish regiment. Naval forces totaled 43,700 (3,300 women), with units stationed on Gibraltar and the Falkland Islands. Naval reserves number almost 26,300. The Royal Air Force has a strength of 55,200 (5,164 women), with units deployed in Germany, Gibraltar, Cyprus, Belize, and the Falkland Islands. Combat aircraft number 462.

The defense budget for 1998–99 was an estimated $36.7 billion, or 2.6% of gross domestic product (GDP). British troops are based in several peacekeeping missions.

17 ECONOMY

The United Kingdom lives by manufacture and trade. It has few natural resources apart from coal and low-grade iron ore, some timber, building materials, hides and skins, natural gas, and North Sea oil. Farming provides nearly two-thirds of the food needed. The rest of the United Kingdom's food and most raw materials for its industries have to be imported and paid for largely through exports of manufactured goods.

By the early 1990s, the United Kingdom had far lower dependence on oil imports than in the past. Inflation averaged 6.3% a year during 1988–92 before falling to 1.6% in 1993. In 1998, inflation was 2.7%. The unemployment rate was 6.1% at the end of 1998.

18 INCOME

In 1998, the United Kingdom's gross domestic product (GDP) was $1.25 trillion, or about $21,200 per person. In 1999, the average inflation rate was 5.1%, resulting in a growth rate in GDP of 2.1%. Average weekly earnings increased by 3.4% in 1995 and by 4% in 1996.

19 INDUSTRY

The United Kingdom is one of the most highly industrialized countries in the world. Since World War II, some traditional industries have become far less important—such as cotton textiles, steel, shipbuilding, locomotives—and their place has been taken by newer industries, such as electronics, offshore oil and gas products, and synthetic fibers.

Metals, engineering, and allied industries—including steel, nonferrous metals, vehicles, and machinery—employ nearly half of all workers in manufacturing. Steel production was 18.95 million ingot tons in 1998. The United Kingdom is one of the world's largest exporters of commercial motor vehicles, with an output of 836,963 in 1995. Production of passenger cars was 1.5 million. Britain's aerospace industry is among the world's greatest.

The United Kingdom continues to produce high-quality woolen textiles. Certain smaller industries are noted for the quality of their products—for example, pottery, jewelry, goldware, and silverware. Other sectors are the cement industry (which focuses on the manufacture of Portland cement, a British invention); the rubber industry, the world's oldest; paper industries; and leather and footwear.

20 LABOR

The total working population of the United Kingdom in 1998 was nearly 28.8 million. Unemployment was 1.7 million (6.1%) in 1998.

Public administration, business services, trade, and commerce together accounts for 73% of all employment, with some 17.9 million workers. Employment in manufacturing, mining, utilities, and construction accounted for 26% of the work force. Agriculture engaged 2% of the work force.

About 10.1 million persons were members of trade unions in 1994. Equal pay for men and women doing the same work has been required by law since the end of 1975. A minimum wage was finally set in April 1999.

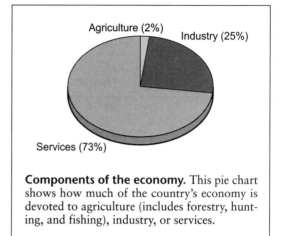

Components of the economy. This pie chart shows how much of the country's economy is devoted to agriculture (includes forestry, hunting, and fishing), industry, or services.

21 AGRICULTURE

Just more than 26% of Great Britain's land area was devoted to agriculture in 1997, roughly 70% of the farms being privately owned. Most British farms produce a variety of products. Chief crops (with estimated 1998 production in tons) were barley, 6.5 million; wheat, 15.4 million; potatoes, 6.5 million; sugar beets, 9.8 million; oats, 588,000; and rapeseed (canola) oil, 1.5 million.

22 DOMESTICATED ANIMALS

Livestock continues to be the largest segment of the farming industry. The United Kingdom raises some of the world's finest pedigreed livestock and is the leading exporter of pedigreed breeding animals. Most of the internationally famous breeds of cattle, sheep, hogs, and farm horses originated in the United Kingdom.

In 1999 there were nearly 11.3 million head of cattle (including 2 million dairy cows), 31 million sheep and goats, 7.5

million hogs, and 153 million chickens. Estimated output of livestock products for 1998 included 695,000 tons of beef and veal, 382,000 tons of mutton and lamb, 1.1 million tons of pork, 1.5 million tons of poultry, 13.9 million tons of milk, 137,000 tons of butter, 370,000 tons of cheese, and 110,000 tons of nonfat dry milk.

In March 1996, the British government reported its concern over the disease called bovine spongiform encephalopathy (BSE, commonly known as "mad cow" disease). There was concern that a new variant of Creutzfeldt-Jakob disease could appear in humans through consumption of beef tainted with BSE. As a result, the consumption of beef dropped and many countries banned imports of British beef and cattle.

In 2001, a rampant outbreak of foot and mouth disease ravaged the livestock industry in the UK. It is a highly contagious disease, and required the slaughter of millions of cattle and sheep, which then required burning and burial. The disease also had greatly affected tourism, as walkers were banned from using the paths that traverse thousands of miles of both public and private lands, because of the risk of further spread of the disease from farm to farm.

23 FISHING

The waters surrounding the British Isles are excellent fishing grounds and breeding grounds for fish. The fishing industry has been declining, but it remains important to Scotland, which catches 67% by weight of all fish caught in the United Kingdom. The total catch of fish in the United Kingdom was more than one million tons in 1997. Leading commercial species are mackerel, herring, haddock, and cod. Salmon farming takes place mainly in Scotland.

24 FORESTRY

The estimated total area of woodland in 1999 was 2.54 million hectares (6.28 million acres), or more than 10% of Great Britain's land area. Roughly 40% of the area is in England, 49% in Scotland, and 11% in Wales. The lumber industry supplies the United Kingdom with 13% of its timber demand. Almost 90% of the national requirements in wood and wood products are met by imports.

25 MINING

Except for North Sea oil deposits, the United Kingdom has comparatively few mineral resources. Traditionally, coal has been by far the most important. In 1996, an estimated 51.5 million tons of coal were mined.

Other minerals mined in quantity are sand and gravel, 96 million tons in 1996; limestone and dolomite, 16.2 million tons; crushed igneous rock, 50 million tons; kaolin (fine white clay, also known as "China clay"), 2.5 million tons; ball clay, 866,000 tons; potash, 580,000 tons; dimensional sandstone, 200,000 tons; gypsum and anhydrite, 65 million tons; fluorspar, 60,000 tons; and chalk, 10 million tons. Lead, zinc, and tungsten are worked on a small scale. The output of iron ore dropped from 916,000 tons in 1980 to 1,180 tons in 1996. The United Kingdom is the leading world producer and exporter of ball clay, and is the largest exporter and second-largest producer after the United States of kaolin.

26 FOREIGN TRADE

The United Kingdom, the world's fifth-largest trading nation, is highly dependent on foreign trade. It must import almost all its copper, ferrous metals, lead, zinc, rubber, and raw cotton; most of its tin, raw wool, hides and skins, and many other raw materials; and about one-third of its food. Principal exports in 1999 were chemicals and related products; food, beverages, and tobacco; office machines and computers; road vehicles; and petroleum and petroleum products. Principal imports that year were consumer goods, machinery, fuels, and food products.

Membership in the European Union has resulted in some adjustment of United Kingdom trade patterns. The United States was the United Kingdom's leading market through 1989. It was then replaced by Germany, which has been the largest supplier since 1982. In 1995, Germany accounted for 13.4% of total United Kingdom trade, and the United States accounted for 12.2%. Trade with the nations of the European Union increased from 43% to 52.6% between 1980 and 1995. Other principal trade partners in 1995 were France, the Netherlands, Italy, Belgium-Luxembourg, Ireland, and Japan. In 1998, the United States moved back into the position of leading trade partner with the UK.

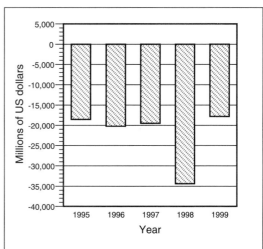

Yearly balance of trade measured in millions of US dollars. The balance of trade is the difference between what a country sells to other countries (its exports) and what it buys (its imports). If a country imports more than it exports, it has a negative balance of trade (a trade deficit). If exports exceed imports there is a positive balance of trade (a trade surplus).

27 ENERGY AND POWER

Coal supplied 22% of the United Kingdom's primary energy consumption in 1995; oil, 37%; natural gas, 30%; nuclear energy and hydroelectricity, 11%.

The United Kingdom's proven oil reserves from the North Sea totaled 5 billion barrels as of 1999. Production reached 130.3 million tons in 1995, when the United Kingdom was the ninth-largest oil producer in the world. In 1996, natural gas reserves were estimated at more than 700 billion cubic meters (25 trillion cubic feet). Production in 1995 was 71.5 billion cubic meters (2.5 trillion cubic feet), fourth highest in the world.

Selected Social Indicators

The statistics below are estimates for the period 1996 to 2000. For comparison purposes, data for the United States and averages for low-income countries and high-income countries are also given.

Indicator	United Kingdom	Low-income countries	High-income countries	United States
Per capita gross national product (GNP)†	$22,220	$1,870	$25,690	$31,910
Population growth rate	0.1%	2.1%	0.7%	1.1%
People per square kilometer of land	246	73	29	30
Life expectancy in years	77	59	78	77
Number of physicians per 1,000 people	1.5	1.0	2.5	2.5
Number of pupils per teacher (primary school)	19	41	17	14
Illiteracy rate (15 years and older)	1%	34%	<5%	3%
Television sets per 1,000 people	652	85	693	844
Energy consumed per capita (kg of oil equivalent)	3,930	550	5,366	7,937

† The GNP is the total dollar value of all goods and services produced by a country in a year. The per capita GNP is calculated by dividing a country's GNP by its population and adjusting for relative purchasing power. About 15% of the world's 6.1 billion people live in high-income countries, while 40% live in low-income countries.

n.a. = data not available   > = greater than   < = less than

Sources: World Bank. *World Development Indicators.* Washington, D.C.: The World Bank, 2001; Central Intelligence Agency. *The World Factbook.* Washington, D.C.: Government Printing Office, 2000.

Most of the United Kingdom's electricity is produced by coal-fired steam generating stations. About 25% of the public electricity supply was generated by nuclear power stations in 1998. The UK was the first country to have a nuclear power station supplying electricity to a national network.

28 SOCIAL DEVELOPMENT

A system of social security, placed in full operation in 1948, provides national insurance, industrial injuries insurance, family allowances, and national assistance throughout the United Kingdom, although the system is administered separately in Northern Ireland. The National Insurance scheme provides benefits for sickness, unemployment, maternity, and widowhood, as well as guardian's allowances, retirement pensions, and death grants.

Financial assistance for the poor is provided through supplementary benefits, in the form of either a pension or an allowance. For needy families in which the head of the household has full-time employment, a family income supplement is paid.

Women's career progress in most sectors of the economy continues, although employed women earned about 21% less in 1995 than their male counterparts (despite the 1975 law requiring equal pay). Sexual harassment is a continuing problem in the workplace.

People of Asian and African origin are sometimes subject to discrimination, even though racial discrimination is prohibited by law.

29 HEALTH

Life expectancy has increased from about 50 years in 1900–10 to about 77 years in 1999. Deaths from infectious diseases have been greatly reduced, although the proportion of deaths from circulatory diseases—including heart attacks and strokes—and cancer has risen. Since 1982, to help control the spread of AIDS, the government has begun measures for blood testing, research, public education, and other social services relating to the disease. In 1990–97, the United Kingdom had 4.7 hospital beds and 1.5 doctors per 1,000 people. Availability of beds is below demand. This results in long waits for treatment made worse by an aging population, budget cuts, and costlier treatments.

A comprehensive National Health Service (NHS), established in 1948, provides full medical care to all residents of the United Kingdom. Included are general medical, dental, pharmaceutical, and optical services; hospital and specialist services (in patients' homes when necessary) for physical and mental illnesses; and local health authority services (maternity and child welfare, vaccination, prevention of illness, health visiting, home nursing, and other services).

The NHS costs Britain's taxpayers more than $73 billion per year. An aging population, more expensive treatments, and a budget crisis have forced some NHS centers to cancel nonemergency treatment.

30 HOUSING

The United Kingdom is less crowded than most European countries. In the mid-1990s there were 23 million dwellings in the United Kingdom. About 50% of families now live in a dwelling built after 1945, usually a two-story house with a garden.

Most homeowners finance their purchase through a home mortgage loan from a building society, bank, insurance company, or other financial institution. The main providers of new subsidized housing are housing associations, which own, manage, and maintain more than 600,000 homes in England alone and completed more than 30,000 new homes for rent or shared ownership in 1994–96.

31 EDUCATION

Although responsibility for education in the United Kingdom rests with the central government, schools are mainly administered by local education authorities. Nearly the entire adult population is literate. Education is compulsory for all children between the ages of 5 and 16. In 1997, about 5.4 million children attended Britain's nearly 24,000 primary schools. Of the 2,500 registered independent schools, the largest and most important (Winchester, Eton, Harrow, for example) are known in England as "public schools." Many have centuries of tradition behind them and are world famous.

In 1991, Britain had 47 universities. In 1996, enrollment in these universities

Row houses in the Welsh countryside.

reached more than 1.8 million students, with almost 90,000 lecturers. The Universities of Oxford and Cambridge date from the twelfth and thirteenth centuries, respectively. Nearly 1.5 million students are taking full-time, postsecondary courses. National policy states that no person should be excluded from higher education by lack of money. More than 90% of students in higher education hold awards from public or private funds. In 1997, the government began to change the policy of cost-free tuition by announcing that students would have to start paying for part of the expense.

32 MEDIA

The Post Office, founded in 1635, was the first in the world to use adhesive stamps as proof of payment for mail. British Telecommunications (Telecom) encompasses a system of some 30 million telephone exchange lines.

The British Broadcasting Corporation (BBC) broadcasts on two television channels: the Independent Television Commission on ITV; and Channel Four, which began operating in 1982. The BBC has 39 local radio stations, and there are 140 independent local radio stations. In September 1992, the first national commercial radio station, Classic FM, began broadcasting. There were an estimated 1,445 radios and 652 television sets registered per 1,000 population in 2000, and 575,000 Internet hosts in 1996.

Although circulation totals have been decreasing, United Kingdom newspaper readership per person was the second highest in the world in 1995. As of that year there were about 101 daily and Sunday newspapers, some 2,000 weekly papers, numerous specialized papers, and about 7,000 periodicals. Nine Sunday papers and 12 daily morning papers are "national" in the sense of circulating throughout Britain.

Leading national dailies, with their average daily circulations in 1999, include *The Sun* (3.7 million); *The Daily Mirror* (2.3 million); *The Daily Mail* (2.4 million); *The Daily Express* (1.1 million); *The Daily Telegraph* (1 million); *The Daily Star* (650,400); *The Guardian* (393,900); *The Times* (766,900); and *The Financial Times* (384,900).

Wales has one morning daily, the *Western Mail*, with a 1999 circulation of 58,700, and four evening dailies with a circulation range between 30,500 and 76,000. Scotland has seven morning, four evening, and three Sunday papers, plus the Scottish editions of the *Daily Mail* and the *Sunday Express*. Northern Ireland has two morning papers, one evening paper, and

one Sunday paper with circulations ranging from 34,000 to 103,000, plus a number of weeklies.

Britain's ethnic minorities publish more than 60 newspapers and magazines, most of them weekly, fortnightly (once every two weeks), or monthly. These include the Chinese *Sing Tao* and *Wen Wei Po,* the Urdu *Daily Jang,* and the Arabic *Al-Arab* (all dailies), as well as newspapers in Gujarati, Bengali, Hindi, and Punjabi. The *Weekly Journal,* aimed at Britain's black community, was begun in 1992.

The 7,000 periodicals published weekly, monthly, or quarterly cover a huge range of special interests. *The Times Literary Supplement* is highly influential in cultural affairs. The chief news agency is Reuters.

33 TOURISM AND RECREATION

The world's seventh most popular tourist destination in 1994, the United Kingdom is rich in historic and cultural attractions. Among the many historic dwellings open to the public are medieval castles in Wales; 10-century-old Traquair House, the oldest continuously inhabited house in Scotland; the Palace of Holyroodhouse in Edinburgh; and Warwick Castle, near Stratford-upon-Avon, the birthplace of William Shakespeare.

Distinguished cathedrals include St. Paul's in London and those in Canterbury, Exeter, Norwich, Winchester, and York. At Bushmills, in Northern Ireland, is the oldest distillery in the world. Some of Scotland's 100 malt whiskey distilleries also offer tours.

Among London's attractions are Buckingham Palace, the Tower of London, and Westminster Abbey. London is particularly noted for its theater, including the Royal Shakespeare Company. Traditional community gatherings for music and dancing, called *ceilidhs*, are held in Scotland, and Edinburgh is the site of many music festivals.

Scotland, where golf developed in the fifteenth century, has many superb golf courses, as does the rest of the United Kingdom. Other popular sports include fishing, riding, sailing, rugby, cricket, and football (soccer). Wimbledon is the site of perhaps the world's best-known tennis competition.

Tourism brings in a great deal of money from overseas. In 1997, some 25 million foreign visitors spent $20 billion in the United Kingdom. The opening of the Channel Tunnel (under the English Channel) in 1994 has boosted travel to and from the continent.

34 FAMOUS BRITONS

Well-known English rulers include William I (the Conqueror, 1027–87), duke of Normandy, who conquered England (1066–70); Henry VIII (1491–1547), who separated the Anglican Church from the Roman Catholic Church; and Victoria (1819–1901), who greatly expanded the British Empire.

Sir Winston Leonard Spencer Churchill (1874–1965) was prime minister during World War II, and won the Nobel Prize for literature in 1953. In 1979, Margaret (Hilda Roberts) Thatcher (b.1925) became the nation's first woman prime minister. The reigning monarch since 1952 has been Queen Elizabeth II (b.1926). The heir to the throne is Charles, prince of Wales (b.1948).

Noted anthropologists include husband and wife Louis Seymour Bazett Leakey (1903–72) and Mary Leakey (1913–96), who discovered important fossil remains of early hominids in Tanzania.

Important British scientists and inventors include Sir Isaac Newton (1642–1727), who discovered gravity; German-born physicist Gabriel Daniel Fahrenheit (1686–1736), who introduced the temperature scale named after him; and Charles Darwin (1809–82), who advanced the theory of evolution.

Geoffrey Chaucer (1340?–1400), author of the *Canterbury Tales* and other works, is the best-known medieval English poet. William Shakespeare (1564–1616), is one of many fine poets and playwrights.

The mathematician Lewis Carroll (Charles Lutwidge Dodgson, 1832–98) became world-famous for two children's books, *Alice in Wonderland* and *Through the Looking Glass*. Rudyard Kipling (1865–1936), author of novels, stories, and poems, received the Nobel Prize for literature in 1907. Sir Arthur Conan Doyle (1859–1930) is known throughout the world as the creator of Sherlock Holmes. Novelist Charles Dickens (1812–70) is known for such works as *David Copperfield* and *Great Expectations*.

Important twentieth-century fiction writers include George Bernard Shaw (1856–1950), Dublin-born playwright, essayist, critic, and humorist.

Major contributors to the cinema have included the comic actor and director Charlie (Sir Charles Spencer) Chaplin (1889–1977); the director Sir Alfred Hitchcock (1899–1980); and actors Cary Grant (Archibald Alexander Leach, 1904–86), Sir Alec Guinness (1914–2000), Welsh-born Richard Burton (1925–84), Irish-born Peter O'Toole (b.1932), and Vanessa Redgrave (b.1937).

Significant twentieth-century composers include Ralph Vaughan Williams (1872–1958); Sir William Walton (1902–83); Edward Benjamin Britten (Baron Britten, 1913–76); and, in popular music, John Winston Lennon (1940–80) and James Paul McCartney (b.1942) of the Beatles.

Notable British athletes include Sir Roger Bannister (b.1929), who on 6 May 1954 became the first person to run a mile in under four minutes.

Two natives of Northern Ireland—Betty Williams (b.1943), a Protestant, and Mairead Corrigan (b.1944), a Roman Catholic—received the Nobel Peace Prize (awarded in 1977) for their leadership of a peace movement in Ulster. In 1998, the Nobel Peace Prize was shared by two Irish leaders, John Hume and David Trimble, who were similarly recognized for their efforts to bring peace to Northern Ireland.

35 BIBLIOGRAPHY

Arnold, Helen. *Great Britain*. Austin, Tex.: Raintree Steck-Vaughn, 1995.

Calcutt, Andrew. *Brit Cult: An A-Z of British Pop Culture*. London: Prion, 2000.

Cannon, John, and Ralph Griffiths. *The Oxford Illustrated History of the British Monarchy*. New York: Oxford University Press, 1988.

Dunlop, Eileen. *Websters' Leap*. New York: Holiday House, 1995.

Flint, David. *The United Kingdom*. Austin, Tex.: Raintree Steck-Vaughn, 1994.

Jenkins, Philip. *A History of Modern Wales, 1536–1990*. New York: Longman, 1992.

Kearney, Hugh F. *The British Isles: A History of Four Nations*. Cambridge; New York: Cambridge University Press, 1989.

Lace, William W. *Scotland*. San Diego, CA: Lucent Books, 2001.

Levy, Patricia. *Scotland*. New York: Marshall Cavendish, 2001.

Lyle, Garry. *England*. Philadelphia: Chelsea House, 2000.

MacLean, Fitzroy. *Scotland: A Concise History*. New York: Thames and Hudson, 1993.

Nagel, Rob, and Anne Commire. "Elizabeth I." In *World Leaders, People Who Shaped the World*. Volume II: Europe. Detroit: U*X*L, 1994.

Nagel, Rob, and Anne Commire. "Mary, Queen of Scots." In *World Leaders, People Who Shaped the World*. Volume II: Europe. Detroit: U*X*L, 1994.

Nagel, Rob, and Anne Commire. "Victoria." In *World Leaders, People Who Shaped the World*. Volume II: Europe. Detroit: U*X*L, 1994.

Nagel, Rob, and Anne Commire. "Winston Churchill." In *World Leaders, People Who Shaped the World*. Volume II: Europe. Detroit: U*X*L, 1994.

Speck, W. A. *A Concise History of Modern Britain, 1707–1975*. New York: Cambridge University Press, 1993.

Steele, Philip. *Great Britain*. New York: Crestwood House, 1994.

UNITED STATES OF AMERICA

CAPITAL: Washington, D.C. (District of Columbia).

FLAG: The flag consists of 13 alternate stripes, 7 red and 6 white; these represent the 13 original colonies. Fifty 5-pointed white stars, representing the present number of states in the Union, are placed in 9 horizontal rows alternately of 6 and 5 against a blue field in the upper left corner of the flag.

ANTHEM: *The Star-Spangled Banner.*

MONETARY UNIT: The dollar ($) of 100 cents is a paper currency with a floating rate. There are coins of 1, 5, 10, 25, and 50 cents and 1 dollar, and notes of 1, 2, 5, 10, 20, 50, and 100 dollars. Although issuance of higher notes ceased in 1969, a limited number of notes of 500, 1,000, 5,000, and 10,000 dollars remain in circulation.

WEIGHTS AND MEASURES: The imperial system is in common use; however, the use of metrics in industry is increasing, and the metric system is taught in public schools throughout the United States. Common avoirdupois units in use are the avoirdupois pound of 16 ounces or 454 grams; the long ton of 2,240 pounds or 35,840 ounces; and the short ton, more commonly used, of 2,000 pounds or 32,000 ounces. (Unless otherwise indicated, all measures given in tons are in short tons.) Liquid measures: 1 gallon = 231 cubic inches = 4 quarts = 8 pints. Dry measures: 1 bushel = 4 pecks = 32 dry quarts = 64 dry pints. Linear measures: 1 foot = 12 inches; 1 statute mile = 1,760 yards = 5,280 feet. Metric equivalent: 1 meter = 39.37 inches.

HOLIDAYS: New Year's Day, 1 January; Birthday of Martin Luther King Jr., 3d Monday in January; Presidents' Day, 3d Monday in February; Memorial or Decoration Day, last Monday in May; Independence Day, 4 July; Labor Day, 1st Monday in September; Columbus Day, 2d Monday in October; Election Day, 1st Tuesday after the 1st Monday in November; Veterans or Armistice Day, 11 November; Thanksgiving Day, 4th Thursday in November; Christmas, 25 December.

TIME: Eastern, 7 AM = noon GMT; Central, 6 AM = noon GMT; Mountain, 5 AM = noon GMT; Pacific (includes the Alaska panhandle), 4 AM = noon GMT; Yukon, 3 AM = noon GMT; Alaska and Hawaii, 2 AM = noon GMT; western Alaska, 1 AM = noon GMT.

1 LOCATION AND SIZE

Located in the Western Hemisphere on the continent of North America, the United States is the fourth-largest country in the world. Its total area, including Alaska and Hawaii, is 9.4 million square kilometers (3.6 million square miles). The contiguous United States has a total boundary length of 17,563 kilometers (10,913 miles).

Alaska, the 49th state, has an area of nearly 1.5 million square kilometers (570,374 square miles), with a total boundary length of 13,161 kilometers (8,178 miles). The 50th state, Hawaii, consists of islands in the Pacific Ocean with a total area of 16,636 square kilometers (6,423 square miles) and a combined coastline of 1,207 kilometers (750 miles).

2 TOPOGRAPHY

The northeastern coast, known as New England, is rocky, but along the rest of the eastern seaboard the Atlantic Coastal Plain rises gradually from the shoreline, merging with the Gulf Coastal Plain in Georgia. To the west is a plateau, bounded by the Appalachian Mountains, which extend from southwest Maine into central Alabama.

Between the Appalachians and the Rocky Mountains, more than 1,600 kilometers (1,000 miles) to the west, lies the vast interior plain of the United States. Its eastern reaches are bounded on the north by the Great Lakes—Lake Superior, Lake Michigan, Lake Huron, Lake Erie, and Lake Ontario—thought to contain about half the world's total supply of fresh water. The interior plain consists of two major divisions: the fertile Central Plains to the east and the drier Great Plains extending westward to the foothills of the Rocky Mountains. Running south through the center of the interior plain, and draining almost two-thirds of the area of the contiguous United States, is the Mississippi River.

The Continental Divide runs along the crest of the Rocky Mountains. The Rock-

---

Geographic Profile

Geographic Features

Size ranking: 4 of 192
Highest elevation: 6,194 meters (20,320 feet) at Mount McKinley
Lowest elevation: –86 meters (–282 feet) at Death Valley

Land Use†

Arable land:	19%
Permanent crops:	0%
Permanent pastures:	25%
Forests:	30%
Other:	26%

Weather††

Average annual precipitation: 112.3 centimeters (44.2 inches)
Average temperature in January: 0.9°C (33.6°F)
Average temperature in July: 24.9°C (76.8°F)

†*Arable land:* Land used for temporary crops, like meadows for mowing or pasture, gardens, and greenhouses. *Permanent crops:* Land cultivated with crops that occupy its use for long periods, such as cocoa, coffee, rubber, fruit and nut orchards, and vineyards. *Permanent pastures:* Land used permanently for forage crops. *Forests:* Land containing stands of trees. *Other:* Any land not specified, including built-on areas, roads, and barren land.

††The measurements for precipitation and average temperature were taken at weather stations closest to the country's largest city. Precipitation and average temperature can vary significantly within a country, due to factors such as latitude, altitude, coastal proximity, and wind patterns.

---

ies and the ranges to the west—the Sierra Nevada, the Coast, and Cascade ranges—are parts of a larger system of mountains that extends through the western part of Central and South America. Between the Rockies and the Pacific ranges lies a group of vast plateaus containing most of the nation's desert areas, known as the Great Basin. The coastal plains along the Pacific Ocean are narrow, and in many places the mountains plunge directly into the sea. The greatest rivers of the far west are the

---

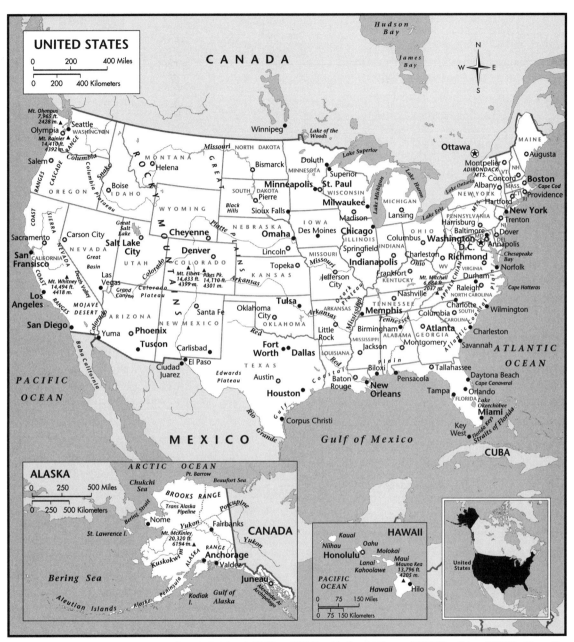

LOCATION: Conterminous US: 66°57′ to 124°44′w; 24°33′ to 49°23′N. Alaska: 130°w to 172°28′E; 51° to 71°23′N. Hawaii: 154°48′ to 178°22′w 18°55′ to 28°25′N. **BOUNDARY LENGTHS:** Conterminous US: Canada, 6,416 kilometers (3,987 miles); Atlantic Ocean, 3,330 kilometers (2,069 miles); Gulf of Mexico coastline, 2,625 kilometers (1,631 miles); Mexico, 3,111 kilometers (1,933 miles); Pacific coastline, 2,081 kilometers (1,293 miles). Alaska: Arctic Ocean coastline, 1,706 kilometers (1,060 miles); Canada, 2,475 kilometers (1,538 miles); Pacific coastline, including the Bering Sea and Strait and Chukchi coastlines, 8,980 kilometers (5,580 miles). Hawaii: coastline, 1,207 kilometers (750 miles).

Colorado in the south and the Columbia in the northwest.

Separated from the contiguous United States by Canada, the state of Alaska occupies the extreme northwest portion of North America. A series of steep mountain ranges separates the Pacific Ocean coast on the south from Alaska's broad central basin, bounded on the north by the Brooks Range, which slopes down gradually to the Arctic Ocean. The Yukon River flows from Canada in the east through the Central Basin to the Bering Sea in the west. The state of Hawaii consists of a group of Pacific islands formed by volcanoes rising sharply from the ocean floor. The largest of the islands, Hawaii, still has active volcanoes.

The lowest point in the United States is Death Valley in California, at 86 meters (282 feet) below sea level. At 6,194 meters (20,320 feet), Mt. McKinley in Alaska is the highest peak in North America. These topographic extremes show how unstable the Pacific Coast region is geologically. Major earthquakes caused great destruction in San Francisco in 1906 and Anchorage, Alaska, in 1964.

3 CLIMATE

The East Coast is affected mostly by masses of air moving from west to east across the continent. Its climate is basically continental, with clear contrasts between seasons. However, because Florida has the Gulf of Mexico lying to its west, it experiences only moderate differences between summer and winter temperatures. Mean annual temperatures vary considerably between north and south,

ranging from 11°C (51°F) in Boston to 24°C (76°F) in Miami. Annual rainfall is generally more than 100 centimeters (40 inches). The Gulf and South Atlantic states are often hit by severe tropical storms in late summer and early autumn.

The prairie lands in the middle of the country have more drought than heavy rainfall. The average midwinter temperature in the extreme north—Minnesota and North Dakota—is about –13°C (9°F) or less, while the average July temperature is 18°C (65°F). In the Texas prairie region to the south, January temperatures average 10–13°C (50–55°F) and July temperatures 27–29°C (80–85°F). Rainfall in this region is as low as 46 centimeters (18 inches).

The Great Plains are semiarid. Rainfall in the southern plains averages about 50 centimeters (20 inches) per year and in the northern plains about 25 centimeters (10 inches). The contrast between summer and winter temperatures is extreme throughout the Great Plains. Maximum summer temperatures of more than 43°C (110°F) have been recorded, while the average minimum temperature for January is –19°C (–3°F).

The higher reaches of the Rockies and the other western ranges have an alpine climate. The climate of the Western desert region varies considerably from north to south. In New Mexico, Arizona, and southeastern California, mean annual rainfall ranges from 8 centimeters (3 inches) to 76 centimeters (30 inches), while some of the mountainous areas of central Washington and Idaho receive at least 152 centimeters (60 inches) of rain per year. Phoenix, Arizona, has a mean annual temperature of 22°C (71°F).

The Pacific Coast has a maritime climate, with mild winters and moderately warm, dry summers. Los Angeles in the south has an average temperature of 13°C (56°F) in January and 21°C (69°F) in July; Seattle in the north has an average temperature of 4°C (39°F) in January and 18°C (65°F) in July. Precipitation ranges from an annual average of 4.52 centimeters (1.78 inches) at Death Valley in California (the lowest in the United States) to more than 356 centimeters (140 inches) in Washington's mountain regions.

Alaska has varied climatic conditions. The Aleutian Islands and the coastal panhandle strip have a moderate maritime climate. The interior is characterized by short, hot summers and long, bitterly cold winters. In the region bordering the Arctic Ocean a polar climate prevails, the soil hundreds of feet below the surface remaining frozen year-round.

Northeast ocean winds give Hawaii a mild, stable climate. The mean temperature in Honolulu is 23°C (73°F) in January and 27°C (80°F) in July. Rainfall is moderate—about 71 centimeters (28 inches) per year—but much greater in the mountains.

The lowest temperature recorded in the United States was −62°C (−79.8°F) in Alaska at Prospect Creek Camp on 23 January 1971; the highest, 57°C (134°F) in California at Greenland Ranch in Death Valley on 10 July 1913. The record annual rainfall is 1,468 centimeters (578 inches) on Maui in Hawaii in 1950.

4 PLANTS AND ANIMALS

At least 7,000 species and subspecies of native United States plants have been categorized. Wildflowers bloom in all areas, from the seldom-seen blossoms of rare desert cacti to the hardiest alpine species. The eastern forests contain a mixture of softwoods and hardwoods that includes pine, birch, maple, and hickory. The central hardwood forest—still an important timber source—contains oak, ash, and walnut among others. Tupelo, pecan, and sycamore are found in the southern forest that stretches along the coast of the Gulf of Mexico into the eastern half of Texas. The forest along the Pacific Ocean coast is spectacular with its enormous redwoods and Douglas firs. In the southwest are saguaro (giant cactus), yucca, candlewood, and the Joshua tree.

Mesquite grass covers parts of west Texas, southern New Mexico, and Arizona. Short grass may be found in the highlands of the latter two states, while tall grass covers large portions of Texas and Louisiana. The Western desert supports sagebrush, creosote, and—near the Great Salt Lake and in Death Valley—saltbrush. Coniferous forests are found on the lower mountain slopes. The central part of the Yukon Basin in Alaska also is a region of softwood forests, while the rest of the state is heath or tundra. Hawaii has extensive forests of bamboo and ferns.

An estimated 1,500 species and subspecies of mammals are found in the continental United States. Among the larger game animals are the white-tailed deer, moose, mountain goat, black bear, and

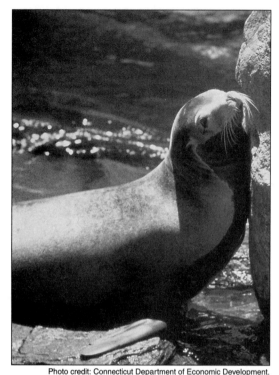

Photo credit: Connecticut Department of Economic Development.

A seal relaxing under the sun's rays at the Mystic Marinelife Aquarium in Connecticut.

grizzly bear. The Alaskan brown bear often reaches a weight of 540–635 kilograms (1,200–1,400 pounds). Some 25 important furbearers are common, including the muskrat, red and gray foxes, mink, raccoon, and beaver. The American buffalo (bison), millions of which once roamed the plains, is now found only on select reserves.

Year-round and migratory birds abound. Loons, wild ducks, and wild geese are found in lake country; terns, gulls, sandpipers, and other seabirds live along the coasts. Wrens, owls, hummingbirds, sparrows, woodpeckers, swallows, and finches appear in large numbers, along with the robin, cardinal, Baltimore oriole, and various blackbirds. Wild turkey, ruffed grouse, and ring-necked pheasant (introduced from Europe) are popular game birds.

Lakes, rivers, and streams are full of trout, bass, perch, carp, catfish, and pike. Sea bass, cod, snapper, and flounder are abundant along the coasts, along with such shellfish as lobster, shrimp, clams, oysters, and mussels. Four poisonous snakes survive, of which the rattlesnake is the most common. Alligators appear in southern waterways, and the Gila monster makes its home in the southwest.

5 ENVIRONMENT

The Environmental Protection Agency (EPA), created in 1970, is the main federal government agency responsible for control of air and noise pollution, water and waste management, and control of toxic substances.

Landmark federal laws protecting the environment include the Clean Air Act Amendments of 1970 and 1990, controlling automobile and electric utility emissions; and the Endangered Species Act of 1973, protecting wildlife near extinction.

The most influential environmental lobbies and conservation groups (with 2001 membership) include the National Wildlife Federation (4.4 million); the National Audubon Society (600,000); the Sierra Club (550,000); and the Nature Conservancy (1 million). Greenpeace USA (250,000 members) has gained international attention by trying to stop whale and seal hunts.

Among the environmental movement's most notable successes have been the creation of recycling programs; the banning in the United States of the insecticide dichlorodiphenyltrichloroethane (DDT); the protection of more than 40 million hectares (100 million acres) of Alaska lands; and the gradual elimination of chlorofluorocarbon (CFC) production by the year 2000.

A continuing environmental problem is pollution of the nation's water by dumping of raw or partially treated sewage from major cities into United States waterways. In addition, runoffs of agricultural pesticides are deadly to fishing streams and very difficult to regulate. The amount of land suitable for farming has decreased due to erosion, depletion of the soil, and urbanization.

Facilities for solid waste disposal are still inadequate, and the United States nuclear industry has expanded without having a good way to dispose of radioactive wastes. Other environmental issues include acid rain (precipitation contaminated from burning coal); the contamination of homes by radon (a radioactive gas that is produced by the decay of underground deposits of radium and that can cause cancer); and the lack of available water in many western states due to overpopulation in naturally drier areas.

As of 1996, the United States Fish and Wildlife Service listed 752 endangered species in the United States, including 432 plants. There also were 207 threatened species, including 93 plants. The agency listed another 522 endangered and 42

threatened foreign species by international agreement.

6 POPULATION

According to census figures for 2000, the population of the United States (including the 50 states and Washington, D.C.) was 281.4 million (up from 226.5 million in 1980), of whom 50.9% were female and 49.1% male. The median age of the population increased from 16.7 years in 1820 to 22.9 years in 1900, and to 35.3 years in 2000. The United States Bureau of the Census projected a population of 288.3 million for the year 2005. Population density varies greatly from region to region; the average is 30.7 persons per square kilometer (19 per square mile).

Suburbs have absorbed most of the shift in population distribution since 1950. In 2000 there were nine cities with more than 1 million population each.

7 MIGRATION

Between 1840 and 1930, some 37 million immigrants, most of them Europeans, arrived in the United States. In 1924 a quota system was established that favored immigrants from northern and western Europe. The quota system was radically reformed in 1965 and abandoned in 1978, when all specific limits by nationality were replaced by a simple total limit of 290,000. A major 1990 overhaul of immigration laws raised the annual ceiling to 675,000 in 1995.

Between 1990 and 1997, international migration increased the country's population by an estimated 5.63 million. In 1997

Photo credit: Oklahoma Tourism Photo by Fred W. Marvel.

American Indian Exposition, Anadarko, Oklahoma.

alone, about 827,000 immigrants entered the United States. In 1994, some 36.4% came from Asia, 39.8% from the Americas, 20% from Europe, 3.3% from Africa, and 0.5% from Pacific Island nations. The changes in immigration law have resulted in a sharp rise in the number of Asian immigrants (primarily Chinese, Filipinos, Indians, Japanese, and Koreans).

Between 1975 and 1978, following the defeat of the American-backed Saigon government in South Vietnam, several hundred thousand Vietnamese refugees came to the United States. Under the Refugee Act of 1980, a limit to the number of refugees allowed to enter the United States is set annually. More than 500,000

Cubans were living in southern Florida by 1980, when another 125,000 Cuban refugees arrived. In 1995, 99,490 immigrants were admitted under the various refugee acts.

In November 1986, Congress passed a bill allowing illegal aliens who had lived and worked in the United States since 1982 the opportunity to become permanent residents. By the end of fiscal year 1992, nearly 2.7 million persons had become permanent residents under this bill. In 1996 the number of illegal alien residents was estimated at 5 million, of whom 2 million were believed to be in California.

The major migratory trends within the United States in the twentieth century have been an exodus of southern blacks to the cities of the North and Midwest, especially after World War I (1914–18); a shift of whites from central cities to surrounding suburbs since World War II (after 1945); and, also during the post–World War II period, a massive shift from the North and East to the South and Southwest.

8 ETHNIC GROUPS

The majority of the population of the United States is of European origin. The largest groups in 1990 trace their ancestry to the United Kingdom (31.4 million), Germany (45.6 million), and Ireland (22.7 million). Many Americans have mixed ancestries. Major racial and national minority groups include blacks (either of United States or Caribbean parentage), Chinese, Filipinos, Japanese, Mexicans, and other Spanish-speaking peoples of the Americas. Whites comprised 75.1% of the United States population in 2000; blacks, 12.2%; Asians and Pacific Islanders, 3.6%; Native Americans (Amerindians—more commonly known as Indians, Eskimos, and Aleuts), 0.9%. The 2000 census reports that 2.4% of Americans claimed two or more races.

In 2000, 12.5% of Americans were of Hispanic origin: Mexican, 7.3%; Puerto Rican, 1.2%; Cuban, 0.4%; and other Hispanic or Latino, 3.6%. People of Hispanic origin can be of any race.

In 2000, there were 2.47 million Amerindians in the United States, found mostly in the southwestern states of Oklahoma, Arizona, New Mexico, and California.

The black population in 2000 totaled 34.6 million. More than three out of four black Americans live in cities.

Included in the population of the United States in 2000 were 10.2 million persons who are of Asian and Pacific descent, chiefly Chinese, 1.7 million; Filipino, 1.4 million; Japanese, 866,160; Indian, 786,694; Korean, 797,304; and Vietnamese, 593,213. The proportion of Asians and Pacific Islanders in Hawaii was the highest in the country, making Hawaii the only state with an Asian and Pacific Islander majority. The Japanese population of Hawaii accounted in 2000 for 16.7% of the state's residents. As of 2000 there were nearly 35.5 million Hispanic Americans.

9 LANGUAGES

The primary language of the United States is English, enriched by words borrowed from the languages of Native Americans and immigrants, mostly European.

The 1990 census recorded that of 229.9 million Americans five years of age or over, 198.1 million spoke only English at home; the remaining 31.8 million spoke a language other than English. The principal foreign languages and their speakers were as follows: Spanish, 17.3 million; French, 1.9 million; German, 1.5 million; Chinese, 1.3 million; and Italian, 1.3 million. Refugee immigration has greatly increased the number of foreign-language speakers from Latin America and Asia.

Educational problems raised by the presence of large numbers of non-English speakers led to the passage in 1976 of the

Bilingual Educational Act, allowing children to study basic courses in their first language while they learn English. A related school issue is that of black English, a Southern dialect variant that is spoken by many black students now in northern schools.

10 RELIGIONS

United States religious traditions are predominantly Judeo-Christian, and most Americans identify themselves as Protestants (of various denominations), Roman Catholics, or Jews. As of 1995, 163 million Americans, or 63% of the total population, reported association with a religious group.

The largest Christian denomination is the Roman Catholic Church, with 59.9 million members in 19,787 parishes in 1995. Immigration from western Europe and the Caribbean accounts for the large number of Roman Catholics in the Northeast, Northwest, and some parts of the Great Lakes region. Hispanic traditions and more recent immigration from Mexico and other Latin American countries account for the historical importance of Roman Catholicism in California and throughout the Southwest. Jewish immigrants settled first in the Northeast, where the largest Jewish population remains; in 1994, nearly 6 million American Jews were affiliated with more than 3,400 local congregations served by 6,500 clergy.

As of 1992, Protestant groups in the United States had at least 94.6 million members. By far the nation's largest Protestant group, the Southern Baptist Convention, had 15.4 million members in 1992; the American Baptist Churches in the USA claimed a membership of some 1.5 million. A concentration of Methodist groups extends westward in a band from Delaware to eastern Colorado; the largest of these groups, the United Methodist Church, had 8.6 million members in 1992.

Lutheran denominations, reflecting in part the patterns of German and Scandinavian settlement, are most highly concentrated in the north-central states, especially Minnesota and the Dakotas. Two Lutheran synods, the Lutheran Church in America and the American Lutheran Church merged in 1987 to form the Evangelical Lutheran Church in America, with 5.2 million members in 1992. In 1999 the Evangelical Lutheran Church in America adopted an agreement to establish a closer relationship with the Episcopal Church.

In June 1983, the two major Presbyterian churches, the northern-based United Presbyterian Church in the USA and the southern-based Presbyterian Church in the US, formally merged as the Presbyterian Church (USA), ending a division that began with the Civil War. This denomination had 3.8 million members in 1992.

Other Protestant denominations and their estimated memberships in 1992 were the Episcopal Church, 2.5 million; Church of Christ, 1.7 million; and the United Church of Christ (Congregationalist), 1.5 million. One Christian-based group, the Church of Latter-day Saints (Mormon), which claimed 4.7 million members in 1992, was organized in New York in 1830 and, since migrating westward, has played a leading role in Utah's political, economic, and religious life. During the 1970s and early 1980s there was a rise in the fundamentalist, evangelical, and Pentecostal movements.

Many native Americans continue to follow their traditional religions. Several million Muslims, Eastern Orthodox Christians, followers of various Asian religions, a number of small Protestant groups, and a sizable number of cults also participate in United States religious life. During the last two decades of the twentieth century, there was a rise in feminist spirituality, New Age, earth-centered, and Neo-Pagan movements.

11 TRANSPORTATION

The United States has well-developed systems of railroads, highways, inland waterways, oil pipelines, and domestic airways. Despite an attempt to encourage more people to travel by train through the development of a national network (Amtrak) in the 1970s, rail transport has continued to experience heavy financial losses. In 1993, 21.8 million people rode on Amtrak. Railroads carried more than 1.8 billion tons of cargo through 27.3 million rail-carloads handled in 1995.

The most widely used form of transportation is the automobile, and the extent and quality of the United States road-transport system are the best in the world. More than 204 million vehicles—a record number—were registered in 1997, including more than 128.5 million passenger cars and some 65.5 million trucks and buses. In 1995, 31% of the world's motor vehicles were registered in the United States, down from 36% in 1985. The United States has a vast network of public roads, whose total length as of 31 December 1995 was 6.3 million kilometers (3.9 million miles).

Major ocean ports or port areas are New York, Philadelphia, Baltimore, Norfolk, New Orleans, Houston, and the San Francisco Bay area. The inland port of Duluth on Lake Superior handles more freight than all but the top-ranking ocean ports. In 1998, the United States had a registered merchant shipping fleet of 385 vessels, with a total of 11.1 million gross registered tons.

In 1995, the United States had 26 international scheduled airlines. Passengers carried by the airlines in 1997 totaled 590 million. The United States in 1998 had 14,459 air facilities, of which 5,167 were public. An estimated 187,312 general aviation aircraft (excluding commuters) flew a total of 26.1 million hours in 1996. As of 2000 the busiest airport was Hartsfield in Atlanta, Georgia, which surpassed O'Hare in Chicago, Illinois.

12 HISTORY

Origins

The first Americans—distant ancestors of the American Indians—probably crossed the Bering Strait from Asia at least 12,000 years ago. By the time Christopher Columbus came to the New World (as America was known) in 1492 there were probably about 2 million Native Americans living in the land that was to become the United States.

The Spanish established the first permanent settlement at St. Augustine in the future state of Florida in 1565, and another in New Mexico in 1599. During the early seventeenth century, the English founded Jamestown in present-day Virginia (1607) and Plymouth Colony in present-day Massachusetts (1620). The Dutch and Swedish also established settlements in the seventeenth century, but the English eventually took over settlement of the East Coast except for Florida, where the Spanish ruled until 1821. In the Southwest, California, Arizona, New Mexico, and Texas also were part of the Spanish empire until the nineteenth century.

The American Revolution

The colonies enjoyed a large measure of self-government until the end of the French and Indian War (1745–63), which resulted in the loss of French Canada to the British. To prevent further troubles with the Indians, the British government in 1763 prohibited the American colonists from settling beyond the Appalachian Mountains. The British also enacted a series of tax measures, which the colonists protested, setting off a struggle between colonial and British authority.

A series of conflicts led to the colonists' decision to separate from British rule and set up their own independent government. George Washington was appointed commander-in-chief of the new American army, and on 4 July 1776, the 13 American colonies adopted the Declaration of Independence. The American Revolution was officially begun.

Photo credit: Delaware Tourism Office.

Liberty Bell in front of Legislator Hall, in Dover, the state capital of Delaware.

British and American forces met in their first organized encounter near Boston on 17 June 1775. Numerous battles up and down the East Coast followed. The entry of France into the war on the American side eventually tipped the balance. On 19 October 1781, the British commander, Charles Cornwallis, surrendered his army at Yorktown, Virginia. American independence was acknowledged by the British in a treaty of peace signed in Paris on 3 September 1783.

The Beginnings of American Government

The first constitution uniting the 13 original states—the Articles of Confederation—denied Congress power to raise taxes or regulate commerce, and many of its authorized powers required the approval of a minimum of nine states. In 1787 Congress passed the Northwest Ordinance, providing for the establishment of new territories on the frontier. In that same year, a convention assembled in Philadelphia to revise the articles. The convention adopted an altogether new document, the present Constitution of the United States, which greatly increased the powers of the central government at the expense of the states.

This document was ratified by the states with the understanding that it would be amended to include a bill of rights guaranteeing certain fundamental freedoms. These freedoms—including the rights of free speech, press, and assembly, freedom from unreasonable search and seizure, and the right to a speedy and public trial by an impartial jury—are assured by the first ten amendments to the constitution, known as the "Bill of Rights," adopted on 5 December 1791. The constitution did recognize slavery, and did not provide for universal suffrage. On 30 April 1789 George Washington was inaugurated as the first president of the United States.

The Federalist Party, to which Washington belonged, was opposed to the French Revolution (1789), while the Democratic-Republicans (an anti-Federalist party led by Thomas Jefferson) supported it. This division of the nation's leadership was the beginning of the two-party system, which has been the dominant characteristic of the United States political scene ever since.

Westward Expansion

In 1803, President Thomas Jefferson purchased the Louisiana Territory from France, including all the present territory of the United States west of the Mississippi drained by that river and its tributaries. Exploration and mapping of the new territory, particularly through the expeditions of Meriwether Lewis and William Clark, began almost immediately.

To make room for the westward expansion of European American settlement, the federal government in 1817 began a policy of forcibly resettling the Indians. They were moved to what later became known as Indian Territory (now Oklahoma); those Indians not forced to move were restricted to reservations. This "removal" of Native Americans to make way for European American settlement was a form of genocide (the deliberate destruction of a whole race, culture, or group of people).

The Missouri Compromise (1820) provided for admission of Missouri into the Union as a slave state but banned slavery in territories to the west that lay north of 36°30′. And in 1823 President James Monroe declared the Western Hemisphere closed to further colonization by European powers.

Development of Farming and Industry

Farming expanded with westward migration. The cotton gin, invented by Eli Whit-

Lewis and Clark monument at Fort Benton in Montana.

New States and the Slavery Question

In 1836, United States settlers in Texas revolted against Mexican rule and established an independent republic. Texas was admitted to the Union as a state in 1845. War with Mexico over a boundary dispute led in 1848 to the addition of California and New Mexico to the growing nation. A dispute with Britain over the Oregon Territory was settled in 1846 by a treaty that established the 49th parallel as the boundary with Canada.

Westward expansion increased the conflict over slavery in the new territories. The Kansas-Nebraska Act of 1854 repealed the Missouri Compromise and left the question of slavery in the territories to be decided by the settlers themselves. Finally, the election of Abraham Lincoln to the presidency in 1860 led strong supporters of slavery to decide to secede from the United States altogether.

ney in 1793, greatly simplified cotton production, and the growing textile industry in New England and Great Britain needed a lot of cotton. So the South remained an agricultural society based mostly on a one-crop economy. Large numbers of field hands were required for cotton farming, and black slavery became a significant part of the southern economy.

The successful completion of the Erie Canal (1825), linking the Great Lakes with the Atlantic, began a canal-building boom. Railroad building began in earnest in the 1830s, and by 1840 about 5,300 kilometers (3,300 miles) of track had been laid.

The Civil War

Between December 1860 and February 1861, the seven states of the Deep South—South Carolina, Mississippi, Florida, Alabama, Georgia, Louisiana, and Texas—withdrew from the Union and formed a separate government. They were known as the Confederate States of America, under the presidency of Jefferson Davis. On 12 April 1861, the Confederates opened fire on Fort Sumter in the harbor of Charleston, South Carolina, beginning the United States Civil War. Arkansas, North Carolina, Virginia, and Tennessee quickly joined the Confederacy.

For the next four years, war raged between the Confederate and Union forces, largely in southern territories. An estimated 360,000 men in the Union forces lost their lives, including 110,000 killed in battle. Confederate dead were estimated at 250,000, including 94,000 killed in battle. The North, with more fighters and resources, finally won. With much of the South in Union hands, Confederate General Robert E. Lee surrendered to Union General Ulysses S. Grant at Appomattox Courthouse in Virginia on 9 April 1865.

The Post-Civil War Era

President Lincoln's Emancipation Proclamation of 1863 was the first step in freeing some four million black slaves. Their liberation was completed soon after the war's end by amendments to the Constitution. Five days after General Lee's surrender, Lincoln was assassinated by John Wilkes Booth. During the Reconstruction era (1865–77), the defeated South was governed by Union Army commanders. The resulting bitterness of southerners toward northern Republican rule, which gave blacks the rights of citizens, including the right to vote, lasted for years afterward. By the end of the Reconstruction era, whites had reestablished their political domination over blacks in the southern states and had begun to enforce rules of segregation that lasted for nearly a century.

Outside the South, the age of big business dawned. Pittsburgh, Chicago, and New York emerged as the nation's great industrial centers. The American Federation of Labor, founded in 1886, established a nationwide system of organized labor that remained dominant for many decades. During this period, too, the woman's rights movement began to organize to fight for the right to vote. It took women until 1920 to win their constitutional right of suffrage.

The 1890s marked the closing of the United States frontier for settlement and the beginning of United States overseas expansion. (Alaska had already been acquired from Russia for $7.2 million in 1867.) In 1898, at its own request, Hawaii was annexed as a territory by the United States. In the same year, as a result of the Spanish-American War, the United States added the Philippines, Guam, and Puerto Rico to its territories. A newly independent Cuba became a United States near-protectorate until the 1950s. In 1903, the United States leased the Panama Canal Zone and started construction of a 68-kilometer (42-mile) canal, completed in 1914.

World War I to World War II

United States involvement in World War I marked the country's emergence as one of the great powers of the world. By late 1917, when United States troops joined the Allied forces in the fighting on the western front, the European armies were approaching exhaustion. American intervention may well have been a key element in the eventual victory of the Allies. Fighting ended with the armistice (truce) of 11 November 1918. President Woodrow Wilson played an active role in drawing up the 1919 Versailles peace treaty.

The 1920s saw a major business boom, followed by the great stock market crash of October 1929, which ushered in the longest and most serious economic depression the country had ever known. The election of Franklin D. Roosevelt, in March 1933, began a new era in United States history, in which the federal government took a much greater role in the nation's economic affairs. Relief measures were instituted, work projects established, and the federal Social Security program was set up. The National Labor Relations Act established the right of employees' organizations to bargain collectively with employers.

Following German, Italian, and Japanese aggression, World War II broke out in Europe during September 1939. In 1940, Roosevelt, ignoring a tradition dating back to Washington that no president should serve more than two terms, ran again for reelection. He easily defeated his Republican opponent, Wendell Willkie.

The United States was brought actively into the war by the Japanese attack on the Pearl Harbor naval base in Hawaii on 7 December 1941. United States forces waged war across the Pacific, in Africa, in Asia, and in Europe. Germany was successfully invaded in 1944 and conquered in May 1945. After the United States dropped the world's first atomic bombs on Hiroshima and Nagasaki in Japan, the Japanese surrendered in August.

Korean War and Civil Rights Movement

The United States became an active member of the new world organization, the United Nations, during President Harry S Truman's administration. In 1949 the North Atlantic Treaty Organization (NATO) established a defensive alliance among a number of West European nations and the United States. Following the North Korean attack on South Korea on 25 June 1950, the United Nations Security Council decided that members of the United Nations should go to the aid of South Korea. United States naval, air, and ground forces were immediately sent by President Truman. An undeclared war followed, which eventually was ended by a truce signed on 27 June 1953.

During President Dwight D. Eisenhower's administration, the United States Supreme Court's decision in *Brown v. Board of Education of Topeka* (1954) outlawed segregation of whites and blacks in public schools. In the early 1960s, sit-ins, freedom rides, and similar expressions of nonviolent resistance by blacks and their sympathizers—known collectively as the Civil Rights Movement—led to the end of some segregation practices.

In the early 1960s, during the administration of President Eisenhower's Democratic successor, John F. Kennedy, the Cold War heated up as Cuba, under the regime of Fidel Castro, aligned itself with the Soviet Union. In October 1962, President Kennedy successfully forced a showdown with the Soviet Union over Cuba in demanding the withdrawal of Soviet-supplied missiles from the nearby island. On 22 November 1963, President Kennedy was assassinated while riding in a motorcade through Dallas, Texas. Hours later, Vice President Lyndon B. Johnson was inaugurated president. President Johnson's ambitious "Great Society" program sought to ensure black Americans' rights in voting and public housing, to give the underprivileged job training, and to provide persons 65 and over with hospitalization and other medical benefits.

The Vietnam War and Watergate

In 1965, President Johnson sent American combat troops to support anti-communist forces in South Vietnam and ordered United States bombing raids on communist North Vietnam. But American military might was unable to defeat the Vietnamese guerrillas, and the American people were badly divided over continuing the undeclared war.

Under President Richard M. Nixon (elected in 1968), the increasingly unpopular and costly war continued for four more years before a cease-fire was finally signed on 27 January 1973 and the last American soldiers were withdrawn. Two years later, the South Vietnamese army collapsed, and the North Vietnamese communist regime united the country. In 1972, President Nixon opened up relations with the People's Republic of China, which had been closed to Westerners since 1949. He also signed a strategic arms limitation agreement with the Soviet Union. (Earlier, in July 1969, American technology had achieved a national triumph by landing the first astronaut on the Moon.)

The Watergate scandal began on 17 June 1972 with the arrest of five men associated with Nixon's reelection campaign during a break-in at Democratic Party headquarters in the Watergate office building in Washington, D.C. Although Nixon was reelected in 1972, further investigations by the press and by a Senate investigating committee revealed a pattern of political "dirty tricks" and illegal wiretapping and other methods of spying on his opponents throughout his first term. The House voted to begin impeachment proceedings. On 9 August 1974, Nixon became the first president to resign the office. The American people's trust in their government leaders was seriously damaged.

The Reagan Era

Gerald R. Ford was appointed vice president in October 1973 to succeed ousted Vice President Spiro T. Agnew. Ford became president in August 1974 when Nixon resigned. Less than a month after taking office, President Ford granted a full pardon to Nixon for any crimes he may have committed as president. Ford's pardon of Nixon probably contributed to his narrow defeat by a Georgia Democrat, Jimmy Carter, in 1976. During 1978–79, President Carter convinced the Senate to pass treaties ending United States sovereignty over the Panama Canal Zone. He also mediated a peace agreement between Israel and Egypt, signed at the Camp David, Maryland, retreat in September 1978. But an economic recession and a prolonged quarrel with Iran over more than 50 United States hostages seized in Tehran on 4 November 1979 caused the American public to doubt his leadership. Exactly a year after the hostages were taken, former California governor Ronald Reagan defeated Carter in the 1980 presi-

Photo credit: Photo by South Dakota Tourism.

Mount Rushmore, Black Hills, South Dakota.

dential election. The hostages were released on 20 January 1981, the day of Reagan's inauguration.

President Reagan used his popularity to push through significant policy changes. He made cuts in income tax and more than doubled the military budget between 1980 and 1989, which resulted in a doubling of the national debt. In an effort to balance the federal budget, Reagan cut welfare and Medicare benefits, reduced allocations for food stamps, and slashed the budget of the Environmental Protection Agency.

Reagan's appointment of Sandra Day O'Connor as the first woman justice of the Supreme Court was widely praised and won unanimous confirmation from the Senate. Protests were raised, however, about his decisions to help the government of El Salvador in its war against leftist rebels, to aid groups in Nicaragua trying to overthrow the leftist Sandinista government in their country, and to send American troops to Grenada in October 1983 to overthrow a leftist government there.

Presidents Bush and Clinton

Reagan was succeeded in 1988 by his vice president, George Bush. President Bush used his personal relationships with foreign leaders to bring about peace talks between Israel and its Arab neighbors, to encourage a peaceful unification of Germany, and to negotiate significant arms cuts with the Russians. Bush sent 400,000 American soldiers to lead the way in forming a multinational coalition to oppose Iraq's invasion of Kuwait in 1990. The multinational forces destroyed Iraq's main force within seven months.

One of the biggest crises that the Bush administration encountered was the collapse of the savings and loan industry in the late 1980s. The federal government was forced by law to rescue the savings and loan banks, under the Federal Savings and Loan Insurance Corporation (FSLIC), costing taxpayers more than $100 billion.

In the 1992 presidential election, Democrat Bill Clinton (b.1946), governor of Arkansas, defeated Bush, winning 43% of the vote to Bush's 38% and third-party candidate Ross Perot's 18%. Clinton's major achievements as president included the passage of a budget designed to raise revenue and thereby lower the deficit, which had ballooned during the Reagan and Bush years. Clinton also persuaded Congress to approve the North American Free Trade Agreement (NAFTA), which removed or reduced tariffs on most goods moving across the borders of the United States, Canada, and Mexico.

In the 1994 midterm elections, the Republican Party gained control of both houses of Congress for the first time in more than 40 years. The elections indicated popular disappointment with the Clinton administration and the Democrat-controlled Congress.

The nation's economic recovery from the 1990–91 recession gained strength as the decade advanced, with healthy growth, falling unemployment, and moderate interest rate and inflation levels. Between 1995 and 1997, the value of the stock market increased 60%. Clinton's faltering popularity rebounded in 1996 when he was reelected, becoming the first Democratic president elected to a second term since Franklin D. Roosevelt. The Republicans retained control of both houses of Congress.

In 1994, Attorney General Janet Reno appointed Kenneth Starr to the position of special prosecutor. His job was to investigate allegations of financial wrongdoing by President Clinton and his wife, Hillary Rodham Clinton. In 1998, Starr submitted a report to Congress that charged President Clinton with potentially impeachable offenses. These offenses related to testimony given in a sexual harassment lawsuit brought against Clinton for actions allegedly taken while Clinton was governor of Arkansas. Starr's report, and public and Congressional reaction to it, seriously hindered Clinton's ability to carry out his leadership as president.

In one of the closest and most controversial presidential elections in history, Republican George W. Bush, son of a former president, was elected after defeating Democrat Vice President Al Gore. Bush took office on 20 January 2001.

13 FEDERAL GOVERNMENT

The Constitution of the United States, signed in 1787, is the nation's governing document. In the first ten amendments to

Photo credit: EPD/The White House.

Name:	George W. Bush
Position:	President of a federal republic
Took office:	20 January 2001
Birthplace:	Midland, Texas
Birth date:	6 July 1946
Religion:	Methodist
Education:	Yale University; Harvard Business School, master's of business administration (MBA)
Spouse:	Laura Welch Bush
Children:	Twin daughters, Barbara and Jenna
Of interest:	Bush served as an F-102 pilot for the Texas Air National Guard before beginning his career in the oil and gas business in 1975. He was co-owner of the Texas Rangers baseball franchise. He also owns two dogs, Spot and Barney, and a cat, India.

the Constitution, ratified in 1791 and known as the Bill of Rights, certain rights are guaranteed to United States citizens. In all, there have been 26 amendments to the Bill of Rights, including the 13th Amendment (1865) which banned slavery, and the 19th (1920), which gave women the right to vote. Suffrage is universal beginning at age 18, as set by the 26th Amendment (1971).

The United States has a federal form of government, with the distribution of powers between federal and state governments constitutionally defined. The legislative powers of the federal government rest in Congress, which consists of the House of Representatives and the Senate. There are 435 members of the House of Representatives. Each state is given a number of representatives in proportion to its population. Representatives are elected for two-year terms in every even-numbered year. The Senate consists of two senators from each state, elected for six-year terms. One-third of the Senate is elected in every even-numbered year.

A bill that is passed by both houses of Congress in the same form is then given to the president, who may sign it or veto (reject) it. The president must be a citizen born in the United States, at least 35 years old, and must have been a resident of the United States for 14 years. Under the 22nd Amendment to the Constitution, adopted in 1951, a president may not be elected more than twice.

The vice president, elected at the same time and on the same ballot as the president, serves as president of the Senate. The vice president assumes the power and duties of the presidency on the president's removal from office or as a result of the president's death, resignation, or inability to perform his duties. Both the president and the vice president can be removed from office after impeachment by the House and conviction at a Senate trial for "treason, bribery, or other high crimes and misdemeanors."

The president nominates and, with the approval of the Senate, appoints ambassadors, consuls, and all federal judges, including the justices of the Supreme Court. As commander in chief, the president is ultimately responsible for the management of the land, naval, and air forces, but the power to declare war belongs to Congress. The president conducts foreign relations and makes treaties with the advice and consent of the Senate. No treaty is binding unless it wins the approval of two-thirds of the Senate. The president's independence also is limited by the House of Representatives, where all money bills originate.

The president also appoints his cabinet, subject to Senate confirmation. The cabinet consists of the secretaries who head the departments of the executive branch. As of 1997, the executive branch included the following cabinet departments: Agriculture, Commerce, Defense, Education, Energy, Health and Human Services, Housing and Urban Development, Interior, Justice, Labor, State, Transportation, Treasury, and Veterans' Affairs.

Each state is divided into counties, municipalities, and special districts such as those for water, education, sanitation, highways, parks, and recreation. There are more than 3,000 counties in the United States and more than 19,000 municipalities, including cities, villages, towns, and boroughs.

14 POLITICAL PARTIES

Two major parties, Democratic and Republican, have dominated national, state, and local politics since 1860. Minority parties have been formed at various periods in American political history, but none has had any lasting national impact. The most successful minority party in recent decades was that of Texas billionaire Ross Perot in 1992. Independent candidates have won state and local office, but no candidate has won the presidency without major party backing.

Traditionally, the Republican Party is more sympathetic to business interests and gets greater support from business than does the Democratic Party. A majority of blue-collar workers, by contrast, have generally supported the Democratic Party, which favors more lenient labor laws, particularly as they affect labor unions. Republicans promote private business and an increased role for state government, while Democrats generally support greater federal government participation and regulatory authority.

In 1984, Geraldine A. Ferraro, a Democrat, became the first female vice-presidential nominee of a major United States political party. Also in 1984, presidential candidate Jesse L. Jackson was the first black ever to win a plurality in a state primary election.

15 JUDICIAL SYSTEM

The Supreme Court, established by the United States Constitution, is the nation's highest judicial body, consisting of the chief justice of the United States and eight associate justices. All justices are appointed for life by the president with the approval of the Senate.

The Supreme Court acts as an appeals court for federal district courts, circuit courts of appeals, and the highest courts in the states. The Supreme Court also exercises the power of judicial review, determining the constitutionality of any state laws, state constitutions, congressional statutes, and federal regulations that are specifically challenged.

The United States Congress establishes all federal courts lower than the Supreme Court. On the lowest level and handling the most federal cases are the district courts—including one each in Puerto Rico, Guam, the Virgin Islands, the Northern Mariana Islands, and the District of Columbia. District courts have no appeals jurisdiction; their decisions may be carried to the courts of appeals, organized into 13 circuits. For most cases, this is usually the last stage of appeal, except where the court rules that a statute of a state conflicts with the Constitution of the United States, with federal law, or with a treaty. Special federal courts include the Court of Claims, Court of Customs and Patent Appeals, and Tax Court.

State courts operate independently of the federal judiciary. Most states have a court system that begins on the lowest level with a justice of the peace and includes courts of general trial jurisdiction and appeals courts. At the highest level of the system is a state supreme court. The court of trial jurisdiction (sometimes called the county or superior court) has both original and appeals jurisdiction; all criminal cases and some civil cases are tried in this court. The state supreme court interprets the constitution and the laws of the state.

16 ARMED FORCES

The armed forces of the United States of America in 2000 numbered 1.37 million on active duty and 1.27 million in the Ready Reserve. The Standby and Retired Reserve includes about 278,000 experienced officers and members who can be recalled in a national emergency. Membership in all of these forces is voluntary and has been since 1973 when the draft expired at the end of the Vietnam War. However, all male citizens must still register for the draft at age 18. The active duty force includes 199,900 women.

The United States Army numbers 469,300 soldiers (71,000 women) on active duty, divided roughly between 6 heavy (armored or mechanized) divisions, 4 light (infantry airborne, airmobile) divisions, 3 independent brigades, 3 armored cavalry regiments, 5 aviation brigades, and 11 air defense battalions. The Army National Guard numbers 362,400 (35,700 women) and the Army Reserve 421,500 (49,700 women).

The United States Navy (369,800; 52,800 women) combines three combat elements: air, surface, and subsurface. The navy has 24 nuclear-powered attack submarines with 1 configured for special operations. The United States Marine Corps (171,000; 9,800 women) trains for a wide range of maneuvers.

The United States Air Force (361,400; 66,300 women) operates more than 3,500 aircraft. Air Force personnel manage the United States radar and satellite early-warning and intelligence effort. The Air Force Reserve and Air National Guard (roughly 106,300 active reserves) provide a wide range of flying and support units.

The United States Coast Guard (42,200) is a separate branch of the armed forces under the Department of Transportation. It is the principal law enforcement agency on coastal waters.

About one-third of active duty personnel are assigned to overseas stations (one to three years) or serve in air, naval, and ground units that serve short tours on a rotating basis. The United States has one battalion in Egypt and participates in four other peacekeeping missions. In 1997 defense spending was around $267.2 billion a year, or 3.4% of Gross Domestic Product (GDP). The 2000 budget called for $112 billion rise in military spending for 2000–2004. Purchases for new weapons were budgeted at $62 billion in 2001.

17 ECONOMY

The United States probably has a greater variety and quantity of natural resources than any other nation, with the possible exception of Russia. However, because of its vast economic growth, the United States depends increasingly on foreign sources for a long list of raw materials.

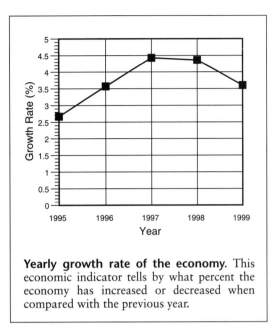

Yearly growth rate of the economy. This economic indicator tells by what percent the economy has increased or decreased when compared with the previous year.

American dependence on oil imports was dramatically demonstrated during the 1973 Arab oil embargo, when serious fuel shortages developed in many sections of the country.

Industrial activity within the United States expanded southward and westward for much of the twentieth century, most rapidly since World War II. Louisiana, Oklahoma, and especially Texas are centers of industries based on petroleum refining; aerospace and other high technology industries are the basis of the new wealth of Texas and California, the nation's leading manufacturing state. The industrial heartland of the United States consists of Ohio, Indiana, Illinois, Michigan, and Wisconsin, with steelmaking and automobile manufacturing among the leading industries. The Middle Atlantic states (New Jersey, New York, and Pennsylvania) and the Northeast also are highly industrialized.

In 1999, unemployment, which had fallen steadily through the mid-1990s, reached a new low of 4.2%, although in 2000 it had begun to creep up.

Inflation is an ever-present factor in the United States economy, although the United States inflation rate, estimated at 2.2% in 1999, tends to be lower than that of the majority of industrialized countries.

18 INCOME

Total earned income was $3.42 trillion in 1995. The gross national product (GNP) in 1995 amounted to about $28,020 per person, according to the World Bank. The average annual inflation rate during 1985–95 was 3.2%.

The median household income in 1995 was $34,076. In 1999, 12.7% of all United States families lived in poverty, down from 13.5% in 1997. By race, 28% of all blacks in the United States were below the federal poverty level, comprising 28% of the total number of impoverished United States citizens. About 10.5% of the white population lived in poverty, making up 66% of all citizens living in poverty.

19 INDUSTRY

Although the United States remains one of the world's top industrial powers, manufacturing no longer plays as dominant a role in the economy as it once did. Between 1979 and 1995, manufacturing employment fell from 21.8% to 14.8% of

national employment. Throughout the 1960s, manufacturing accounted for about 29% of total national income; by 1993, the proportion was down to about 18%. The Midwest leads all other regions in heavy industry, including the manufacturing of automobiles, trucks, and other vehicles.

Leading manufacturing industries of durable goods include nonelectrical machinery, electric and electronic equipment, motor vehicles and equipment, and other transportation equipment. The principal manufacturing industries of nondurable goods are chemicals and allied products, food, printing and publishing, and petroleum and coal products. Large corporations are dominant especially in areas such as steel, automobiles, pharmaceuticals, aircraft, petroleum refining, computers, soaps and detergents, tires, and communications equipment.

Advances in chemistry and electronics have revolutionized many industries through new products and methods. Industries that have been best able to make use of new technology have done well, and the economies of some states—in particular California and Massachusetts—are largely based on it. On the other hand, certain industries—especially clothing and steelmaking—have suffered from outmoded facilities that force the price of their products above the world market level.

Automobile manufacturing was an ailing industry in the 1980s, but rebounded slightly in the 1990s. Passenger car production, which had fallen from 7.1 million

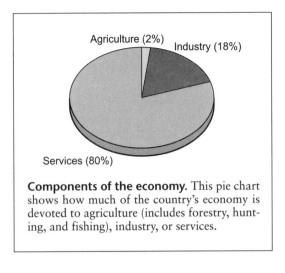

Agriculture (2%) Industry (18%)

Services (80%)

Components of the economy. This pie chart shows how much of the country's economy is devoted to agriculture (includes forestry, hunting, and fishing), industry, or services.

in 1987 to 5.4 million in 1991, rose to 8.3 million by 1999.

20 LABOR

The country's civilian and military labor force in 1999 numbered about 139 million persons. During 1992, a recession year, the unemployment rate reached 7.4%; by 1999 it had fallen to 4.2%. As of January 1997, services employed 46 million people; retail trade, 21 million; manufacturing, 20.6 million; finance, insurance and real estate, 8 million; wholesale trade, 4.8 million; transportation and public utilities, 8.7 million; construction, 7.8 million; agriculture and mining, 3.5 million; and public administration, 5.7 million.

Earnings of workers vary considerably with type of work and section of country. The national average wage was $13.24 per hour for nonagricultural workers in 1999. There were 39 national labor unions with more than 100,000 members, the largest being the National Education Association with 2 million members. In 1995, 14.9%

of the nonagricultural work force belonged to labor unions, down from 20.1% in 1983. The most important federation of organized workers in the United States is the American Federation of Labor–Congress of Industrial Organizations (AFL–CIO), whose affiliated unions had 13 million members in 1995, down from 14.1 million in 1992. In the mid-1990s, 19 states had right-to-work laws, forbidding forced union membership as a condition of employment.

21 AGRICULTURE

In 1998, the United States produced a huge share of the world's agricultural commodities, including soybeans, 47%; corn for grain (maize), 41%; cotton, 16%; wheat, 12%; and tobacco, 10%.

About 19% of the total United States land area was actively used for crops; another 25% was grassland pasture. The total amount of farmland declined from 479 million hectares (1.18 billion acres) in 1959 to 386 million hectares (954 million acres) in 1998. The farm population, which comprised 35% of the total United States population in 1910, declined to 25% during the Great Depression of the 1930s and dwindled to less than 2% by 1998.

A remarkable increase in the use of farm machinery took place during and after World War II. Tractors, trucks, milking machines, grain combines, corn pickers, and pickup bailers became near-necessities in farming. In 1920 there was less than one tractor in use for every 400 hectares (1,000 acres) of cropland harvested; by 1991 there were 15. Two other

Photo credit: Candace Cochrane, State of New Hampshire Tourism.

Maple sugaring is a popular activity as the sap begins to run in New Hampshire.

elements essential to United States farm productivity are chemical fertilizers and irrigation.

Substantial quantities of corn, the most valuable crop produced in the United States, are grown in almost every state. Its yield and price are important factors in the economies of the regions where it is grown.

22 DOMESTICATED ANIMALS

The livestock population in 1998 included an estimated 98.5 million head of cattle (approximately 9% were milk cows), 62.2 million hogs, 7.2 million sheep and lambs, 1.77 billion chickens, and 95 million turkeys.

Milk production totaled 70.6 million metric tons (155.6 billion pounds) in 1995. United States butter production totaled 1.3 million metric tons (6.7 billion pounds) in 1994; in that year, the United States produced more than 3 million metric tons (6.7 billion pounds) of cheese.

23 FISHING

The 1997 commercial catch was 5.5 million metric tons (9.9 billion pounds). Fish for food make up 78% of the catch, and nonfood fish (processed for fertilizer and oil), 22%.

Alaska pollock was the most important species in terms of quantity, followed by salmon, crab, flounder, cod, and shrimp. Domestic aquaculture (fish farming) produced 23,700 metric tons (52.1 million pounds) of trout and 295.1 million catfish.

24 FORESTRY

United States forest and woodlands covered about 30% of land area in 2000. Major forest regions include the eastern, central hardwood, southern, Rocky Mountain, and Pacific coast areas. The National Forest System accounts for approximately 19% of the nation's forestland. As of 30 September 1992, the United States Forest Service managed 77.2 million hectares (191 million acres) of forest, including 13.8 million hectares (34 million acres) of designated wilderness.

Domestic production of roundwood during 1997 amounted to 490.7 million cubic meters, of which softwoods accounted for roughly 60%. The United States, the world's second-leading producer of newsprint, produced 7 million metric tons in 1995. Other forest products in 1995 included 89.3 million metric tons of paper and paperboard (excluding newsprint), 67.1 million metric tons of wood pulp, 17.1 million cubic meters (22.4 million cubic yards) of plywood, and 15.4 million cubic meters (20.2 million cubic yards) of particleboard. Rising petroleum prices in the late 1970s caused an increase in the use of wood as home heating fuel, especially in the Northeast. Fuelwood and charcoal production amounted to 14.8 million cubic meters (19.4 million cubic yards) in 1995.

25 MINING

Rich in a variety of mineral resources, the United States is a world leader in the production of many important mineral commodities such as aluminum, cement, copper, pig iron, lead, molybdenum, phosphates, potash, salt, sulfur, uranium, and zinc. The leading mineral-producing states are: Texas, Louisiana, Oklahoma, and New Mexico, which are important for petroleum and natural gas; and Kentucky, West Virginia, and Pennsylvania, important for coal. Iron ore supports the nation's most basic nonagricultural industry, iron and steel manufacture.

In 1994, the United States' share in world production of mica was 51%; magnesium, 48%; molybdenum, 45%; phosphate, 33%; and lead, 24%. Selected mineral production (excluding fossil fuels) in 1995 (in tons) was as follows: iron ore, 62 million; phosphate, 46 million; salt,

Yearly balance of trade measured in millions of US dollars. The balance of trade is the difference between what a country sells to other countries (its exports) and what it buys (its imports). If a country imports more than it exports, it has a negative balance of trade (a trade deficit). If exports exceed imports there is a positive balance of trade (a trade surplus).

39.2 million; elemental sulfur, 3 million; potash, 1.5 million; copper, 1.9 million; zinc, 600,000; and lead, 374,000. (Figures for salt and cement include Puerto Rico.) Some 76.1 billion short tons of cement also were produced that year.

26 FOREIGN TRADE

The United States led the world in value of exports and imports in 1998. Exports of domestic merchandise, raw materials, agricultural and industrial products, and military goods amounted in 1998 to $663 billion. General imports were valued at more than $912 billion, a record high, leaving a trade deficit of more than $249 billion. Electric machinery and machines accounted for 8.8% of exports in 1995.

Road vehicles accounted for nearly 13.5% of imports that year. A rapidly growing export category was computers, which rose from $1.2 billion in 1970 to $33.5 billion in 1995.

Principal purchasers of United States exports in 1998 were Canada (23%), Mexico (12%), Japan (8%), the United Kingdom (6%), Germany (4%), France (3%), and the Netherlands (3%). Principal suppliers of imports to the United States were Canada (19%), Japan (13%), Mexico (10%), China (8%), Germany (5%), Taiwan (4%), and the United Kingdom (4%).

27 ENERGY AND POWER

The United States, with about 4.6% of the world's population, consumed 24.3% of the world's energy in 1995. The United States also is the world's leading energy producer, accounting for 19.1% of the world's primary energy production in 1995. (Primary energy is all energy consumed by the final users, excluding electricity but including the energy used at electric utilities to generate electricity.) Based on the amount of potential heat it could create, coal supplied about 31.8% of total energy production in 1995; crude oil, 20.1%; liquefied natural gas, 3.5%; nuclear electric power, 10.4%; water-power, 4.8%; and geothermal, wood, waste, wind, photovoltaic, and solar thermal energy, 1.4%.

In 1999, proved recoverable reserves of crude oil totaled an estimated 22.5 billion barrels; reserves of natural gas were about 4.7 trillion cubic meters (167 trillion cubic feet); and in 1998 recoverable coal reserves amounted to 275.1 billion tons (44% anthracite and bituminous). Mineral fuel production in 1995 included an estimated 636.1 million tons of hard coal (second in the world after China) and 393.5 million tons of lignite (first in the world); 538.5 billion cubic meters (18.9 trillion cubic feet) of natural gas (second after Russia); and 382.5 million tons of crude oil (second after Saudi Arabia).

In 1998, public utilities and private industrial plants generated nearly 3.62 trillion kilowatt hours of electricity. That year, coal-fired generation produced 50.9% of the electricity generated, and natural gas, 14.8%. Because of cost and safety problems, the future of the nuclear power industry in the United States came into doubt in the late 1980s.

During the 1980s, attention was focused on the development of solar power, synthetic fuels, geothermal resources, and other energy technologies. The federal government promoted energy conservation measures such as mandatory automobile fuel-efficiency standards and tax incentives for home insulation. Petroleum imports have risen since the mid-1980s, reaching nearly 7.1 million barrels per day in 1994. This amount, however, is still below the record level of almost 8.6 million barrels per day in 1977.

28 SOCIAL DEVELOPMENT

Social welfare programs in the United States depend on both the federal government and the state governments for resources and administration. The old age, survivors', disability, and Medicare (health) programs are administered by the

Selected Social Indicators

The statistics below are estimates for the period 1996 to 2000. For comparison purposes, data for the United States and averages for low-income countries and high-income countries are also given.

Indicator	United States of America	Low-income countries	High-income countries	United States
Per capita gross national product (GNP)†	$31,910	$1,870	$25,690	$31,910
Population growth rate	0.8%	2.1%	0.7%	1.1%
People per square kilometer of land	30	73	29	30
Life expectancy in years	77	59	78	77
Number of physicians per 1,000 people	n.a.	1.0	2.5	2.5
Number of pupils per teacher (primary school)	n.a.	41	17	14
Illiteracy rate (15 years and older)	3%	34%	<5%	3%
Television sets per 1,000 people	844	85	693	844
Energy consumed per capita (kg of oil equivalent)	7,937	550	5,366	7,937

† The GNP is the total dollar value of all goods and services produced by a country in a year. The per capita GNP is calculated by dividing a country's GNP by its population and adjusting for relative purchasing power. About 15% of the world's 6.1 billion people live in high-income countries, while 40% live in low-income countries.

n.a. = data not available   > = greater than   < = less than

Sources: World Bank. World Development Indicators. Washington, D.C.: The World Bank, 2001; Central Intelligence Agency. The World Factbook. Washington, D.C.: Government Printing Office, 2000.

federal government. Unemployment insurance, dependent child care, and a variety of other public assistance programs are state administered, although the federal government contributes to all of them through grants to the states.

In 1995, nearly 13.7 million Americans received $22 billion under the Aid to Families with Dependent Children (AFDC) program. The Food and Nutrition Service of the United States Department of Agriculture oversees several food assistance programs, including the food stamp program, school lunch and breakfast programs, and nutrition programs for the elderly. In 1996, the United States government replaced the open-ended AFDC entitlement program with Temporary Assistance for Needy Families (TANF), a limited system of assistance funded through grants given to communities. The program provides $16.4 billion in block grants each year during 1997–2002.

The present Social Security program differs greatly from that created by the Social Security Act of 1935. Since 1939, Congress has attached a series of amendments to the program, including provisions for workers who retire at age 62, widows, dependent children under 18 years of age, and children who are disabled prior to age 18. Disabled workers between 50 and 65 years of age also are entitled to monthly benefits. In 1998, monthly Social Security benefits totaled $375 billion, including $232.3 billion in monthly retirement benefits and $43.5 billion in disability benefits.

In January 1974, the Social Security Administration took on responsibility for helping the aged, blind, and disabled under the Supplemental Security Income program. By the end of 1995, some 4.2 disabled Americans were receiving $3.2 billion in monthly benefits. Medicare, another program administered under the Social Security Act, provides hospital insurance and voluntary medical insurance for persons 65 and over, with reduced benefits available at age 62. Medicare hospital insurance covered some 40 million Americans in 1996, who received benefit payments of $191.2 billion. Medicaid is a program that helps the needy meet the costs of medical, hospital, and nursing-home care; its 33.3 million recipients received benefits averaging $3,311 per person in 1995.

29 HEALTH

The United States health care system is among the most advanced in the world. In 1995, health expenditures were to have reached $1 trillion. National health care spending was estimated at $3,510 per person in 1994. Medical facilities in the United States included 6,374 hospitals in 1994, with 1.1 million beds. During the mid-1990s, there was an average of 2.5 doctors per 1,000 people. During 1994, the United States Census Bureau estimated that 41 million United States residents (16.1% of the population) were without any form of health insurance.

Life expectancy in 1998 was 76.8 years. Males could expect to live 73.5 years, females 80.2 years.

Leading causes of death (with percent of total deaths) in 1998 were: heart disease (31.9%); cancer (23.3%); cerebrovascular diseases (6.8%); chronic obstructive pulmonary diseases (4.5%); accidents and adverse effects (4%); pneumonia and influenza (3.6%); diabetes mellitus (2.6%); human immunodeficiency virus (HIV) infection (1.9%); suicide (1.4%); and homicide and legal intervention (1%).

Other leading causes of death in 1995 included chronic liver disease and cirrhosis, nephritis, and arteriosclerosis. About 20% of all deaths in the United States were attributed to cigarette smoking in 1990. First identified in 1981, HIV infection and AIDS (acquired immune deficiency syndrome) have spread rapidly; by 1999, there were between 650,000–900,000 AIDS cases reported in the United States. About 40,000 new cases of AIDS are reported annually.

30 HOUSING

The housing resources of the United States far exceed those of any other country, with 102.2 million housing units as of April 1990, 91.9 million of which were occupied. Construction of housing following World War II set a record-breaking pace; 1986 was the 38th successive year during which construction of more than one million housing units was begun.

After 1986, housing starts dropped for five years in succession, hitting 946,000 in

1991 and then climbing to 1.4 million in 1996. Most dwellings are one-family houses. Perhaps the most significant change in the housing scene has been the shift to the suburbs made possible by the widespread ownership of automobiles.

31 EDUCATION

The literacy rate is estimated to be 97%. Education is compulsory in all states and a responsibility of each state and local government. Generally, formal schooling begins at the age of 6 and continues up to age 17. Government spending (state and federal) on all educational institutions accounts for one-third of all government spending.

Elementary schooling is from grade 1 to grade 8. High schools cover grades 9 through 12. Colleges include junior or community colleges, offering two-year associate degrees; regular four-year colleges and universities; and graduate or professional schools.

In 1996, public schools had 45.8 million students, while private schools had 8.9 million. Students in grades 9–12 numbered 14.4 million in 1996, with 13 million enrolled in public schools. In the same year, public colleges had 11.3 million students, while private college enrollment was 3.1 million. In 1995, there were 3,688 two-year and four-year colleges and universities.

32 MEDIA

All major electronic communications systems are privately owned but regulated by the Federal Communications Commission.

In 1995, more than 98% of all United States households had telephones. In 1999, broadcasting stations on the air comprised 10,000 radio stations (both AM and FM) and 1,500 television stations. More than 98% of all American households owned at least one TV set. The expanding cable television industry, with 11,220 cable systems as of 1996, served 63.2 million subscribers.

In 1995 there were 1,586 daily newspapers in the United States. The following newspapers reported average daily circulations of one million or more in 1995: *USA Today* (2 million); *The Wall Street Journal* (1.8 million); *The Chicago Tribune* (1.3 million); *The New York Times* (1.2 million); and *The Los Angeles Times* (1.1 million). *The Washington Post* (1995 circulation 852,260), which gained national recognition for its coverage of the Watergate affair in the early 1970s, is another influential daily newspaper.

The three magazines with the greatest circulation in 2000 were *Modern Maturity*, 22 million; *Reader's Digest,* 17 million; and *TV Guide,* 15 million. *Time* and *Newsweek* were the leading news magazines, with a weekly circulation of 4.6 million and 3.1 million, respectively. In 1994, 51,863 book titles were published in the United States.

33 TOURISM AND RECREATION

Foreign visitors to the United States numbered approximately 46 million in 1998. Of these visitors, 32% came from Canada, 22% from Mexico, 20% from Europe, and 9% from Central and South America

Photo credit: The Wagner Perspective.

Bullriding at the Cheyenne Frontier Days rodeo in Wyoming, the largest professional outdoor rodeo in the world.

and the Caribbean. In 1997, travelers to the United States from all foreign countries spent $73.3 billion. With a few exceptions, such as Canadians entering from the Western Hemisphere, all visitors to the United States are required to have passports and visas.

The United States had a total of 54 national parks as of 1995. Among the most striking scenic attractions in the United States are the Grand Canyon in Arizona; Carlsbad Caverns in New Mexico; Yosemite National Park in California; Yellowstone National Park in Idaho, Montana, and Wyoming; Niagara Falls,

partly in New York; and the Everglades in Florida.

Historical attractions include the Liberty Bell and Constitution Hall in Philadelphia; the Statue of Liberty in New York City; the White House, the Capitol, and the monuments to Washington, Jefferson, and Lincoln in Washington, D.C.; the Williamsburg historical restoration in Virginia; the Alamo in San Antonio, Texas; and Mt. Rushmore in South Dakota.

Among many other popular tourist attractions are the movie and television studios in Los Angeles; the cable cars in San Francisco; casino gambling in Las Vegas, Nevada, and in Atlantic City, New Jersey; the Grand Ole Opry in Nashville, Tennessee; the many jazz clubs of New Orleans; and such amusement parks as Disneyland (Anaheim, California) and Walt Disney World (near Orlando, Florida). For amount and variety of entertainment—theater, movies, music, dance, and sports—New York City has few rivals.

Americans' recreational activities range from the major spectator sports—professional baseball, football, basketball, ice hockey, soccer, horse racing, and college football and basketball—to home gardening. Participant sports are a favorite form of recreation, including jogging, tennis, and golf. Skiing is a popular recreation in New England and the western mountain ranges. Sailing, power boating, and rafting are popular water sports. In 1994, the United States hosted the World Cup Soccer Championship. The United States hosted the Summer Olympics in 1904, 1932, 1984, and 1996. The Winter Olympics were held in the United States in 1960 and 1980. The United States was scheduled to host the 2002 Winter Olympics in Salt Lake City, Utah.

34 FAMOUS AMERICANS

Political and Military Figures

Printer, inventor, scientist, and statesman, Benjamin Franklin (1706–90) was America's outstanding figure of the colonial period. George Washington (1732–99), military leader in the American Revolution and first president of the United States, is known as the father of his country. Chief author of the Declaration of Independence and third president was Thomas Jefferson (1743–1826). His leading political opponents were John Adams (1735–1826), second president; and Alexander Hamilton (b.West Indies, 1755–1804), first secretary of the treasury. James Madison (1751–1836), a leading figure in drawing up the United States Constitution, served as fourth president.

Abraham Lincoln (1809–65) led the United States through its most difficult period, the Civil War, in the course of which he issued the Emancipation Proclamation. Jefferson Davis (1808–89) served as the only president of the short-lived Confederacy. Among the foremost presidents of the 20th century were Nobel Peace Prize winner Theodore Roosevelt (1858–1919); Woodrow Wilson (1856–1924), who led the nation during World War I; and Franklin Delano Roosevelt (1882–1945), elected to four terms spanning the Great Depression and World War II.

Outstanding military leaders of the Civil War were Union general Ulysses Simpson Grant (1822–85), who later served as the eighteenth president; and Confederate general Robert Edward Lee (1807–70). Douglas MacArthur (1880–1964) commanded the United States forces in Asia during World War II, oversaw the postwar occupation and reorganization of Japan, and directed United Nations forces in the first year of the Korean conflict. Dwight D. Eisenhower (1890–1969) served as supreme Allied commander during World War II, later becoming the thirty-fourth president.

John Marshall (1755–1835), chief justice of the United States from 1801 to 1835, established the power of the Supreme Court through the principle of judicial review. Other important chief justices included Earl Warren (1891–1974), whose period as chief justice from 1953 to 1969 saw important decisions on desegregation, reapportionment, and civil liberties.

Native American chiefs renowned for their resistance to white invasion were Tecumseh (1768–1813), Geronimo (1829?–1909), Sitting Bull (1831?–90), and Crazy Horse (1849?–77). Historical figures who have become part of American folklore include pioneer Daniel Boone (1734–1820); silversmith, engraver, and patriot Paul Revere (1735–1818); frontiersman David "Davy" Crockett (1786–1836); scout and Indian agent Christopher "Kit" Carson (1809–68); William Frederick "Buffalo Bill" Cody (1846–1917); and the outlaws Jesse Woodson James (1847–

82) and Billy the Kid (William H. Bonney, 1859–81).

Inventors and Scientists

Outstanding inventors were Robert Fulton (1765–1815), who developed the steamboat; Samuel Finley Breese Morse (1791–1872), who invented the telegraph; and Elias Howe (1819–67), who invented the sewing machine. Alexander Graham Bell (b.Scotland, 1847–1922) invented the telephone. Thomas Alva Edison (1847–1931) was responsible for hundreds of inventions, among them the incandescent electric lamp, the phonograph, and a motion picture camera and projector. Two brothers, Wilbur Wright (1867–1912) and Orville Wright (1871–1948), designed, built, and flew the first successful motor-powered airplane. Amelia Earhart (1898–1937) and Charles Lindbergh (1902–74) were aviation pioneers. Pioneers in the space program include John Glenn (b.1921), the first American astronaut to orbit Earth; and Neil Armstrong (b.1930), the first man to set foot on the Moon.

Outstanding botanists and naturalists include George Washington Carver (1864–1943), known especially for his work on industrial applications for peanuts; and John James Audubon (1785–1851) who won fame as an ornithologist and artist.

Albert Abraham Michelson (b.Germany, 1852–1931) measured the speed of light and became the first of a long line of United States Nobel Prize winners. The theory of relativity was conceived by Albert Einstein (b.Germany, 1879–1955), generally considered one of the greatest minds in the physical sciences. Enrico Fermi (b.Italy, 1901–54) created the first nuclear chain reaction and contributed to the development of the atomic and hydrogen bombs. Also prominent in the splitting of the atom were J. Robert Oppenheimer (1904–67) and Edward Teller (b.Hungary, 1908). Jonas Edward Salk (1914–95) developed an effective vaccine for polio, and Albert Bruce Sabin (1906–93) contributed oral, attenuated live-virus polio vaccines.

Social Reformers

Social reformers of note include Frederick Douglass (Frederick Augustus Washington Bailey, 1817–95), a prominent abolitionist; Elizabeth Cady Stanton (1815–1902) and Susan Brownell Anthony (1820–1906), leaders in the women's suffrage movement; Clara Barton (1821–1912), founder of the American Red Cross; Eugene Victor Debs (1855–1926), labor leader and an organizer of the Socialist movement in the United States; and Martin Luther King Jr. (1929–68), a central figure in the black civil rights movement and winner of the Nobel Peace Prize in 1964.

Religious leaders include Roger Williams (1603–83), an early advocate of religious tolerance in the United States; Jonathan Edwards (1703–58), New England preacher and theologian; Joseph Smith (1805–44), founder of the Church of Jesus Christ of Latter-day Saints (Mormon), and his chief associate, Brigham Young (1801–77); and Mary Baker Eddy

(1821–1910), founder of the Christian Science Church.

Literary Figures

The first American author to be widely read outside the United States was Washington Irving (1783–1859). James Fenimore Cooper (1789–1851) was the first popular American novelist. The writings of two men of Concord, Massachusetts—Ralph Waldo Emerson (1803–82) and Henry David Thoreau (1817–62)—influenced philosophers, political leaders, and ordinary men and women in many parts of the world. The novels and short stories of Nathaniel Hawthorne (1804–64) explore New England's Puritan heritage. Herman Melville (1819–91) wrote the novel *Moby-Dick,* a symbolic work about a whale hunt that has become an American classic. Mark Twain (Samuel Langhorne Clemens, 1835–1910) is the best-known American humorist.

Other leading novelists of the later 19th and early 20th centuries were Henry James (1843–1916), Edith Wharton (1862–1937), Stephen Crane (1871–1900), Willa Cather (1873–1947), and Sinclair Lewis (1885–1951), first American winner of the Nobel Prize for literature (1930). Later Nobel Prize–winning United States novelists include William Faulkner (1897–1962) in 1949; Ernest Hemingway (1899–1961) in 1954; John Steinbeck (1902–68) in 1962; Saul Bellow (b.Canada, 1915), in 1976; and Isaac Bashevis Singer (b.Poland, 1904–91) in 1978. Among other noteworthy writers are James Thurber (1894–1961), Francis Scott Key Fitzgerald (1896–1940), Elwyn Brooks White (1899–1985), Richard Wright (1908–60), Eudora Welty (1909–2001), James Baldwin (1924–87), Toni Morrison (b.1931), and John Updike (b.1932).

Noted American poets include Henry Wadsworth Longfellow (1807–82), Edgar Allan Poe (1809–49), Walt Whitman (1819–92), Emily Dickinson (1830–86), and Robert Frost (1874–1963). Allen Ginsberg (b.1926), Maya Angelou (b.1928), and Sylvia Plath (1932–63) are among the best-known poets since World War II. Carl Sandburg (1878–1967) was a noted poet, historian, novelist, and folklorist. The foremost United States playwrights include Eugene (Gladstone) O'Neill (1888–1953), who won the Nobel Prize for literature in 1936; Tennessee Williams (Thomas Lanier Williams, 1911–83); and Arthur Miller (b.1915). Neil Simon (b.1927) is among the nation's most popular playwrights.

Artists

Two renowned painters of the early period were John Singleton Copley (1738–1815) and Gilbert Stuart (1755–1828). Outstanding 19th-century painters were James Abbott McNeill Whistler (1834–1903) and John Singer Sargent (b.Italy, 1856–1925). More recently, Edward Hopper (1882–1967), Georgia O'Keeffe (1887–1986), Norman Rockwell (1894–1978), and Andrew Wyeth (b.1917) have achieved wide recognition.

Entertainment Figures

The first great American "showman" was Phineas Taylor Barnum (1810–91). Outstanding figures in the motion picture industry are Sir Charles Spencer "Charlie" Chaplin (b.England, 1889–1978), Walter Elias "Walt" Disney (1906–66), and George Orson Welles (1915–85). Sir Alfred Hitchcock (b.England, 1899–1980) was a famous motion picture director; George Lucas (b.1944), Steven Spielberg (b.1947), and Spike Lee (b.1957) have achieved remarkable popular success with their films, as has Woody Allen (Allen Konigsberg, b.1935).

World-famous American actors and actresses include Humphrey Bogart (1899–1957); Clark Gable (1901–60); Cary Grant (Alexander Archibald Leach, b.England, 1904–86); John Wayne (Marion Michael Morrison, 1907–79); Judy Garland (Frances Gumm, 1922–69); Marlon Brando (b.1924); Marilyn Monroe (Norma Jean Mortenson, 1926–62); Jane Fonda (b.1937); and Dustin Hoffman (b.1937). Among other great entertainers are W. C. Fields (William Claude Dukenfield, 1880–1946); Jack Benny (Benjamin Kubelsky, 1894–1974); Fred Astaire (Fred Austerlitz, 1899–1987); Bob (Leslie Townes) Hope (b.England, 1903); Frank (Francis Albert) Sinatra (1915–98); Elvis Aaron Presley (1935–77); and Barbra (Barbara Joan) Streisand (b.1942).

Composers and Musicians

The songs of Stephen Collins Foster (1826–64) have achieved folk-song status. Among the foremost composers are Edward MacDowell (1861–1908), Aaron Copland (1900–90), and Leonard Bernstein (1918–90). Leading composers of popular music are John Philip Sousa (1854–1932), George Gershwin (1898–1937), and Woody Guthrie (1912–67). Prominent in the blues tradition are Leadbelly (Huddie Ledbetter, 1888–1949), Bessie Smith (1898?–1937), and Muddy Waters (McKinley Morganfield, 1915–83). Leading jazz figures include the composers Scott Joplin (1868–1917), Edward Kennedy "Duke" Ellington (1899–1974), and William "Count" Basie (1904–84), and performers Louis Armstrong (1900–1971), Billie Holiday (Eleanora Fagan, 1915–59), John Birks "Dizzy" Gillespie (1917–93), and Charlie "Bird" Parker (1920–55).

Sports Figures

Among the many noteworthy sports stars are baseball's Tyrus Raymond "Ty" Cobb (1886–1961) and George Herman "Babe" Ruth (1895–1948); football's Jim Brown (b.1936); and golf's Mildred "Babe" Didrikson Zaharias (1914–56). Billie Jean (Moffitt) King (b.1943) starred in tennis; Joe Louis (Joseph Louis Barrow, 1914–81) and Muhammad Ali (Cassius Marcellus Clay, b.1942) in boxing; Wilton Norman "Wilt" Chamberlain (b.1936) and Michael Jordan (b.1963) in basketball; Mark Spitz (b.1950) in swimming; Eric Heiden (b.1958) in speed skating; and Jesse Owens (1913–80) in track and field.

35 BIBLIOGRAPHY

Altman, Linda Jacobs. *The Decade That Roared: America During Prohibition.* New York: Twenty-First Century Books, 1997.

Baines, John D. *The United States.* Austin, Tex.: Raintree Steck-Vaughn, 1994.

Barone, Michael. *The Almanac of American Politics.* Washington, D.C.: National Journal, 1992.

Bennett, Lerone. *Before the Mayflower: A History*

of Black America. 6th ed. New York: Penguin, 1993.

Brown, Gene. The Nation in Turmoil: Civil Rights and the Vietnam War (1960–1973). New York: Twenty-First Century Books, 1993.

Burg, David F. The Great Depression. New York: Facts On File, 1996.

Collier, Christopher. Andrew Jackson's America, 1821–1850. New York: Benchmark Books, 1998.

Frank, Nicole. Welcome to the USA. Milwaukee, WI: Gareth Stevens, 2000.

Grossman, James R. A Chance to Make Good: African Americans, 1900–1929. New York: Oxford University Press, 1997.

Hakim, Joy. An Age of Extremes. New York: Oxford University Press, 1999.

Hakim, Joy. The New Nation. New York: Oxford University Press, 1999.

Harvard Encyclopedia of American Ethnic Groups. Cambridge: Harvard University Press, 1980.

Hicks, Roger. The Big Book of America. Philadelphia: Courage Books, 1994.

Josephy, Alvin M., Jr. Now that the Buffalo's Gone: A Study of Today's American Indians. Norman, Okla.: Univ. of Oklahoma Press, 1984.

Kallen, Stuart A. The 1950s. San Diego: Lucent Books, 1999.

Kallen, Stuart A. The 1980s. San Diego: Lucent Books, 1999.

Kallen, Stuart A. The 1990s. San Diego: Lucent Books, 1999.

Katz, William Loren. Exploration to the War of 1812, 1492–1814. Austin, TX: Raintree Steck-Vaughn, 1993.

Katz, William Loren. The Westward Movement and Abolitionism, 1815–1850. Austin, TX: Raintree Steck-Vaughn, 1993.

Kronenwetter, Michael. America in the 1960s. San Diego: Lucent Books, 1998.

Lindop, Edmund. James K. Polk, Abraham Lincoln, Theodore Roosevelt. New York: Twenty-first Century Books, 1995.

Lindop, Edmund. Woodrow Wilson, Franklin D. Roosevelt, Harry S. Truman. New York: Twenty-First Century Books, 1995.

Littlefield, Daniel C. Revolutionary Citizens: African Americans, 1776–1804. New York: Oxford University Press, 1997.

Mettger, Zak. Reconstruction—America After the Civil War. New York: Lodestar Books, 1994.

Nickelson, Harry. Vietnam. San Diego, Calif.: Lucent Books, 1989.

Sandak, Cass R. The United States. Austin, Tex.: Raintree Steck-Vaughn, 1997.

Smith-Baranzini, Marlene. USKids History: Book of the New American Nation. Boston: Little, Brown, 1995.

Stein, R. Conrad. The United States of America. Chicago: Children's Press, 1994.

Steins, Richard. A Nation Is Born: Rebellion and Independence in America, 1700–1820. New York: Twenty-First Century Books, 1993.

Steins, Richard. The Postwar Years: The Cold War and the Atomic Age (1950–1959). New York: Twenty-First Century Books, 1993.

Stewart, Gail. The 1970s. San Diego: Lucent Books, 1999.

Tocqueville, Alexis de. Democracy in America. New York: A. Knopf, 1994.

Trotter, Joe William. From a Raw Deal to a New Deal?: African Americans, 1929–1945. New York: Oxford University Press, 1996.

Uschan, Michael V. The 1910s. San Diego: Lucent Books, 1999.

Uschan, Michael V. The 1940s. San Diego: Lucent Books, 1999.

Webb, Marcus. The United States of America. San Diego: Lucent Books, 2000.

Woog, Adam. The 1900s. San Diego: Lucent Books, 1999.

URUGUAY

Oriental Republic of Uruguay
República Oriental del Uruguay

CAPITAL: Montevideo.

FLAG: The flag, approved in 1830, has four azure blue horizontal stripes on a white background; on a white canton is a golden sun, alternately straight and wavy. This "Sun of May" symbolizes Uruguay's independence.

ANTHEM: *Himno Nacional,* which begins "Orientales, la patria o la tumba" ("Easterners [Uruguayans], our country or death").

MONETARY UNIT: The Uruguayan peso (UP), of 100 centésimos replaced the new peso in 1993 at the rate of UP1=1,000 new pesos. There are coins of 10, 20, and 50 centésimos and 1, 2, 5, and 10 new pesos, and notes of 1, 5, 10, 20, and 50 Uruguayan pesos. UP1 = $0.08819 ($1 = UP11.339).

WEIGHTS AND MEASURES: The metric system is the legal standard, but some traditional measures also are used.

HOLIDAYS: New Year's Day, 1 January; Epiphany, 6 January; Landing of the 33, 19 April; Labor Day, 1 May; Battle of Las Piedras, 18 May; Birthday of Artigas, 19 June; Constitution Day, 18 July; Independence Day, 25 August; Columbus Day, 12 October; All Souls' Day, 2 November; Blessing of the Waters, 8 December; Christmas Day, 25 December.

TIME: 9 AM = noon GMT.

1 LOCATION AND SIZE

The second-smallest South American country, Uruguay is situated in the southeastern part of the continent. It has an area of 176,220 square kilometers (68,039 square miles), slightly smaller than the state of Washington. Uruguay has a total boundary length of 2,063 kilometers (1,282 miles). Uruguay's capital city, Montevideo, is located in the southern part of the country on the Atlantic coast.

2 TOPOGRAPHY

Southern Uruguay consists mostly of rolling plains and is an eastward extension of the *pampas* (grass-covered plain) of Argentina. The Atlantic coastline is fringed with tidal lakes and sand dunes. Low, unbroken stretches of level land line the banks of the two border rivers, the Uruguay and the Rio de la Plata. The northern section is broken by occasional highlands *(cuchillas)*, alternating with broad valleys. The highest point in the country, Mount Catedral, is 513 meters (1,683 feet) above sea level. The most noteworthy features of the northwest landscape are the highlands known as Cuchilla de Haedo. The Cuchilla Grande runs northeastward from the southern region to the Brazilian border.

Geographic Profile

Geographic Features

Size ranking: 88 of 192
Highest elevation: 513 meters (1,683 feet) at Mount Catedral
Lowest elevation: Sea level at the Atlantic Ocean

Land Use

Arable land:	7%
Permanent crops:	0%
Permanent pastures:	77%
Forests:	5%
Other:	11%

Weather

Average annual precipitation: 109 centimeters (43 inches)
Average temperature range in January: 25°C (77°F)
Average temperature range in June: 15°C (59°F)

3 CLIMATE

The climate is temperate; the average temperatures are 15°C (59°F) in June and 25°C (77°F) in January. Rainfall is evenly distributed throughout the year; it averages about 109 centimeters (43 inches), varying from 97 centimeters (38 inches) in Montevideo to nearly 127 centimeters (50 inches) farther north. Frost is virtually unknown.

4 PLANTS AND ANIMALS

Uruguay is primarily a grass-growing land, and the vegetation is essentially a continuation of the Argentine pampas (grass-covered plain). Forest areas are relatively small. The most useful hardwoods are algarobo, guayabo, quebracho, and urunday; other hardwoods include arazá, coronilla, espinillo, lapacho, lignum vitae, and nandubay. The acacia, alder, aloe, eucalyptus (imported from Australia), ombú, poplar, and willow are common softwoods. Palms are native to the valleys. Rosemary, myrtle, scarlet-flowered ceibo, and mimosa are common. Most of the valleys are covered with aromatic shrubs, and the rolling hills with white and scarlet verbena.

Large animals have practically disappeared from the eastern regions. The carpincho (water hog), fox, deer, nutria, otter, and small armadillo roam the northern foothills. On the pampas are the hornero (ovenbird), quail, partridge, and crow. The avestruz (a small ostrich similar to the Argentine rhea), swan, and royal duck are found at lagoons.

Fish include pompano, salmon, and corvina. The principal reptiles are cross vipers and tortoises. Seals are found on Lobos Island, near Maldonado.

5 ENVIRONMENT

Air pollution is a problem, particularly in the larger population centers. Its primary sources are its own industry and an energy plant in Brazil. Pollution from mining and industrial sources threatens the nation's water supply; 95% of the nation's rural dwellers do not have pure water.

The nation's cities produce 0.5 million tons of solid waste per year; 40% of the urban population does not have adequate waste disposal facilities. As of 1994, five of Uruguay's mammal species and 11 of its bird species were endangered, and 14 types of plants were threatened with extinction.

6 POPULATION

According to 2000 estimates, the population of Uruguay was 3.3 million, and the projection for the year 2005 was 3.45 million. In 2000, an estimated 91% of the population lived in urban areas. The population of the capital city Montevideo in 2000 was estimated at 1.3 million. The estimated population density in 1998 was 19 persons per square kilometer (49 per square mile).

7 MIGRATION

There were 103,002 foreign-born people in 1985. Immigration came to 1,471 in 1990. Substantial emigration by Uruguayans for political or economic reasons occurred during the mid-1970s and early 1980s. Official figures suggest that about 180,000 Uruguayans left between 1963 and 1975 and 150,000 between 1975 and 1985. Most of them were young and, on average, better educated than the total population. Argentina and Brazil were the main destinations.

8 ETHNIC GROUPS

The inhabitants of Uruguay are primarily (about 88%) white and of European origin, mostly Spanish and Italian; a small percentage is descended from Portuguese, English, and other Europeans. Mestizos (mixed white and Amerindian lineage) represent 8% of the population, and blacks and mulattoes (mixed black and white) about 4%.

9 LANGUAGES

Spanish is the official language. Uruguayan Spanish, like Argentine Spanish,

LOCATION: 30°06′ to 35°02′s; 53°05′ to 59°29′w.
BOUNDARY LENGTHS: Brazil, 1,003 kilometers (623 miles); Atlantic coastline, 565 kilometers (351 miles); Argentina, 495 kilometers (308 miles). **TERRITORIAL SEA LIMIT:** 200 miles.

has been somewhat modified by the Italians who migrated in large numbers to both countries.

10 RELIGIONS

Uruguay is the only Latin American nation that approaches religious diversity. Con-

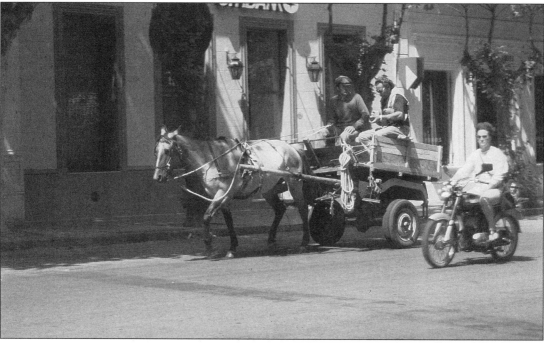

Contrasting modes of transportation in Colonia, Uruguay.

trasting with the 90% formal Roman Catholic affiliation in other Latin American countries, only 52% of Uruguayans identified themselves as Roman Catholics. Many (30%) claimed no church membership. Only 16% of the population was Protestant, and 2.4%, Jewish.

11 TRANSPORTATION

Four main lines connect the western and northern areas with Montevideo. In 1997 there were 2,994 kilometers (1,860 miles) of standard-gauge, government-owned track. Highways have surpassed railroads as the principal means of transport for passengers and freight. In 1998 there were 8,420 kilometers (5,232 miles) of roads. In 1995, there were 491,000 motor vehicles, of which 444,800 were passenger cars.

Montevideo is the major Uruguayan port. There are some 1,600 kilometers (994 miles) of inland waterways, of which the most important are the Río de la Plata and the Uruguay. There were two vessels in the merchant fleet in 1998, with gross registered tons of 44,042. Carrasco, an airport outside Montevideo, is used by most international carriers. In 1997, 544,000 passengers were carried on scheduled airline flights.

12 HISTORY

In the sixteenth century, the native Charrúa Indians drove off the few Spanish expeditions that landed on the east bank of the Uruguay river. By 1680, when Portuguese from Brazil founded Colonia do Sacramento as a rival to Buenos Aires, Uruguay became a focal point for Spanish-Portuguese rivalry.

Montevideo was founded in 1726, and Uruguay became part of the viceroyalty of La Plata, which the Spaniards established in Buenos Aires in 1776. During the Napoleonic Wars (1803–15), the British invaded the region of La Plata and captured Buenos Aires and Montevideo (1806–07), but they were forced out in 1807. After Buenos Aires refused to give Uruguay autonomy, the Uruguayan national hero, José Gervasio Artigas, declared Uruguay independent in 1815. A year later, Brazilians attacked Montevideo from the north, and, after four years of fighting, Uruguay was annexed to Brazil in 1821.

On 25 August 1825, Juan Antonio Lavalleja issued a declaration of independence. After a three-year fight, a peace treaty signed on 28 August 1828 guaranteed Uruguay's independence. During the following period of political turmoil and civil war, the two political parties around which Uruguayan history has traditionally revolved, the Colorados (reds) and the Blancos (whites), were founded.

The nineteenth century was largely a struggle between the two factions. Some measure of national unity was achieved in the 1860s. In 1865, Uruguay allied with Brazil and Argentina to defeat Paraguay in the Paraguayan War (1865–70), also known as the War of the Triple Alliance.

The administrations of José Batlle y Ordóñez (1903–7, 1911–15) marked the nation's period of greatest progress. Batlle initiated Uruguay's famed social welfare system, funded primarily by earnings of beef and wool in foreign markets.

After World War II (1939–45), the Colorados ruled, except for an eight-year period from 1958–66. During the administration of President Jorge Pacheco Areco (1967–72), Uruguay entered a period of crisis. Economic and political instability stemming from the decline of wool revenues resulted in the emergence of Uruguay's National Liberation Movement, popularly known as the Tupamaros. A well-organized Marxist (communist) guerrilla movement, the Tupamaros mounted a campaign of kidnapping, assassination, and bank robbery.

Their activities, coupled with the worsening economic situation, aggravated Uruguay's political uncertainty. Gradually, the military assumed a greater role in government and by 1973 was in control of the system, crushing the Tupamaros by the end of that year. The military retained control of the country until 1981, suspending the constitution and, in 1976, naming a new president, Aparicio Méndez Manfredini. In 1979, Amnesty International estimated the number of political prisoners at 6,000.

In September 1981, a "transitional" president, Georgio Álvarez Armellino, was installed, and the moderate government of Colorado candidate Julio María Sanguinetti Cairolo took office in March 1985.

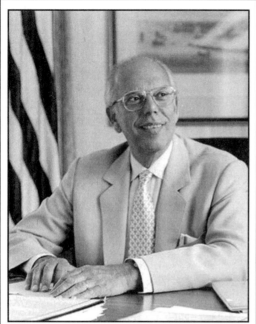

Photo credit: EPD/Office of the President.

Name:	Jorge Batlle
Position:	President of a republic
Took office:	1 March 2000
Birthplace:	Uruguay
Birth date:	25 October 1927
Education:	University of Montevideo, Faculty of Law and Social Sciences, law degree
Spouse:	Mercedes Menafra
Children:	Two children, Three grandchildren
Of interest:	Batlle has spent the bulk of his time as a journalist and editor of various publications.

of state enterprises to private ownership. However, these plans were dealt a serious blow in a 1993 election, when the public failed to ratify a set of proposals for liberalization. In 1994, Sanguinetti returned to office in the closest election ever recorded in Uruguay's history. His administration began a program of economic reforms, including a long-range plan for cutting back on generous social security payments.

In the 1999 elections Jorge Batlle Ibáñez won the runoff in November, calling for a conservative fiscal course. This plan will leave most state-owned companies untouched, despite an 11% unemployment rate in 2000.

13 GOVERNMENT

According to the constitutional revision of 1966, the Congress (or General Assembly) consisted of the 30-member Senate and the 99-member Chamber of Deputies. From June 1973 until March 1985, Uruguay was ruled by executive decree, subject to veto by the military, with legislative functions carried out by the 25-member Council of State, appointed by the executive.

In March 1985, democracy was restored under President Sanguinetti; in July, the government set up a National Constituent Assembly to devise constitutional reforms that would be submitted to the electorate for ratification. Uruguay is divided into 19 departments (provinces).

14 POLITICAL PARTIES

Uruguay has Latin America's oldest two-party system. The Colorados (reds) and

The new government released all political prisoners, declared amnesty for former military and police leaders, and initiated talks between employers and union leaders to reduce social tension. However, slow progress on the economic front led to the 1989 election of the Blanco candidate, Luis Alberto Lacalle. Lacalle emphasized deficit reduction, reforms in education, labor, and the civil service, and the return

Blancos (whites), formed during the conflicts of the 1830s and 1840s, persisted into the 1990s. The Colorados are traditional Latin American liberals, representing urban business interest, and favoring limitation on the power of the Catholic Church. The Blancos (officially called the National Party) are conservatives, defenders of large landowners and the Church.

In 1989, Blanco candidate Lacalle took 37% of the vote. The Blancos also carried a plurality in each house of the legislature, followed respectively by the Colorados, the Broad Front and the "New Space" Coalition.

In 1999, the Colorados and Blancos united under Batlle's leadership to create a coalition to defeat the socialist candidate.

15 JUDICIAL SYSTEM

Below the Supreme Court are appeals courts and lower civil and criminal courts, justices of the peace, electoral and administrative courts, and an accounts court. A parallel military court system operates under its own procedure. When the Supreme Court hears cases involving the military, two military justices join the court. Civilians are tried in the military court only in time of war or insurrection.

16 ARMED FORCES

The armed forces numbered 25,600 in 2000. The active army consists of volunteers between the ages of 18 and 45 who contract for one or two years of service.

The army numbered 17,600, organized in four regional divisions of 10 brigades; the navy (including naval air force and

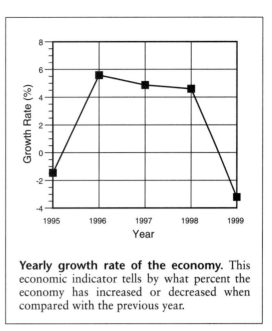

Yearly growth rate of the economy. This economic indicator tells by what percent the economy has increased or decreased when compared with the previous year.

infantry) numbered 5,000 with three frigates and 10 patrol and coastal combatants. The air force had 3,000 men and 27 combat aircraft. Defense spending was $172 million in 1998.

17 ECONOMY

Historically, Uruguay's economy has been based on the production and processing of agricultural commodities. Currently, the services sector, especially tourism and financial services, accounts for more than 60% of the gross domestic product (GDP). Agriculture, especially livestock, is still important in making products for export as well as inputs for other sectors of the economy.

Since 1990, the government has emphasized a free-market economy. The government has lowered tariffs, reduced deficit spending, controlled inflation, reduced the size of government, and entered into the Mercosur free-trade zone with some other South American nations.

18 INCOME

In 1999, the gross domestic product (GDP) was $28.4 billion, or about $8,600 per person. That year, the average inflation rate was 8.6%, resulting in an annual decline rate in GDP of 3%.

19 INDUSTRY

Although foreign trade depends mainly on agricultural production, the production of industrial goods for domestic consumption is increasing, primarily in the fields of textiles, rubber, glass, paper, electronics, chemicals, cement, light metallurgical manufactures, ceramics, and beverages. World War II (1939–45) spurred the industrial growth of Uruguay, and now local industry supplies most of the manufactured products used. Most industry is concentrated in and around Montevideo. Manufacturing output fell by an average of 0.1% per year during 1988–98.

20 LABOR

About 1.23 million Uruguayans, or an estimated 47% of the population, were in the civilian labor force in 1998. In that same year, manufacturing and construction accounted for 19.9% of the labor force; agriculture, 3.8%; and services, 76.3%. The unemployment rate rose from 8.94% in 1991 to 10.1% in 1998.

The eight-hour day and 48-hour week were instituted in 1915. Civil servants and employees of state-run businesses and other public services have a 30-hour week.

Unemployment and dismissal compensation, old age and liability pensions, workers' accident compensation, and family allowances are provided by law.

21 AGRICULTURE

About 77% of Uruguay's land area is devoted to stock raising and 7.4% to the cultivation of crops. In pasturage, large farms predominate, with farms of more than 1,000 hectares (2,500 acres) accounting for two-thirds of all farmland. Crops are grown mainly on small farms of less than 100 hectares (250 acres).

In 1998, production of Uruguay's principal crops (in tons) was as follows: rice, 865,000; wheat, 145,000; barley, 250,000; corn, 226,000; sorghum, 97,000; sunflower seeds, 86,000; and oats, 45,000.

22 DOMESTICATED ANIMALS

Livestock is the basis of the economy. As of 1995, Uruguay had nearly 22.7 million sheep, the lowest number since 1980 but still more than any other South American country. The production costs of stock raising are low, and the quality of the product is generally high.

Uruguay is especially suited to the raising of sheep and cattle. In 1998 there were 10.5 million head of cattle, 500,000 horses, 270,000 pigs, 17.8 million sheep, and 12 million chickens. Milk production was 1.4 billion liters in 1998. The Mercosur free trade agreement has given Uruguay a great advantage in selling its dairy products to Brazil. Meat production in 1998 included 454,000 tons of beef and

53,000 tons of mutton. Beef consumption in Uruguay was 60 kilograms per person in 1998, one of the highest rates in the world.

23 FISHING

Fishing underwent rapid growth in the 1970s. The government-promoted fishing industry made an average annual catch of 136,912 tons in 1997. The main commercial species are Argentine hake, whitemouth croaker, and striped weakfish. Other important sea fish are corvina negra (a kind of bass), mullet, sole, anchovy, mackerel, whiting, and shark. The finest freshwater fish is the dorado, a type of salmon. The southern coastal zone near Maldonado is considered one of the finest fishing areas in the world.

24 FORESTRY

Uruguay has some 930,000 hectares (2.3 million acres) of forestland. About 8,200 hectares (20,300 acres) were reforested annually from 1981 to 1986. The principal species cultivated are eucalyptus and pine; domestic woods are used for windbreaks, fence posts, and firewood. Lumber suitable for building and construction is imported. Roundwood removals totaled 4.1 million cubic meters (5.4 million cubic yards) in 1997, with 75% burned as fuel.

25 MINING

Mineral resources are limited and undeveloped. There are deposits of manganese, iron, lead, and copper, and in the Rivera Department, gold is mined in small quantities. More important are stones, such as the marble quarried for local use, lime-

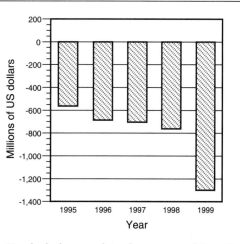

Yearly balance of trade measured in millions of US dollars. The balance of trade is the difference between what a country sells to other countries (its exports) and what it buys (its imports). If a country imports more than it exports, it has a negative balance of trade (a trade deficit). If exports exceed imports there is a positive balance of trade (a trade surplus).

stone, granite, quartz, gypsum, and dolomite. Sand, common stone, and talcum are exported. Agates, opals, and onyx are found in Salto and Artigas.

26 FOREIGN TRADE

Uruguay traditionally relies on foreign sales of wool, hides, meat, and meat products for its export revenues, which have been increasing over the past several years. Recent reforms favoring a free-market economy have stimulated a growth in exports and imports. In 1999, exports amounted to $2.1 billion. Imports totaled $3.4 billion that year. Uruguay's main trading partners were Brazil, Argentina, the United States, and Germany. Exports increased by 1.4% during 1998, and imports rose 2.8%. Principal partners in

Photo credit: Mary A. Dempsey.

Palacio Salvo on Montevideo's Plaza de Independencia.

1998 were Argentina, the United States, France, and Brazil.

27 ENERGY AND POWER

Uruguay's power is provided by hydroelectric and diesel-generating plants. Uruguay's total electrical power output was 9.4 billion kilowatt hours in 1998, of which 90% came from hydroelectric sources.

By a bilateral agreement signed with the United States, Uruguay is entitled to receive atomic equipment and to lease nuclear fuels. In 1995, the state-owned refinery at Montevideo processed 3.6 million barrels of distillate fuel oil, 3 million barrels of residual fuel oil, and 2.1 million barrels of gasoline. Consumption included 38,000 barrels per day of crude petroleum in 1998.

28 SOCIAL DEVELOPMENT

Uruguay has frequently been referred to as South America's first welfare state. The social reform movement began under the leadership of José Batlle y Ordóñez in the early 1900s. Social legislation now provides for a day of rest in every week (plus Saturday afternoon), holidays with pay, minimum wages, annual cash and vacation bonuses, family allowances, compensation for unemployment or dismissal, workers' accident compensation, retirement pensions for rural and domestic workers, old age and disability pensions, and special consideration for working women and minors. The state also provides care for children and mothers, as well as for the blind, deaf, and mute. Free medical attention is available to the poor, as are low-cost living quarters for workers.

The government's social security system is divided into six main funds: civil service and teachers, industrial and commercial, rural workers and domestic servants, family allowances, banking, and the professions.

In 1995, women made up about one-half of the work force but tended to be concentrated in lower paying jobs. Nevertheless, many attend the national university and pursue professional careers.

Selected Social Indicators

The statistics below are estimates for the period 1996 to 2000. For comparison purposes, data for the United States and averages for low-income countries and high-income countries are also given.

Indicator	Uruguay	Low-income countries	High-income countries	United States
Per capita gross national product (GNP)†	$8,750	$1,870	$25,690	$31,910
Population growth rate	0.6%	2.1%	0.7%	1.1%
People per square kilometer of land	19	73	29	30
Life expectancy in years	74	59	78	77
Number of physicians per 1,000 people	2.9	1.0	2.5	2.5
Number of pupils per teacher (primary school)	21	41	17	14
Illiteracy rate (15 years and older)	2.2%	34%	<5%	3%
Television sets per 1,000 people	531	85	693	844
Energy consumed per capita (kg of oil equivalent)	910	550	5,366	7,937

† The GNP is the total dollar value of all goods and services produced by a country in a year. The per capita GNP is calculated by dividing a country's GNP by its population and adjusting for relative purchasing power. About 15% of the world's 6.1 billion people live in high-income countries, while 40% live in low-income countries.

n.a. = data not available   > = greater than   < = less than

Sources: World Bank. *World Development Indicators.* Washington, D.C.: The World Bank, 2001; Central Intelligence Agency. *The World Factbook.* Washington, D.C.: Government Printing Office, 2000.

29 HEALTH

The US Institute of Inter-American Affairs and the Uruguayan Ministry of Public Health created the Inter-American Cooperative Public Health Service, which built four health centers and clinics. The ratios of doctors and beds to the population are exceptionally good. In 1997 there were 2.9 doctors per 1,000 people. In 1995 there were 45 hospital beds per 1,000 people.

For the region, life expectancy is high (74 years in 2000); infant mortality is low (17.5 per 1,000 live births in 1996). The major causes of death are heart disease, cancer, and digestive disorders. Degenerative diseases rank higher as a cause of death in Uruguay than in most other Latin American countries. In 1995, 89% had access to safe water.

30 HOUSING

The housing situation is more favorable in Uruguay than in most Latin American countries. The National Institute of Low-Cost Housing builds low-cost dwellings for low-income workers and pensioners. Nearly all housing units are made of durable materials including stone masonry, wood, zinc, or concrete. Of all housing units, 92% had private toilet facilities and 75% had water piped indoors.

31 EDUCATION

Adult illiteracy in 2000 was approximately 2.2% (males, 2.6%; females,

1.8%), among the lowest in Latin America. Elementary education, which lasts six years, is compulsory. Secondary education is in two stages of three years each. In 1996 there were 2,415 primary schools, with 16,868 teachers and 345,573 students. There were 269,826 students in secondary and technical schools. Enrollment at all institutions of higher learning was 79,691 in 1996.

32 MEDIA

The state owns the telegraph and telephone services. In 1997 there were 767,300 telephones, most of them in the metropolitan Montevideo area. Uruguay in 1999 had 72 radio stations and 26 television stations. The number of radio receivers was about 600 and the number of television sets was 531 per 1,000 population in 2000. In 1996, there were 50 Internet hosts per 1,000 population.

In 1995, Uruguay had 32 daily newspapers, with a combined circulation of more than 750,000. Major Montevideo dailies, with their 1999 circulations, included *El Diario* (170,000); *El País* (100,000); *La Mañana* (40,000); and *La Republica* (unknown).

33 TOURISM AND RECREATION

Tourism, one of Uruguay's major enterprises, enjoys government support. The state owns many hotels along the coast, including some of the more sophisticated resorts in South America. Montevideo has been promoted as the "city of roses" because of its many parks and gardens. In 1997, 2.3 million tourists visited Uruguay, and tourism receipts totaled $759 million.

The most popular sport in Uruguay is soccer; there is an intense rivalry between supporters of the two major teams, the Peñarol and the Nacional. Other popular sports include basketball, cycling, tennis, pelota (handball), golf, and water sports.

34 FAMOUS URUGUAYANS

The national hero of Uruguay is José Gervasio Artigas (1764–1850), who led the fight for independence against Brazil and Portugal. Juan Antonio Lavalleja (1786?–1853) directed the uprising that established Uruguay's independence in 1828. One of Uruguay's greatest citizens was José Batlle y Ordóñez (1856–1929), who served twice as president of the country, and was great-uncle to the current president. Eduardo Acevedo Díaz (1851–1924) won fame as the writer of a gaucho (South American cowboy) novel, *Soledad* (1894). Horacio Quiroga (1878–1937) is regarded as one of Latin America's foremost short-story writers. The poets Julio Herrera y Reissig (1875–1910) and Juana de Ibarbourou (1895–1979) have attained a devoted audience beyond the borders of Uruguay. The painter Juan Manuel Blanes (1830–1901) is best known for his *Episode of the Yellow Fever*. Eduardo Fabini (1883–1951) is Uruguay's best-known composer.

35 BIBLIOGRAPHY

Finch, Martin. *Uruguay.* Santa Barbara, Calif.: Clio, 1989.

Jermyn, Leslie. *Uruguay.* New York: Marshall Cavendish, 1999.

Morrison, Marion. *Uruguay.* Chicago: Children's Press, 1992.

Selby, Anna. *Argentina, Chile, Paraguay, Uruguay.* Austin, Tex.: Raintree Steck-Vaughn, 1999.

UZBEKISTAN

Republic of Uzbekistan
Uzbekiston Respublikasi

CAPITAL: Tashkent (Toshkent).

FLAG: Horizontal bands of blue (top), white, and green separated by narrow red bands; white crescent moon and twelve stars on the blue band.

MONETARY UNIT: The som (SOM) is the official currency, introduced when Uzbekistan left the ruble zone in November 1993. SOM1 = $0.00707 (or $1 = SOM141.40).

WEIGHTS AND MEASURES: The metric system is used.

HOLIDAYS: Independence Day, 1 September.

TIME: 5 PM = noon GMT.

1 LOCATION AND SIZE

Uzbekistan, a republic of the former Soviet Union, is located in central Asia bordering the Aral Sea, between Kazakstan and Turkmenistan. Comparatively, it is slightly larger than the state of California, with a total area of 447,400 square kilometers (172,742 square miles). Uzbekistan's boundary length totals 6,221 kilometers (3,866 miles). Its capital city, Tashkent, is located in the eastern part of the country.

2 TOPOGRAPHY

Uzbekistan consists of mostly flat to rolling sandy desert with dunes. A valley lies in the east surrounded by mountainous Tajikistan and Kyrgyzstan. The Aral Sea lies in the northwest. There is semiarid grassland in the east.

3 CLIMATE

Temperatures in the desert can reach upwards of 32°C (90°F). In the capital city of Tashkent the mean temperature is 32°C (90°F) in the summer and 3°C (37°F) in January. There is very little rainfall in the country.

4 PLANTS AND ANIMALS

Uzbekistan, a republic of the former Soviet Union, suffered damage to its environment by the Soviet agricultural programs of the 1950s. Due to its excessive use of irrigation, the Amu Dar'ya and Syr Dar'ya rivers run dry in places. Half of the Aral Sea is now a dry lake bed, and the land is poisoned from the overuse of fertilizer. Much of the country has no animal life.

5 ENVIRONMENT

Uzbekistan's main environmental problems are soil salt content, land pollution, and water pollution. Chemicals used in farming contribute to the pollution of the soil, and the nation's forestlands are dwindling. The country's water supply also suffers from toxic chemical pollutants. The

Geographic Profile

Geographic Features

Size ranking: 55 of 192
Highest elevation: 4,301 meters (14,112 feet) at
  Adelunga Toghi
Lowest elevation: −12 meters (−39 feet) at Sariqarnish
  Kuli

Land Use

Arable land:	9%
Permanent crops:	1%
Permanent pastures:	46%
Forests:	3%
Other:	41%

Weather

Average temperature in January (Tashkent): 3°C
  (37°F)
Average temperature in July (Tashkent): 32°C (90°F)

nation's cities produce 45.8 million tons of solid waste per year.

In 1994, 20 of Uzbekistan's mammal species were endangered and 38 of its bird species were threatened with extinction.

6 POPULATION

The population of Uzbekistan was estimated at 24.4 million in 2000 and projected at 26.1 million for the year 2005. Tashkent, the capital, had an estimated population of 2.4 million in 2000.

7 MIGRATION

After the breakup of the Soviet Union, about 400,000 ethnic Russians emigrated from Uzbekistan. Most of the 250,000 Crimean Tatars who have left Central Asia for the Ukraine were from Uzbekistan. In 1999, Uzbekistan had an estimated 30,000 Tajik refugees and 8,000 Afghan refugees.

8 ETHNIC GROUPS

In 1996, 80% of the population was Uzbek. Russians constituted 5.5%; Tajiks, 5%; Kazaks, 3%; and others (Tatars, Karakalpaks, and various European groups), 6.5%.

9 LANGUAGES

Uzbek, the state language, was the most widely spoken non-Slavic tongue in the former Soviet Union. It is a Turkic language. In 1993, the government decided to start using the Roman alphabet instead of the Cyrillic alphabet. Russian also is commonly spoken.

10 RELIGIONS

Freedom of religion is guaranteed by the constitution of 1992, adopted after independence. About 88% of the population is Muslim. Ethnic Uzbeks mostly belong to the Hanafi branch of Sunni Islam, but the Wahhabi sect has flourished in recent years. Uzbekistan had a significant Jewish population of some 93,000 in 1999, mostly in the Bukhara area.

11 TRANSPORTATION

Uzbekistan has about 3,380 kilometers (2,100 miles) of railroad and 81,600 kilometers (50,706 miles) of highways. The Zeravshan River is the largest inland waterway. In 1997, more than 1.5 million passengers were carried on scheduled flights.

12 HISTORY

Independent states existed in present-day Uzbekistan in the first millennium (thousand years) BC. The territory was con-

LOCATION: 41°0′N; 64°0′E. **BOUNDARY LENGTHS:** Afghanistan, 137 kilometers (85 miles); Kazakstan, 2,203 kilometers (1,369 miles); Kyrgyzstan, 1,099 kilometers (683 miles); Tajikistan, 1,161 kilometers (722 miles); Turkmenistan, 1,621 kilometers (1,007 miles).

quered by Alexander the Great in 329–327 BC. After a series of other conquests, Arabs won control of the region in the eighth century and introduced Islam.

Genghis Khan's Mongols invaded in 1219, and a series of Mongol kingdoms ruled Uzbekistan. In the sixteenth century, the region was divided into separate principalities. Bukhara (Bukhoro) was conquered by Persia in 1740, and soon afterwards by the Mangyt dynasty, which

ruled until 1920. In the early nineteenth century the Kokand Khanate (kingdom ruled by a khan, or local chieftain) grew powerful in the eastern part of present-day Uzbekistan.

Concern about British expansion in India and Afghanistan led eventually to Russian conquest, which began in the 1860s and ended in the 1880s, when Uzbekistan became part of Turkestan, with Bukhara (Bukhoro) administered as a

Photo credit: EPD/Embassy of the Republic of Uzbekistan.

Name: Islam Karimov
Position: President of a republic
Took office: 24 March 1990
Birthplace: Samarkand, Uzbekistan
Birth date: 30 January 1938
Education: Central Asian Polytechnic Institute, degree in mechanical engineering
Of interest: In the mid-1960s, Karimov worked at an aviation production association.

separate emirate (Islamic territory) under Russian protection.

During the Bolshevik revolution of 1917–20, the Muslim Congress attempted to form an Autonomous Government of Turkestan. Red Army (communist) forces intervened savagely, but armed resistance continued as late as 1924. The Uzbek Soviet Socialist Republic was created in 1925. Under the leadership of long-time leader S. Rashidov, Uzbekistan was politically conservative during the 1970s and early 1980s. In the mid-1980s, considerable fraud was discovered in the cotton industry.

In March 1990, Islam Karimov was elected to the newly created post of president by the Uzbek Supreme Soviet. Uzbekistan declared independence on 1 September 1991. Karimov was reelected in December 1991, but he has opposed moving Uzbekistan towards democracy. Opposition parties were banned in 1992 and political reformers were either put in jail or fled the country. Karimov was once again reelected in 1999.

Karimov opposes the fundamentalist Islamic military and political movements in Afghanistan and Tajikistan. Uzbekistan supplies arms to the secular forces in those countries' civil wars.

13 GOVERNMENT

The executive branch consists of the president and his appointed prime minister and Cabinet of Ministers. The legislative branch consists of a single-chamber Supreme Soviet of 150 seats. The judicial branch is appointed by the president.

14 POLITICAL PARTIES

The ruling National Democratic Party is the renamed Communist Party. In 1992, opposition parties were banned.

15 JUDICIAL SYSTEM

There are three levels of courts: district courts (people's courts) at the lowest level, regional courts, and the Supreme Court.

16 ARMED FORCES

Uzbekistan has an army of 50,000, an air force of 4,000 with 150 combat aircraft,

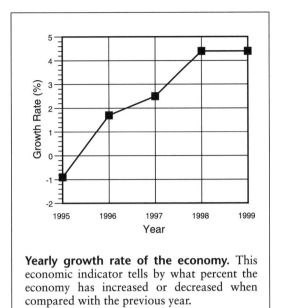

Yearly growth rate of the economy. This economic indicator tells by what percent the economy has increased or decreased when compared with the previous year.

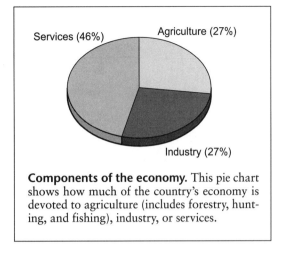

Components of the economy. This pie chart shows how much of the country's economy is devoted to agriculture (includes forestry, hunting, and fishing), industry, or services.

and about 19,000 internal security personnel.

17 ECONOMY

Uzbekistan has one of the lowest per person incomes in Central Asia. The world's third-largest cotton producer, it is evolving from a mainly agricultural economy to include more industry. Agriculture and agricultural processing industries accounted for 27% of the economy in 1999. Government measures toward establishing a market economy have been more cautious than in many other post-Soviet countries. The domestic economy shrank by 17% between 1991 and 1994. When the government realized that the slow pace of reforms wasn't working, it stepped up the efforts to move from a command-driven to a market-driven economy. As a result, the economic decline slowed to just 1% in 1996, and the inflation rate fell to 35% (compared to 1,300% in 1994).

18 INCOME

In 1998, Uzbekistan's gross domestic product (GDP) was $59.2 billion, or about $2,500 per person. In 1999, the average inflation rate was 40%, and the annual growth in the GDP was about 4.5%.

19 INDUSTRY

Manufacturing is concentrated in Tashkent and the Fergana Valley. The main manufactured items are cotton, wool, silk fiber, and processed foods (including cottonseed oil, meat, dried fruit, wines, and tobacco).

Uzbeklegprom, the state association for light industry, produces 90% of Uzbekistan's textiles. Total textile production in 1995 was 650 million square meters (777 million square yards), valued at $510 million. Most textile mills use outdated machinery from the 1970s.

Uzbekistan is the primary producer of machines and heavy equipment in Central Asia. The country's automotive industry has joint ventures with Daimler-Benz of Germany and Daewoo of South Korea. The Chkalov Tashkent Aircraft Production Co. is the largest aircraft assembly plant in Central Asia.

20 LABOR

The labor force was estimated at 10 million in 1998. Agriculture and forestry engaged 43% of the labor force; industry and construction, 20%; and other services, 36%. There are large numbers of underemployed workers.

21 AGRICULTURE

Uzbekistan was the world's fifth-largest producer of cotton in 1998 (after the United States, India, China, and Pakistan), accounting for 5.3% of world supply. Rice, wheat, barley, and corn are important grain crops. In 1998, 3.7 million tons of cereal grains were produced.

22 DOMESTICATED ANIMALS

The livestock population in 1998 included 8 million sheep, 5.3 million cattle, 800,000 goats, 195,000 pigs, and about 12 million chickens. Meat production that year totaled 529,000 tons (76% beef). Wool production was estimated at 18,000 tons that year. The Uzbeks have bred silkworms to produce silk since the fourth century.

23 FISHING

Fishing occurs mainly in the eastern valley between Kazakstan and Tajikistan. The total catch in 1997 was 10,565 tons. The Aral Sea in the north has become too salty for fishing.

24 FORESTRY

Forests and woodlands make up only about 3% of the total land area. Commercial forestry is not a significant part of the economy.

25 MINING

Copper, lead-zinc, and molybdenum are mined, as well as gold and fluorspar. Uzbekistan was one of the world's largest producers of gold in 1999, which provided much of the country's foreign currency earnings.

26 FOREIGN TRADE

Trade involves mainly the export of light industry products and machinery along with the import of food items, light industry products, and chemicals. In 1999, exports totaled $2.9 billion, while imports amounted to $3.1 billion. Cotton accounted for 75% of export earnings that year.

Russia, Switzerland, the United Kingdom, Belgium, Kazakstan, and Tajikistan were the leading buyers of Uzbekistan's exports in 1999. Germany, South Korea, the United States, Turkey, and Russia were the leading sources of imports that year. Uzbekistan depends on trade with other former Soviet republics for grain, food, machinery, and industrial items.

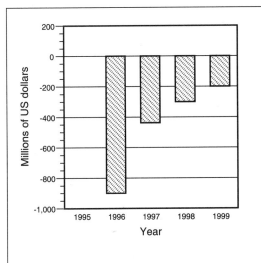

Yearly balance of trade measured in millions of US dollars. The balance of trade is the difference between what a country sells to other countries (its exports) and what it buys (its imports). If a country imports more than it exports, it has a negative balance of trade (a trade deficit). If exports exceed imports, there is a positive balance of trade (a trade surplus).

27 ENERGY AND POWER

Uzbekistan is the eighth-largest producer of natural gas in the world. In 1990, production totaled 55.5 billion cubic meters (1.9 trillion cubic feet). Crude oil production that year was about 213,000 barrels per day. In 1998, electricity production came to 43.4 billion kilowatt hours.

28 SOCIAL DEVELOPMENT

The current social security system was developed in 1994, and includes pensions for old age, disability, and survivorship. There also are sickness, maternity, work injury, and unemployment benefits. Traditional customs decree that women generally marry young and confine their activities to the home. Some political prisoners are being held. A person can be put in jail for three days without a charge, and some are mistreated.

29 HEALTH

The average life expectancy was 70 years in 2000. Uzbekistan had 3.3 doctors and 8.3 hospital beds per 1,000 people that year.

Uzbekistan's health care system provides services mostly free of charge. However, the system is inefficient and is under pressure to change its organization and financing.

30 HOUSING

In 1990, Uzbekistan had an average of 12.1 square meters (130 square feet) of housing space per person.

31 EDUCATION

The estimated adult illiteracy rate in 2000 was 1%. In recent years, there has been an increased emphasis on teaching Uzbek literature, culture, and history. There are three universities: Tashkent State University; Nukus State University; and Samarkland Alisher Naroi State University. In 1992, all higher level institutions had a total of 638,200 students.

32 MEDIA

Radio Tashkent broadcasts in Uzbek, English, Urdu, Hindi, Farsi, Arabic, and Uighur. There also is a television station. In 1995 there were 279 newspapers and 93 periodicals. Although the constitution

Selected Social Indicators

The statistics below are estimates for the period 1996 to 2000. For comparison purposes, data for the United States and averages for low-income countries and high-income countries are also given.

Indicator	Uzbekistan	Low-income countries	High-income countries	United States
Per capita gross national product (GNP)†	**$2,230**	$1,870	$25,690	$31,910
Population growth rate	**1.9%**	2.1%	0.7%	1.1%
People per square kilometer of land	**59**	73	29	30
Life expectancy in years	**70**	59	78	77
Number of physicians per 1,000 people	**3.3**	1.0	2.5	2.5
Number of pupils per teacher (primary school)	**21**	41	17	14
Illiteracy rate (15 years and older)	**1%**	34%	<5%	3%
Television sets per 1,000 people	**276**	85	693	844
Energy consumed per capita (kg of oil equivalent)	**1,930**	550	5,366	7,937

† The GNP is the total dollar value of all goods and services produced by a country in a year. The per capita GNP is calculated by dividing a country's GNP by its population and adjusting for relative purchasing power. About 15% of the world's 6.1 billion people live in high-income countries, while 40% live in low-income countries.

n.a. = data not available   > = greater than   < = less than

Sources: World Bank. *World Development Indicators.* Washington, D.C.: The World Bank, 2001; Central Intelligence Agency. *The World Factbook.* Washington, D.C.: Government Printing Office, 2000.

allows freedom of expression, the government controls the flow of information.

33 TOURISM AND RECREATION

Uzbekistan tourist attractions include the ancient cities of Samarkand, Bukhara, Khiva, and Kokand, with their palaces, mosques, religious schools, and pre-Islamic remains.

34 FAMOUS UZBEKISTANIS

Islam A. Karimov (b.1938) has been president of Uzbekistan since 1990. Mir Alishar Navai (1441–1501) is considered the father of the Uzbek language and the national poet. Abdullah Quaisi (1894–1939) wrote the historical novels *Days Gone By* and the *Scorpion from the Pulpit*, published in the 1920s. Ilyas Malayev (b.1936) is a popular poet and musician.

35 BIBLIOGRAPHY

Critchlow, James. *Nationalism in Uzbekistan: A Soviet Republic's Road to Sovereignty.* Boulder, Colo.: Westview Press, 1991.

Gippenreiter, Vadim Evgenevich. *Fabled Cities of Central Asia: Samarkand, Bukhara, Khiva.* New York: Abbeville Press, 1989.

MacLeod, Calum. *Uzbekistan: The Golden Road to Samarkand.* New York: Odyssey Publications, 1999.

Nazarov, Bakhtiyar A., and Denis Sinor, eds. *Essays on Uzbek History, Culture, and Language.* Bloomington, Ind.: Indiana University, Research Institute for Inner Asian Studies, 1993.

Uzbekistan. Minneapolis: Lerner, 1993.

VANUATU

Republic of Vanuatu

[French:] *République de Vanuatu* [Bislama:] *Ripablik blong Vanuatu*

CAPITAL: Port-Vila.

FLAG: Red and green sections are divided horizontally by a gold stripe running within a black border and widening at the hoist into a black triangle on which is a pig's tusk enclosing two crossed yellow mele leaves.

ANTHEM: *Yumi, Yumi, Yumi (We, We, We)*.

MONETARY UNIT: As of 1 January 1981, the vatu (VT) replaced at par value the New Hebridean franc as the national currency. There are coins of 100 vatu and notes of 100, 500, 1,000, and 5,000 vatu. VT1 = $0.0077 (or $1 = VT129.76).

WEIGHTS AND MEASURES: The metric standard is used.

HOLIDAYS: New Year's Day, 1 January; May Day, 1 May; Independence Day, 30 July; Assumption, 15 August; Constitution Day, 5 October; National Unity Day, 29 November; Christmas Day, 25 December; Family Day, 26 December. Movable religious holidays include Good Friday, Easter Monday, and Ascension.

TIME: 11 PM = noon GMT.

1 LOCATION AND SIZE

Vanuatu is an irregular Y-shaped chain of some 80 South Pacific islands, with a total land area of about 14,760 square kilometers (5,699 square miles)—slightly larger than the state of Connecticut—and a total coastline of 2,528 kilometers (1,571 miles). The island chain is about 800 kilometers (500 miles) long.

Vanuatu's capital city, Port-Vila, is located on the island of Éfaté.

2 TOPOGRAPHY

The islands are of coral and volcanic origin; there are active volcanoes on several islands, including Ambrym, Loopévi, and Tanna. The highest peak, Mount Tabwemasana, on Espiritu Santo, rises 1,879 meters (6,165 feet) above sea level. Most of the islands are forested and mountainous, with narrow coastal strips.

3 CLIMATE

Average midday temperatures in Port-Vila range from 25°C (77°F) in July to 29°C (84°F) in January. Humidity averages about 74%, and rainfall on Éfaté is about 230 centimeters (90 inches) a year.

4 PLANTS AND ANIMALS

Despite its tropical forests, Vanuatu has a limited number of plant and animal spe-

Geographic Profile

Geographic Features

Size ranking: 155 of 192
Highest elevation: 1,879 meters (6,165 feet) at Mount Tabwemasana
Lowest elevation: Sea level at the Pacific Ocean

Land Use†

Arable land:	2%
Permanent crops:	10%
Permanent pastures:	2%
Forests:	75%
Other:	11%

Weather††

Average annual precipitation: 230 centimeters (90 inches)
Average temperature in January: 29°C (84°F)
Average temperature in July: 25°C (77°F)

†*Arable land:* Land used for temporary crops, like meadows for mowing or pasture, gardens, and greenhouses. *Permanent crops:* Land cultivated with crops that occupy its use for long periods, such as cocoa, coffee, rubber, fruit and nut orchards, and vineyards. *Permanent pastures:* Land used permanently for forage crops. *Forests:* Land containing stands of trees. *Other:* Any land not specified, including built-on areas, roads, and barren land.

††Precipitation and average temperature can vary significantly within a country, due to factors such as latitude, altitude, coastal proximity, and wind patterns.

cies. The region is rich in sea life, with more than 4,000 species of marine mollusks.

5 ENVIRONMENT

Urban water is polluted due to inadequate sanitation systems. The logging industry threatens the forests and contributes to the problem of soil erosion. Coral reefs, homes to the country's marine life, are threatened by harmful fishing methods. The green sea and hawksbill turtles are endangered species. In 1987, the government formed a committee on the environment to address the nation's developing environmental concerns.

6 POPULATION

Estimated population in 2000 was 192,848, and the projection for 2005 was 212,000. As of 2000, the population of the capital, Port-Vila, on Éfaté, was estimated at 23,000. The population is unevenly distributed, with the vast majority in some 2,000 small villages.

7 MIGRATION

Adverse economic conditions have encouraged emigration to Fiji, New Zealand, and the United States.

8 ETHNIC GROUPS

Nearly 94% of the total population is of Melanesian origin. Minority groups include Europeans, mostly French (4%), and other Pacific Islanders, Chinese, and Vietnamese (2%).

9 LANGUAGES

More than 100 languages and dialects are spoken in Vanuatu. Melanesian, the principal language, is related to Fijian and New Caledonian speech. Pidgin English, known as Bislama or Bichelama, is recognized by the constitution as the common language, although English and French also are official languages.

10 RELIGIONS

About 80% of the population is considered to be Christian; other Vanuatuans follow native traditional religions.

11 TRANSPORTATION

In 1996 there were 1,070 kilometers (665 miles) of roads and 7,000 registered motor vehicles, including 4,200 passenger cars.

The chief airports are Bauerfield, on Éfaté, and Pekoa, on Espiritu Santo. Air Vanuatu, the national airline operated by Ansett Airlines of Australia, maintains regular service to Australia. Port-Vila and Luganville are the chief seaports. As of 1998, there were 82 ships in the Vanuatuan merchant fleet, with a total capacity of 1.3 million gross registered tons.

12 HISTORY

The British Captain James Cook discovered, named, and charted most of the southern New Hebrides islands, as Vanuatu was known, in 1774. The next century brought British and French missionaries, planters, and traders.

A joint Anglo-French naval commission was established in 1887 to protect the lives and interests of the islanders. In 1906, the Anglo-French Condominium (joint rule by nations) was established, largely to settle land claims.

In 1975, a representative assembly replaced the nominated advisory council under which the New Hebrides had been governed. Two years later, the National Party (Vanua'aku Pati) demanded independence, and self-government was agreed on for 1978, to be followed by a 1980 referendum on independence.

In May 1980, however, a dissident French-speaking group, based on Espiritu

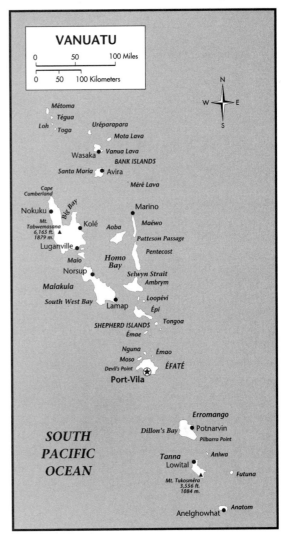

LOCATION: 13° to 21°s; 166° to 171°E. **TOTAL COASTLINE:** 2,528 kilometers (1,571 miles). **TERRITORIAL SEA LIMIT:** 12 miles.

Santo, attempted to break away and declare an independent government. This attempt was suppressed by the presence of British and French troops sent to Luganville on 24 July, although no shots were fired. The soldiers remained until Vanuatu's formal declaration of independence on 30 July 1980. They were then replaced, at the new government's request, by forces from Papua New Guinea, who were assisted by the local police in putting down the rebellion.

Since independence, Vanuatu has been the only South Pacific nation to follow a nonaligned foreign policy. In January 1987 it signed a controversial fishing agreement with the Soviet Union.

In the last election results available, the chief of state was President Father John Bani, and the head of state was Prime Minister Edward Natapei.

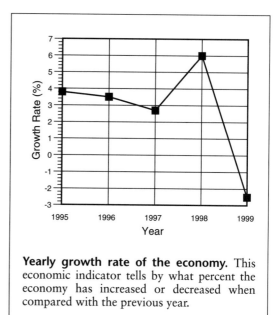

Yearly growth rate of the economy. This economic indicator tells by what percent the economy has increased or decreased when compared with the previous year.

13 GOVERNMENT

Vanuatu is an independent republic within the Commonwealth of Nations. The head of state is the president; the head of government is the prime minister. The single-chamber legislature consists of 50 members elected by universal adult suffrage to four-year terms. Vanuatu is divided into six administrative districts.

14 POLITICAL PARTIES

The Union of Moderate Parties (UMP), led by Maxime Carlot Korman, is the largest single party in the legislature. Its coalition partner in governing is the National United Party (NUP). In opposition are the Vanua'aku Pati (VPÑ—Our Land Party), Melanesian Progressive Party (MPP), National United Party (NUP), and Fren Melanesian Party (FMP).

15 JUDICIAL SYSTEM

The constitution establishes a Supreme Court, with a chief justice and three other judges, as well as an appeals court. Village and island courts have jurisdiction over customary and other matters.

16 ARMED FORCES

Vanuatuan cadets train in Papua New Guinea for a mobile defense force under the direction of the Australian Ministry of Defense.

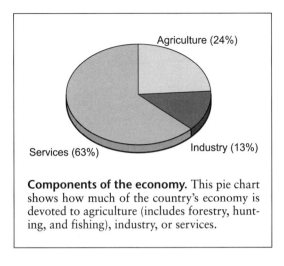

Components of the economy. This pie chart shows how much of the country's economy is devoted to agriculture (includes forestry, hunting, and fishing), industry, or services.

17 ECONOMY

Agriculture supports about 75% of the population and makes up 24% of the economy, but the service industry is playing an increasingly important role in the economy. The absence of personal and corporate income taxes have made Vanuatu an offshore financial center.

18 INCOME

In 1997, Vanuatu's gross domestic product (GDP) was $240 million, or about $1,300 per person. In 1999, the average inflation rate was 4.3%, resulting in a decline in the GDP of 2.5%.

19 INDUSTRY

Industries include fish freezing, meat canning, sawmilling, and the production of furniture, soft drinks, and fabricated aluminum goods. Native crafts include basketry, canoe building, and pottery.

20 LABOR

About 80% of the people are engaged in farming either for survival or for the production of commercial crops, such as copra.

For persons engaged in government, port work, construction, and certain other jobs, the terms of employment, wages, and union membership are set by legislation.

The nation's first unions were formed in 1984, but by 1999 there were only 1,000 active members.

21 AGRICULTURE

While most crops, including yams, taro, manioc, sweet potato, and breadfruit, are raised for local consumption, cash crops like copra (dried coconut meat), cocoa, and coffee have been increasingly important. Production of copra totaled 40,000 tons in 1998.

22 DOMESTICATED ANIMALS

Hogs and fowl form part of the village economy. Vanuatu is ideal for cattle, and large numbers are raised on plantations; in 1998 there were 151,000 head of cattle. The beef industry is centered on the island of Espiritu Santo.

23 FISHING

Fishing is currently focused on domestic consumption. Vanuatu's catch was 2,689 tons in 1997, and fish exports that year totaled $1.3 million.

24 FORESTRY

About 75% of total land area is forest or bushland. Total roundwood production in 1997 was 63,000 cubic meters, with 38% burned as fuel. Exports of forest products were valued at almost $2.1 million that year.

25 MINING

Vanuatu has few known minerals, although gold deposits have recently been discovered.

26 FOREIGN TRADE

Export commodities in 1999 included: meat, cocoa, coffee, copra, and timber. Vanuatu's main trade partners are Australia, Japan, and Spain.

27 ENERGY AND POWER

Electricity production totaled 32 million kilowatt hours in 1998.

28 SOCIAL DEVELOPMENT

The extended family system ensures that no islanders starve, while church missions and the social development section of the Education Ministry concentrate on rural development and youth activities. A provident fund system provides lump-sum benefits for old age, disability, and death. Women are just beginning to emerge from traditional cultural roles, but there are still no female leaders in the country's civic, business, or religious institutions.

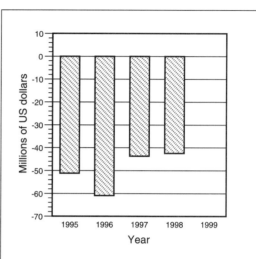

Yearly balance of trade measured in millions of US dollars. The balance of trade is the difference between what a country sells to other countries (its exports) and what it buys (its imports). If a country imports more than it exports, it has a negative balance of trade (a trade deficit). If exports exceed imports, there is a positive balance of trade (a trade surplus).

29 HEALTH

Malaria is the most serious of the country's diseases, which also include leprosy, tuberculosis, filariasis, and venereal diseases. Life expectancy was 65 years in 2000. Medical care is provided by 94 hospitals, health centers, and clinics. The country had 15 physicians in 1991.

30 HOUSING

In urban areas only the emerging middle class can afford government-built housing. Other migrants to the towns buy plots of land and build cheap shacks of corrugated iron and waste materials, principally near

Selected Social Indicators

The statistics below are estimates for the period 1996 to 2000. For comparison purposes, data for the United States and averages for low-income countries and high-income countries are also given.

Indicator	Vanuatu	Low-income countries	High-income countries	United States
Per capita gross national product (GNP)†	**$2,880**	$1,870	$25,690	$31,910
Population growth rate	**1.7%**	2.1%	0.7%	1.1%
People per square kilometer of land	**16**	73	29	30
Life expectancy in years	**65**	59	78	77
Number of physicians per 1,000 people	**n.a.**	1.0	2.5	2.5
Number of pupils per teacher (primary school)	**31**	41	17	14
Illiteracy rate (15 years and older)	**47%**	34%	<5%	3%
Television sets per 1,000 people	**10**	85	693	844
Energy consumed per capita (kg of oil equivalent)	**279**	550	5,366	7,937

† The GNP is the total dollar value of all goods and services produced by a country in a year. The per capita GNP is calculated by dividing a country's GNP by its population and adjusting for relative purchasing power. About 15% of the world's 6.1 billion people live in high-income countries, while 40% live in low-income countries.

n.a. = data not available   > = greater than   < = less than

Sources: World Bank. *World Development Indicators.* Washington, D.C.: The World Bank, 2001; Central Intelligence Agency. *The World Factbook.* Washington, D.C.: Government Printing Office, 2000.

Port-Vila and Luganville. The vast majority of villagers still build their own homes from local materials.

31 EDUCATION

The overall literacy rate is 53%, but is primarily spread among those under age 35. Primary education is available for almost all children except in a few remote tribal areas. In 1992, there were 272 primary schools with 852 teachers and 26,267 students. General secondary schools had 220 teachers and 4,269 students. Education accounted for 20% of the government's budget in 1995.

32 MEDIA

The weekly government newspaper, *The Vanuatu Weekly,* appears in English, French, and Bislama. In 1999, it had a circulation of 2,500. Radio Vanuatu broadcasts daily in English, French, and Bislama. In 2000 there were 254 radios, and 10 television sets per 1,000 population.

33 TOURISM AND RECREATION

The number of tourist arrivals reached 52,085 in 1998; of these, 62% were from Australia alone. Tourist receipts that year totaled $46 million. Popular recreations include marine sightseeing, deep-sea fishing, and sailing.

34 FAMOUS VANUATUANS

Father Walter Hayde Lini (1943–99), ordained as an Anglican priest in 1970, was a major political force in Vanuatu after independence.

35 BIBLIOGRAPHY

Aldrich, Robert. *France and the South Pacific Since 1940*. Honolulu: University of Hawaii Press, 1993.

Bonnemaison, Jokl, ed. *Arts of Vanuatu*. Honolulu: University of Hawaii Press, 1996.

Douglas, Norman. *Vanuatu: A Guide*. Sydney: Pacific Publications, 1987.

Lini, Walter. *Beyond Pandemonium: From the New Hebrides to Vanuatu*. Wellington: Asia Pacific Books, 1981.

VATICAN

The Holy See (State of the Vatican City)

Santa Sede (Stato della Cittá del Vaticano)

FLAG: The flag consists of two vertical stripes, yellow at the hoist and white at the fly. On the white field, in yellow, are the crossed keys of St. Peter, the first pope, surmounted by the papal tiara (triple crown).

ANTHEM: *Pontifical March* (no words).

MONETARY UNIT: In 1930, after a lapse of 60 years, the Vatican resumed issuance of its own coinage—the lira (L)—but it agreed to issue no more than 300 million lire in any year. There are coins of 10, 20, 50, 100, and 500 lire. Italian notes also are in use. The currencies of Italy and the Vatican are mutually convertible. L1 = $0.00059 (or $1 = L1,688.7).

WEIGHTS AND MEASURES: The metric system is in use.

HOLIDAYS: Roman Catholic religious holidays; the coronation day of the reigning pope; days when public consistory is held.

TIME: 1 PM = noon GMT.

1 LOCATION AND SIZE

Located within Rome, Vatican City is the smallest state in Europe and in the world. It is a roughly triangular area of 44 hectares (108.7 acres) lying near the west bank of the Tiber River and to the west of the Castel Sant'Angelo. The Vatican area comprises the following: St. Peter's Square; St. Peter's Basilica, the largest Christian church in the world, to which the square serves as an entrance; an area comprised of administrative buildings and Belvedere Park; the pontifical palaces; and the Vatican Gardens, which occupy about half the acreage.

A number of churches and palaces outside Vatican City itself—including the Lateran Basilica and Palace in the Piazza San Giovanni—are under its jurisdiction, as are the papal villa and its environs at Castel Gandolfo, 24 kilometers (15 miles) southeast of Rome, and an area at Santa Maria di Galeria where a Vatican radio station was established in 1957.

2 TOPOGRAPHY

Vatican City lies on a slight hill not far from the Tiber River.

3 CLIMATE

Winters are mild, and although summer temperatures are high during the day, the evenings are cold. Temperatures in January average 7°C (45°F); in July, 24°C (75°F).

4 PLANTS AND ANIMALS

The gardens are famous for their fine collection of orchids and other exotic plants.

Geographic Profile

Geographic Features

Size ranking: 192 of 192
Highest elevation: 75 meters (246 feet) at an unnamed
   location
Lowest elevation: 19 meters (62 feet) at an unnamed
   location

Weather

Average annual precipitation: 90 centimeters (35.4
   inches)
Average temperature in January: 7°C (45°F)
Average temperature in July: 24°C (75°F)

Vatican City, being entirely urban, does not have distinctive native animals.

5 ENVIRONMENT

The environment of Vatican City is similar to that of Rome (*see Italy*).

6 POPULATION

The resident population is fairly constant at about 1,000 (in 2000), including Italian nationals. About 400 inhabitants have citizenship, including the pope, cardinals resident in Rome, diplomats of the Vatican, and Swiss Guards.

7 MIGRATION

Does not apply.

8 ETHNIC GROUPS

Although the citizenry of the Vatican includes cardinals and other clergymen from all parts of the world, most of the inhabitants are Italian. The members of the Swiss Guard are a notable exception.

9 LANGUAGES

Italian is the official language of Vatican City, but Latin is the official language of the Holy See (the seat of the pope's jurisdiction as spiritual leader) and is employed for most papal encyclicals (letters) and other formal pronouncements. As the ordinary working language, Italian is in greater use.

10 RELIGIONS

Vatican City is the center of the worldwide organization of the Roman Catholic Church and the seat of the pope. Roman Catholicism is the official religion and the primary business of the state itself.

11 TRANSPORTATION

Vatican City is easily reached by the public transportation system of Rome. It has its own railroad station, with 862 meters (2,828 feet) of track, and a helicopter landing pad.

12 HISTORY

Since the time of St. Peter, regarded by the Catholic Church as the first pope, Rome has been the seat of the popes, except in periods of great turbulence, when they were forced to take refuge elsewhere, most notably in Avignon, France, from 1309 to 1377.

The State of the Vatican City and the places over which the Vatican now exercises jurisdiction are the sole remnants of the States of the Church, or Papal States. At various times, beginning in 755, these states included large areas in Italy and, until the French Revolution, even parts of

VATICAN CITY

0   250   500 Feet

0   50   100 Meters

BOUNDARY LENGTHS: Italy, 3.2 kilometers (2 miles).

southern France. Most of the papal domain fell into the hands of King Victor Emmanuel II in 1860 in the course of the unification of Italy. By 1870, Pope Pius IX, supported by a garrison of French troops, retained rule over only the besieged city of Rome and a small territory surrounding it. When the French troops withdrew to take part in the Franco-Prussian War, the walls of Rome were broken through by Italian forces on 20 September, and the city fell. On 2 October, following a referendum, the city was annexed to the kingdom of Italy and made the national capital.

In May 1871, the Italian government passed a Law of Guarantees, which attempted to define the relationship between the Italian kingdom and the papacy (pope's rule). The enactment declared the safety of the pope, guaranteed him full liberty in his religious functions and in the conduct of diplomatic relations; awarded an annual indemnity (payment to compensate for the income lost when the

Photo credit: EPD/Apostolic Nunciature in the United States.

Name:	John Paul II
Nickname:	"Pilgrim Pope"
Position:	Pope of a monarchical-sacerdotal state
Took office:	16 October 1978
Birthplace:	Wadowice, Poland
Birth date:	18 May 1920
Religion:	Roman Catholic
Education:	Jagiellonian University, Krakow, Poland, field of literature; Pontifical Angelicum University, Rome
Of interest:	In school, the Pope had excelled in sports, dramatics, and academic subjects. He once earned a living as a manual laborer in a quarry and a chemical factory. He has recorded an album of religious hymns. He is the first non-Italian pope since the year 1522.

Papal States were annexed), and provided the pope the right of jurisdiction over the Vatican and the papal palaces. Pius IX refused to accept the law or the money allowance; he and his successors chose to become "prisoners of the Vatican." Until 1919, Roman Catholics were prohibited by the papacy from participating in the Italian government.

The so-called Roman Question was brought to an end by the conclusion on 11 February 1929 of three treaties between the Vatican and Italy. One treaty recognized the full sovereignty of the Vatican and established its territorial extent. Another treaty established the Roman Catholic Church as the state church of Italy. The remaining treaty awarded the Vatican financial reparations to settle all financial claims against Italy for annexing the Papal States. In 1962–65, the Vatican was the site of the Second Vatican Council, the first worldwide council in almost a century. Convened by Pope John XXIII and continued under Paul VI, the Council resulted in modernization of the Church's role in spiritual and social matters.

On 13 May 1981, Pope John Paul II was wounded in Vatican Square by a Turkish gunman, who is serving a life sentence for this action. The alleged accomplices, three Bulgarians and three Turks, were acquitted of conspiracy in the assassination attempt on 29 March 1986 because of lack of evidence. The treaties of 1929 were superseded in 1984 by a new agreement under which the pope retains temporal authority over Vatican City but Roman Catholicism is no longer Italy's state religion. In December 1993, the Vatican and the Israeli government concluded a mutual recognition agreement. In Octo-

Photo credit: Corel Corporation.

The detailed front of St. Peter's Church in the Vatican City.

ber 1994, the Vatican established diplomatic ties with the Palestine Liberation Organization (PLO) to balance its ties with Israel. In January 1995, Pope John Paul II offered to recognize official papal authority over China's Catholics. In return, the Vatican would approve the Chinese government's officially sponsored church, the Chinese Patriotic Catholic Association. No progress had been made in this direction at this time.

The pope also traveled to Israel in 2000, where he visited different Holocaust memorials. He also visited Bethlehem to affirm the Vatican's support for an independent Palestinian homeland.

13 GOVERNMENT

The pope is simultaneously the absolute sovereign of the State of the Vatican City and the head of the Roman Catholic Church throughout the world. Since 1984, the pope has been represented by the cardinal secretary of state in the civil governance of Vatican City. In administering the government of the Vatican, the pope is assisted by the Pontifical Commission for the State of the Vatican City. Religious affairs are governed under the pope's direction by a number of ecclesiastical bodies known collectively as the Roman Curia. Much of the work of the Roman Curia is conducted by offices called sacred congregations, each headed by a cardinal appointed for a five-year period.

Under the Pontifical Commission are the following: a central council (heading various administrative offices); the directorships of museums, technical services, economic services (including the postal and telegraph systems), and medical services; the guard; the Vatican radio system and television center; the Vatican observatory; and the directorship of the villa at Castel Gandolfo, the traditional summer residence of popes.

A pope serves from his election until death. After his death, the College of Cardinals meets to choose a successor from among themselves. The usual method is to vote on the succession; in this case, the cardinal who receives two-thirds plus one of the votes of those present is declared elected.

14 POLITICAL PARTIES

Does not apply.

15 JUDICIAL SYSTEM

A tribunal rules on ordinary legal matters occurring within Vatican territory. Criminal cases are tried in Italian courts. There are three tribunals at the Vatican for religious cases. The Apostolic Penitentiary determines questions of penance and absolution from sin. The Roman Rota deals principally with marital issues but also is competent to handle appeals from any decisions of lower ecclesiastical courts. In exceptional cases, the Supreme Tribunal of the Apostolic Signature hears appeals from the Rota.

16 ARMED FORCES

The papal patrol force now consists only of the Swiss Guard, who walk their posts in picturesque striped uniforms supposedly designed by the artist Michelangelo (1475–1564). The force was founded in 1506 and is recruited from several Roman Catholic cantons of Switzerland. It now numbers approximately 100 members. There also is a civilian security force, which protects Vatican personnel and property and the art treasures owned by the Church.

17 ECONOMY

The Vatican, being essentially an administrative center, is dependent for its support on the receipt of charitable contributions, the fees charged those able to pay for the services of the congregations and other ecclesiastical bodies, and interest on investments. Funds also are raised from the sale of stamps, religious literature, and mementos, and from museum admissions.

18 INCOME

Income in 1992 was estimated at $92 million.

19 INDUSTRY

A studio in the Vatican produces mosaic work, and a sewing establishment produces uniforms. There is a large printing plant, the Vatican Polyglot Press.

20 LABOR

The labor force consists mainly of priests, who serve as consultants and counselors; about 3,000 laborers, who live outside the Vatican; the guards; the nuns, who do administrative work as well as the cooking, cleaning, laundering, and tapestry repair; and the cardinals, archbishops, bishops, and other higher dignitaries. Some ecclesiastical (church) officials live outside Vatican City and commute from the secular (not religious) city. The Association of Vatican Lay Workers, a trade union, has 1,800 members. Lay employees have always been required to be Roman Catholic and swear loyalty to the pope.

21 AGRICULTURE

Does not apply.

22 DOMESTICATED ANIMALS

Does not apply.

23 FISHING

Does not apply.

24 FORESTRY

Does not apply.

25 MINING

Does not apply.

26 FOREIGN TRADE

Does not apply.

27 ENERGY AND POWER

Electric power is supplied by Italy, but the Vatican's generating plant had a capacity of 5,000 kilowatts in 1990.

28 SOCIAL DEVELOPMENT

Celibacy (abstention from sexual intercourse) is required of all Roman Catholic clergy, except permanent deacons. The Church upholds the concept of family planning through traditional methods, such as abstinence, but resolutely opposes such "artificial methods" as contraceptive pills and devices, as well as abortion and sterilization. Five important papal encyclicals (letters)—*Rerum Novarum* (1870), *Quadragesimo Anno* (1931), *Mater et Magistra* (1961), *Pacem in Terris* (1963), and *Laborem Exercens* (1981)—have enunciated the Church position on matters of workers' rights and social and international justice.

29 HEALTH

The health services directorate, under the Pontifical Commission for the Vatican City State, is responsible for health matters.

30 HOUSING

Information is not available.

31 EDUCATION

The Vatican is a major center for higher Roman Catholic education, especially of the clergy being trained for important positions. Adult literacy is 100%. About 65 papal educational institutions are scattered throughout Rome; some of the more important (all prefixed by the word "Pontifical") are the Gregorian University, the Biblical Institute, the Institute of Oriental Studies, the Lateran Athenaeum, the Institute of Christian Archaeology, and the Institute of Sacred Music. There were a total of 14,403 students in 1996 with 1,872 teaching staff in all higher level institutions.

32 MEDIA

The state maintains its own telegraph and postal facilities and has a 2,000-line automatic telephone exchange. Radio Vatican operates three AM and four FM stations. Programs in 34 languages are broadcast regularly. The Vatican Television Center, founded in 1983, produces and distributes religious programs.

Vatican City is an important center for publishing. A semiofficial newspaper of wide fame, *L'Osservatore Romano,* is published daily, with an estimated 1999 circulation of 70,000 copies. The international Religious Press Service distributes news of missionary activity. In the mid-1990s, 47 periodicals were published, with a total circulation of almost 60,000. The book publishers for the Vatican are the Vatican Editions, the Vatican Apostolic Library, and the Vatican Polyglot Press (*Tipografia Poliglotta Vaticana*). In 1991, there were 196 titles published.

33 TOURISM AND RECREATION

The Vatican is regularly visited by tourists in Rome, as well as by pilgrims attracted by the jubilees (festivals) proclaimed by the pope every 25 years and by other special occasions. While there are no public accommodations in the Vatican, special inexpensive facilities are often arranged in Rome for pilgrims. No passport or identification is needed ordinarily for admission to the public parts of the Vatican.

34 FAMOUS POPES

Among those who greatly increased the secular (nonreligious) power of the papacy were St. Gregory I (the Great, 540?–604),

pope from 590 to 604, who also was influential in matters of doctrine and missionary work; St. Gregory VII (Hildebrand, 1020?–1085), pope from 1073 to 1085, who engaged in conflict with Holy Roman Emperor Henry IV, who was forced to do public penance at the village of Canossa, but who later drove the pope out of Rome; and Alexander VI (Rodrigo Lanzol y Borja, b. Spain, 1431?–1503), pope from 1492 to 1503, who also divided colonial territories in the New World between Spain and Portugal.

The most significant nineteenth-century pope was Pius IX (Giovanni Maria Mastai-Ferretti, 1792–1878), pope from 1846 to 1878, who lost the Papal States to the kingdom of Italy and convened the First Vatican Council (1869–70). John Paul II (Karol Wojtyla, b.1920), was elevated to the papacy on 16 October 1978. This former archbishop of Krakow was not only the first Polish pope but also the first non-Italian pope since the Renaissance.

35 BIBLIOGRAPHY

Bull, George. *Inside the Vatican.* New York: St. Martin's, 1983.

Hutchinson, Robert J. *When in Rome: A Journal of Life in Vatican City.* New York: Doubleday, 1998.

Martin, Malachi. *Vatican.* New York: Harper & Row, 1986.

McDowell, Bart. *Inside the Vatican.* Washington, D.C.: National Geographic Society, 1991.

Packard, Jerrold M. *Peter's Kingdom: Inside the Papal City.* New York: Scribner, 1985.

Reese, Thomas J. *Inside the Vatican: The Politics and Organization of the Catholic Church.* Cambridge, Mass.: Harvard University Press, 1996.

Wynn, Wilton. *Keepers of the Keys.* New York: Random House, 1988.

VENEZUELA

Republic of Venezuela
República de Venezuela

CAPITAL: Caracas.

FLAG: The national flag, adopted in 1930, is a tricolor of yellow, blue, and red horizontal stripes. An arc of seven white stars on the blue stripe represents the seven original states.

ANTHEM: *Himno Nacional,* beginning "Gloria al bravo pueblo" ("Glory to the brave people").

MONETARY UNIT: The bolívar (B) is a paper currency of 100 céntimos. There are coins of 5, 25, and 50 céntimos and 1, 2, and 5 bolívars, and notes of 5, 10, 20, 50, 100, 500, and 1,000 bolívars. B1 = $0.00153 (or $1 = B652.33).

WEIGHTS AND MEASURES: The metric system is the legal standard.

HOLIDAYS: New Year's Day, 1 January; Declaration of Independence and Day of the Indian, 19 April; Labor Day, 1 May; Army Day and Anniversary of the Battle of Carabobo, 24 June; Independence Day, 5 July; Bolívar's Birthday, 24 July; Civil Servants Day, 4 September; Columbus Day, 12 October; Christmas, 25 December; New Year's Eve, 31 December. Movable holidays are Carnival (Monday and Tuesday before Ash Wednesday), Holy Thursday, Good Friday, and Holy Saturday. Numerous other bank holidays and local festivals are observed.

TIME: 8 AM = noon GMT.

1 LOCATION AND SIZE

Venezuela, located on the northern coast of South America, covers an area of 912,050 square kilometers (352,144 square miles), slightly more than twice the size of the state of California. It has a total boundary length of 7,609 kilometers (4,729 miles). There are 72 offshore islands. Venezuela's capital city, Caracas, is located in the northern part of the country on the Caribbean Sea coast.

2 TOPOGRAPHY

Venezuela has four principal geographical divisions. In the north emerges a low extension of the Andes mountain chain; to the west lies the hot basin of Lake Maracaibo (Lago Maracaibo); to the southeast spread the great plains (*llanos*) and forests; and south of the Orinoco River lie the unoccupied and largely unexplored Guiana Highlands, accounting for about half the country's total area. The Orinoco River, which is more than 2,900 kilometers (1,800 miles) long, drains four-fifths of Venezuela. There are more than 1,000 other rivers.

Outstanding geographical features include Angel Falls (979 meters/3,212 feet high) in the Guiana Highlands of southeastern Venezuela, the highest waterfall in the world, and Bolívar Peak, the highest

Geographic Profile

Geographic Features

Size ranking: 32 of 192
Highest elevation: 5,007 meters (16,427 feet) at
  Bolívar Peak
Lowest elevation: Sea level at the Caribbean Sea

Land Use†

Arable land:	4%
Permanent crops:	1%
Permanent pastures:	20%
Forests:	34%
Other:	41%

Weather††

Average annual precipitation: 85.4 centimeters (33.6
  inches)
Average temperature in January: 19.6°C (67.3°F)
Average temperature in July: 21.9°C (71.4°F)

†*Arable land:* Land used for temporary crops, like
meadows for mowing or pasture, gardens, and greenhouses. *Permanent crops:* Land cultivated with crops
that occupy its use for long periods, such as cocoa,
coffee, rubber, fruit and nut orchards, and vineyards.
Permanent pastures: Land used permanently for forage crops. *Forests:* Land containing stands of trees.
Other: Any land not specified, including built-on
areas, roads, and barren land.

††The measurements for precipitation and average
temperature were taken at weather stations closest to
the country's largest city. Precipitation and average
temperature can vary significantly within a country,
due to factors such as latitude, altitude, coastal proximity, and wind patterns.

peak in Venezuela (5,007 meters/16,427 feet).

3 CLIMATE

Although Venezuela lies entirely within the torrid zone, generally there are four climatic regions, based mainly on altitude. In the tropical region, mean annual temperatures range from 24° to 35°C (75° to 95°F). In the subtropical region, where Caracas is situated, the means range from 10° to 25°C (50° to 77°F). During the wet season (May to October), the llanos and forest areas are swampy, green, and lush. At the beginning of the dry season, the same areas become dry, brown, and parched. The temperate and cold regions are located above elevations of 1,830 meters (6,000 feet). There is perpetual snow on several peaks of the mountain chain, Cordillera de Mérida.

4 PLANTS AND ANIMALS

The natural vegetation of the tropical zone varies from the rainforest regions of the lower Lake Maracaibo Basin to the grasslands of the llanos. The subtropical zone was originally almost covered by a luxuriant forest and is now the nation's principal agricultural region. In the temperate region, wild vegetation is sparse and scrubby. In the higher altitudes, from about 2,740 to 4,880 meters (9,000 to 16,000 feet), vegetation becomes even thinner. Above 3,050 meters (10,000 feet), the only vegetation seen is the espeletia, similar to the century plant, which grows to a height of 1.8–2.1 meters (6–7 feet).

The wild animals of Venezuela are abundant because of their relative isolation from human disturbance. The forests are populated with tapirs, sloths, anteaters, and a variety of monkeys. In the mountains are puma, margay, vampire bats, and deer. Semiwild horses, donkeys, and cattle are found in the plains. The forests are rich in tropical birds such as the cacique, crested coquette, heron, umbrella bird, manakin, cock-of-the-rock, parrot, macaw, and aigrette. Aquatic fowl include the pelican, heron, flamingo, and a muscovy duck weighing up to 9.1 kilograms

VENEZUELA

| 0 | 50 | 100 | 150 | 200 Miles |
| 0 | 50 | 100 | 150 | 200 Kilometers |

LOCATION: 0°35′ to 12°11′N; 60°10′ to 73°25′W. **BOUNDARY LENGTHS:** Total coastline, 2,816 kilometers (1,750 miles); Guyana, 743 kilometers (462 miles); Brazil, 2,000 kilometers (1,243 miles); Colombia, 2,050 kilometers (1,274 miles). **TERRITORIAL SEA LIMIT:** 12 miles.

(20 pounds). More than 32 species of eagles are found in Venezuela. There are numerous reptiles, including the rattle-snake, coral snake, bushmaster, anaconda, and boa. Crocodiles are found in the low-land rivers. Fish, shellfish, tortoises, and sand tortoises also are plentiful.

5 ENVIRONMENT

Power plants, industry, and transportation vehicles contribute to air pollution; Venezuela's waterways have been polluted by untreated industrial wastes and by mining activity. Between 1983 and 1993, Venezuela's forests and woodlands decreased

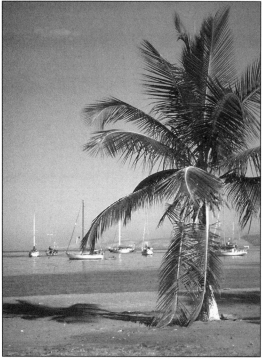

Photo credit: Mary A. Dempsey.

Beach at Puerto La Cruz, Venezuela.

6 POPULATION

An estimated 23.6 million people lived in Venezuela in 2000, up from 18.1 million in 1990. A population of 25.5 million is projected for the year 2005. Venezuela is one of the least densely populated countries in the Western Hemisphere with an estimated population density of 27 persons per square kilometer (70 per square mile). In 2000, 87% of the population was urban. The largest metropolitan areas in 2000 were Caracas, 3.15 million; Maracaibo, 1.8 million; and Valencia, 1.8 million.

7 MIGRATION

In the decades immediately before and after World War II (1939–45), nearly 500,000 Europeans—mostly from Italy, Spain, and Portugal—came to Venezuela. By 1990, however, only 5.7% of the resident population was of foreign birth. In 1989 there were 18,893 immigrants and 9,643 emigrants. An estimated 300,000 illegal immigrants, most of them Colombians, were living in Venezuela in 1985. Internal migration is chiefly eastward from the far northwest. During 1990–97, 1,630 persons in Venezuela were given refugee status by the United Nations.

8 ETHNIC GROUPS

The original inhabitants of Venezuela were Amerindians, mainly Caribs and Arawaks. The bulk (about 68%) of the present population is mestizo (mixed race); an estimated 21% are European, 8–10% black, and 2% Amerindian.

8.2%. In the Andes mountain area, Venezuela loses up to 300 tons of soil per hectare (120 tons per acre) due to land erosion by rivers. Pressing environmental problems led the government in 1976 to establish the Ministry of Environment and Renewable Natural Resources. Measures designed to prevent forest depletion include suspension of logging permits and a large-scale afforestation program.

In 1994, 19 of the nation's mammal species and 34 bird species were endangered, as well as 106 plant types. As of 1994, endangered species in Venezuela included the tundra peregrine falcon, giant otter, and five species of turtle.

9 LANGUAGES

The official language is Spanish, with marked regional variations.

10 RELIGIONS

In 1998, an estimated 75% of the population was Roman Catholic, Protestants constituted about 18%, and about 7% practiced tribal religions or were Afro-American spiritists. There also were small, but influential Muslim and Jewish communitites.

11 TRANSPORTATION

The most important mode of domestic cargo and passenger transport is shipping over the country's more than 16,000 kilometers (9,900 miles) of navigable inland waterways. In 1998, the merchant fleet had 32 vessels weighing more than 1,000 gross tons, for a total of 535,882 gross registered tons. Puerto Cabello handles the most cargo, and Maracaibo is the main port for oil shipments.

Photo credit: Anne Kalosh.

Central Park (Parque Central) *in Caracas, Venezuela's capital city.*

Highway and railroad construction is both costly and dangerous because of the rough mountainous terrain in the areas of dense population. Nevertheless, the government has undertaken massive highway construction projects throughout the country. By 1998, Venezuela had 84,300 kilometers (52,384 miles) of highway, of which 39% were paved. In 1995 there were 1.5 million passenger cars and 511,800 commercial vehicles in Venezuela.

Venezuela's two railroads carry mostly freight. There were 584 kilometers (362 miles) of track in 1998. Much of the equipment is out of date, and the linking of lines is difficult because of the different gauges in use. In the early 1980s, the government planned to build a 3,900-kilometer (2,420-mile) railroad network by the end of the decade; however, the financial crisis that began in 1983 has scaled the program down to 2,000 kilometers (1,200 miles) over 20 years.

Cities and towns of the remote regions are linked principally by air transportation. Venezuela has three main airlines, the

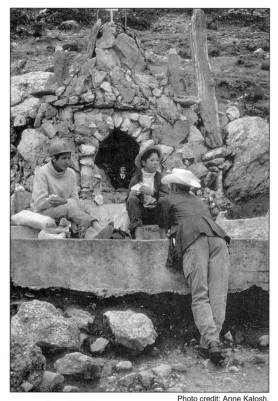

Venezuelans pause for a snack at a shrine on a trail in the Andes.

government-owned Aerovías Venezolanas S.A. (AVENSA), Línea Aeropostal Venezolana (LAV), and Venezolana Internacional de Aviación, S.A. (VIASA). The government has expanded Simón Bolívar International Airport at Maiquetía, near Caracas, to accommodate heavy jet traffic. In 1997, more than four million passengers traveled through Venezuela on scheduled flights.

12 HISTORY

Venezuela received its name, meaning "Little Venice," from Alonso de Ojeda, who sailed into the Gulf of Venezuela (Golfo de Venezuela) in August 1499 and was reminded of the Italian city by the native huts built on stilts over the water. Except for a brief period of control by German commercial interests, Venezuela was a colonial territory of Spain.

Under the Spanish, eastern Venezuela was governed under the audiencia (region under a royal court) of Santo Domingo, and the western and southern regions became a captaincy-general under the viceroyalty of Peru. Settlement of the colony was hampered by constant wars with the Amerindians, which did not stop until after a smallpox epidemic in 1580. In 1717, the western and southern provinces were incorporated into the viceroyalty of New Granada, and in 1783, the area of present-day Venezuela became a captaincy-general of Caracas.

Beginning in 1811, Venezuela struggled for independence from Spain for 10 years, first under Francisco de Miranda, then led by Simón Bolívar. The end of the Venezuelan war of independence came with Bolívar's victory in June 1821. Under Bolívar's leadership, Gran Colombia (Greater Colombia) was formed from Colombia, Ecuador, and Venezuela, with Bolívar as its president and military dictator.

In 1830, Venezuela seceded from Gran Colombia. A period of civil wars lasted from 1846 to 1870, when Antonio Guzmán Blanco assumed power. After this, Venezuela was ruled by dictatorships for nearly a century. When Cipriano Castro, who ruled from 1899 to 1908, refused to repay Venezuela's international loans,

Germany, Great Britain, and Italy sent gunboats to blockade the Venezuelan coast. During the dictatorship of Juan Vicente Gómez (1908–35), agriculture was developed and oil was discovered, making Venezuela one of the richest countries in Latin America. Oil concessions attracted American, British, and Dutch companies, initiating an era of oil wealth that continues today.

After the death of Gómez, Venezuela began to move toward democracy. The first free election for president in Venezuelan history was held in 1947, and Rómulo Gallegos, a distinguished novelist and candidate of Democratic Action (Acción Democrática—AD), was elected overwhelmingly. However, Gallegos was replaced by a military junta, followed by another dictatorship in the 1950s. Venezuela took its last steps toward full democracy in 1958, when Rómulo Betancourt was chosen president. Venezuela has had fair and free elections ever since.

The Betancourt government (1959–64) instituted modest financial and agricultural reforms, built schools, and eliminated illiteracy. In spite of attempts by the military to return to power, and the activities of pro-Castro guerrillas, the AD was reelected in December 1964, when Raúl Leoni won the presidency over five other candidates. In 1968, Venezuela passed another test of democracy by transferring power peacefully from AD to the opposition Social Christian Party.

In 1979, Venezuela received a rude awakening when demand for oil dropped, threatening the foundations of its economic and political systems. The crisis climaxed with the devaluation of the national currency, the bolívar, which dropped to one-third of its previous value against the dollar. Venezuelan consumers responded angrily, and the early 1980s were years of unrest. In the elections of December 1983, the AD returned to power behind presidential candidate Jaime Lusinchi.

While the economy floundered through the 1980s, the government maintained public confidence by stressing a "social pact" with guarantees of housing, education, and public health. Some progress has been made in boosting non-oil exports, particularly in agriculture and mining. The 1988 elections brought back Carlos Andrés Pérez, who had been elected president 15 years earlier. When Pérez removed government subsidies on a number of consumer goods, including gasoline, prices rose and Caracas was rocked by rioting on a scale not seen since 1958. The military was called in to stop the disturbances, but when the trouble finally died down, thousands had been killed or injured.

In 1992, Venezuela was shocked by two military coup attempts, and Pérez was suspended from office on embezzlement and theft allegations. In the regularly scheduled presidential elections of December 1993, Venezuelans chose former president Rafael Caldera, who ran under a coalition of four parties. Even though Venezuela remained one of the wealthiest countries in Latin America, its government is increasingly unstable.

The economy fell into recession in 1993, and President Caldera suspended a number of civil rights in 1994–95. The inflation rate hit 103% in 1995, and poverty affected Venezuela's middle class. Doctors, professors, and national telephone company workers all went on strike in 1997.

In 1994, 108 inmates were killed by National Guard troops in a protest over prison crowding and poor living conditions. In 1996, 25 prisoners at another overcrowded facility were burned to death by National Guard troops.

13 GOVERNMENT

Venezuela is a republic governed under the constitution of 23 January 1961, which stresses social, economic, and political rights. The president (Hugo Rafael Chavez Friaz in 2001) is elected by direct popular vote for a five-year term. Presidential duties include the selection and removal of cabinet ministers and all other administrative officers and employees of the national government, as well as the appointment of state governors. The president is both chief-of-state and head-of-state.

The president is commander-in-chief of the armed forces, directs foreign affairs, and may make and ratify international treaties, conventions, and agreements. He may veto legislation, but a two-thirds majority of Congress can override it. There is no vice-president, and if the president cannot complete a term of office, the Congress, meeting in joint session, must select a new president by secret vote.

The Congress has two chambers, a 47-member Senate and 200-seat Chamber of Deputies. Both houses are elected concurrently with the president for five-year terms. A bill may be introduced in either house but must be passed by both in order to become law. There is compulsory adult voting at age 18.

Venezuela is divided into 21 states, one federal territory, the Federal District, and 72 offshore islands. The states are subdivided into 156 districts and 613 municipalities.

14 POLITICAL PARTIES

Since 1958, the dominant force in Venezuelan politics has been the Democratic Action Party (Acción Democrática—AD), formed from the nationalist and democratic-socialist faction of the socialist movement. The most recent development from the left has been the emergence of the Movement for Socialism (Movimiento al Socialismo—MAS), which took 10% of the vote for the Chamber of Deputies in 1988.

The right has been characterized by small parties, some of which have been able to form coalitions with larger parties to achieve some success within the system. COPEI is a center-right Christian Democratic party that has succeeded as an opposition party to the AD, occasionally taking advantage of splits in the AD's governing coalition or within the AD itself.

Agreements between AD and COPEI in 1970 and 1973 called for cooperation in appointive posts, so that the competition has been controlled. AD and COPEI have dominated the system since, although the 1994 election of Caldera as the candidate of a four-party coalition suggests a movement away from the two-party arrangement.

15 JUDICIAL SYSTEM

The Supreme Court, which organizes and directs the other courts and tribunals of the republic, is the nation's highest tribunal, and there is no appeal of its decisions. It can declare a law, or any part of a law or any regulation or act of the president unconstitutional. The court determines whether there are grounds for the trial of the president, a member of Congress, members of the court itself, or certain executive officials.

The lower branches of the judiciary include courts of appeal and direct courts, whose judges and magistrates are appointed by the Supreme Court. Each state has its own supreme court, superior court, district courts, and municipal courts. The territories have civil and military judges. The jury system is not used. The justice system in general is inefficient, backlogged, and open to corruption.

16 ARMED FORCES

Venezuela's armed forces are professional and well equipped. In principle, all male Venezuelans 18 years of age are required to serve two years (or 30 months in the navy) and then to remain in the reserve until the age of 45. In practice, however, many males, including workers in essential occupations, students, and heads of households, are exempted from service.

Photo credit: EPD/Office of the President.

Name:	Hugo Chavez
Position:	President of a federal republic
Took office:	3 February 1999
Birthplace:	Sabaneta, Venezuela
Birth date:	28 July 1954
Religion:	Roman Catholic
Education:	Military Academy of Venezuela, graduate degree in international relations
Spouse:	Marisabel
Children:	Four children
Of interest:	A devout Roman Catholic, Chavez often quotes passages from the Bible.

Total armed strength in 2000 was 79,000, including 23,000 volunteers in the Fuerzas Armados de Cooperacion, an internal security force. The army had 34,000 regulars, including six infantry divisions and 12 specialized brigades, and 2,000 airmen. The navy had 15,000 mem-

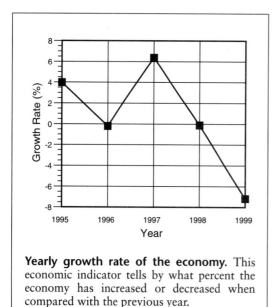

Yearly growth rate of the economy. This economic indicator tells by what percent the economy has increased or decreased when compared with the previous year.

bers, including 5,000 marines; naval strength included two submarines and six frigates. The air force had 7,000 personnel, 124 combat aircraft, and 31 armed helicopters. Defense expenditures in 1998 were $1.1 billion, or 1% of the gross domestic product (GDP).

17 ECONOMY

For more than 40 years the economy has been completely dominated by the petroleum industry; in the mid-1980s, oil exports accounted for 90% of all export value. Weakening world oil prices contributed to economic stagnation in the 1980s, when Venezuela had difficulty meeting its payments on short-term loans accumulated by state-owned enterprises.

After severe adjustments during 1989 and 1990, the main economic indicators improved considerably in 1991 and 1992.

Growth was led by the oil industry, due mainly to the Persian Gulf War (1991). Consumer prices rose by an average of 43.8% per year between 1990 and 1995.

In 1996, the government devalued its currency, got rid of foreign exchange controls, and raised gasoline prices. These moves helped reduce deficits, but brought about more inflation.

18 INCOME

In 1998, Venezuela's gross domestic product (GDP) was $194.5 billion, or approximately $8,500 per person. In 1999, the average inflation rate was 30%, resulting in an annual decline rate in GDP of about 7%.

19 INDUSTRY

Although much of Venezuela's petroleum is exported in crude form, petroleum refining is a major industry. Petroleum products amounted to three billion barrels per day in 1999. The steel industry, operating at 48% of capacity, produced 3.6 million tons of steel in 1995. Other industries include shipbuilding, automobile production (96,403 vehicles in 1995), and fertilizer manufacture.

Valencia is a major new industrial center. A second major industrial development scheme has made Ciudad Guayana the hub of a vast industrial area with a 160-kilometers (100-miles) radius. There is a steel mill with a yearly capacity of 750,000 tons, and a bauxite-processing plant.

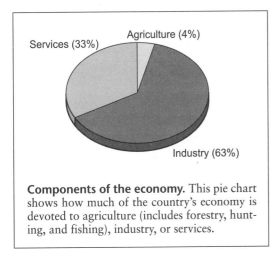

Components of the economy. This pie chart shows how much of the country's economy is devoted to agriculture (includes forestry, hunting, and fishing), industry, or services.

20 LABOR

Venezuela's economically active population in 1997 was 9.5 million. The distribution of employment among major economic areas was as follows: services, 64% (33% of economy); industry, 23% (63%); and agriculture, 13% (4%). The unemployment rate was 11.4% at the end of 1997. In 1996, about 25% of the labor force was unionized.

The constitution provides for a minimum wage, the right to strike, and the right of labor to organize into unions. Labor laws include provisions for an eight-hour day, a paid vacation of at least 15 workdays a year, compulsory profit sharing, severance pay, death and disability payments, medical services, and social security. For children under 16, there are restrictions on the number of hours and working conditions. These restrictions are enforced for formal jobs, but as many as one million children may be working outside the formal economy.

21 AGRICULTURE

Venezuela does not have the rich soil of many other Latin American countries. In 1997, 3.5 million hectares (8.6 million acres), or 4% of the total land area, were used for temporary or permanent crops. The most highly developed agricultural region is a lake basin west of Caracas and inland from Puerto Cabello. The principal crop of this area is coffee.

The main field crops are sugarcane, rice, corn, and sorghum; and the chief fruits are bananas, plantains, oranges, coconuts, and mangoes. The most important agricultural items for industrial use are cotton, tobacco, and sisal. Two varieties of tobacco grow in Venezuela, black and Virginia blond; the latter is used for the most part to make certain popular brands of American cigarettes under license. Sisal is grown and widely used to make cords and sacks for grains and coffee. Thin strings of the fiber also are used in hammocks, household bags, doormats, hats, and sandals.

Agricultural production in 1998 (in tons) included sugarcane, 7.2 million; bananas, 1.1 million; corn, 938,000; rice, 673,000; sorghum, 386,000; plantains, 509,000; oranges, 528,000; potatoes, 349,000; tomatoes, 292,000; cotton, 12,000; and tobacco, 14,000.

22 DOMESTICATED ANIMALS

Since colonial days, cattle raising has been the dominant livestock industry in Venezuela. Chiefly *criollos*, or Spanish longhorns, the cattle are raised on unfenced ranges. Venezuela's livestock population in 1998 included 15.3 million head of cattle, 3.2 million goats, 4.7 million hogs, and 8.2 million sheep. Beef production increased from 147,000 tons in 1963 to 363,000 tons in 1998. In 1998, pork production was 150,000 tons; goat meat, 5,000 tons; mutton, 2,000 tons; and poultry, 495,000 tons. Milk production was more than 1.4 billion tons in 1998. Venezuela is self-sufficient in beef, but it has to import 50% of the milk it consumes.

23 FISHING

With its 2,816 kilometers (1,750 miles) of open coast, Venezuela has vast fishing potential. Fish and fish products currently play a relatively minor role in Venezuela's international trade, but fish are extremely important domestically. Venezuela has the highest per person fish consumption in Latin America, about three times that of the United States. Some of the main fishing areas are La Guaira, the Paraguaná peninsula, and the Cariaco—Margarita–Carúpano area. The total catch in 1997 was 502,764 tons, up from 284,235 tons in 1986.

24 FORESTRY

Partly because of the remoteness of forest areas, exploitation of Venezuela's high-quality wood is underdeveloped. Forest land is misused by small farmers, who clear land for farming by burning trees without replacing them. The greatest concentration of forests lies south of the Orinoco. Cedar and mahogany are the principal trees cut; rubber, dividivi, mangrove bark, tonka beans, oil-bearing palm nuts, and medicinal plants also are pro-

Photo credit: Anne Kalosh.

Picking coffee beans at Mt. Mochima National Park near Pto, La Cruz, Venezuela.

duced. Roundwood output was more than 2.2 million cubic meters (2.9 million cubic yards) in 1997, with 43% used as fuel.

25 MINING

Principal mineral commodities are aluminum, cement, diamonds, ferroalloys, gold, and iron ore. The most important metal mined in Venezuela is iron. Iron ore production was an estimated 18.3 million tons in 1997. Gold, the first metal found in Venezuela, reached its production peak in 1890. Production was 22,322 kilograms in 1997. In the same year, diamond production was an estimated 158,260 carats. Bauxite production was 4.9 million tons in 1997.

Other minerals extracted are sulfur, gypsum, limestone, salt (produced as a government monopoly), granite, clay, and phosphate rock. Minerals known to exist but not yet mined are manganese (with deposits estimated at several million tons), mercury, nickel, magnesite, cobalt, mica, cyanite, and radioactive materials.

26 FOREIGN TRADE

In 1999, exports were officially reported at $20.9 billion, and imports were put at $11.8 billion. Oil accounted for 75% of exports that year. Aluminum, automobiles, iron and steel products, and alcohol were the main non-oil exports. Venezuela's principal imports were industrial supplies, machinery, transportation equipment, and food products.

The country's major export markets in 1999 included Colombia, the United States, the Netherlands, Germany, and Japan. The leading import suppliers that year were the United States, Colombia, Germany, Brazil, and Japan.

After several years of negotiations, the Group of Three (Colombia, Mexico, and Venezuela) signed a freetrade agreement. The agreement went into effect on 1 January 1995 and committed the countries to lift most trade restrictions over a 10-year period.

27 ENERGY AND POWER

With vast petroleum deposits, extensive waterways, and an abundance of natural

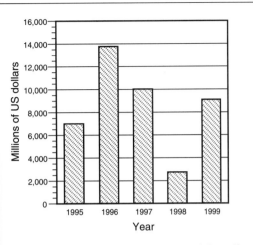

Yearly balance of trade measured in millions of US dollars. The balance of trade is the difference between what a country sells to other countries (its exports) and what it buys (its imports). If a country imports more than it exports, it has a negative balance of trade (a trade deficit). If exports exceed imports there is a positive balance of trade (a trade surplus).

gas, Venezuela possesses great electric power potential. In 1998, total electrical power generation was an estimated 70 billion kilowatt hours. Venezuela was the world's tenth-largest oil producer in 1998. Proven oil reserves were estimated at 72.6 billion barrels in 2000, the largest in the world outside the Middle East. Petroleum production rose to an estimated 3.3 million barrels per day in 1998. The output of natural gas was an estimated 28.3 billion cubic meters in 1998. Proven reserves totaled four trillion cubic meters (141 trillion cubic feet) in 2000.

28 SOCIAL DEVELOPMENT

The social security system covers medical care, maternity benefits, disability, retirement and survivors' pensions, burial costs,

Selected Social Indicators

The statistics below are estimates for the period 1996 to 2000. For comparison purposes, data for the United States and averages for low-income countries and high-income countries are also given.

Indicator	Venezuela	Low-income countries	High-income countries	United States
Per capita gross national product (GNP)†	$5,420	$1,870	$25,690	$31,910
Population growth rate	2%	2.1%	0.7%	1.1%
People per square kilometer of land	27	73	29	30
Life expectancy in years	73	59	78	77
Number of physicians per 1,000 people	1.6	1.0	2.5	2.5
Number of pupils per teacher (primary school)	23	41	17	14
Illiteracy rate (15 years and older)	7%	34%	<5%	3%
Television sets per 1,000 people	185	85	693	844
Energy consumed per capita (kg of oil equivalent)	2,433	550	5,366	7,937

† The GNP is the total dollar value of all goods and services produced by a country in a year. The per capita GNP is calculated by dividing a country's GNP by its population and adjusting for relative purchasing power. About 15% of the world's 6.1 billion people live in high-income countries, while 40% live in low-income countries.

n.a. = data not available   > = greater than   < = less than

Sources: World Bank. *World Development Indicators*. Washington, D.C.: The World Bank, 2001; Central Intelligence Agency. *The World Factbook*. Washington, D.C.: Government Printing Office, 2000.

and a marriage bonus. In July 1982, a reform of the Venezuelan civil code extended women's rights. Women comprise roughly half the student body of most universities, and have advanced in many professions, but women are still underrepresented in political and economic life.

29 HEALTH

Despite strenuous government efforts in the field of public health, Venezuela does not have enough physicians for its booming population. In 2000 there were 1.6 physicians per 1,000 population.

Great strides have been made in improving public health conditions. The infant mortality rate, 50.2 per 1,000 live births in 1971, fell to 22 in 1996. Life expectancy averaged 73 years in 2000. Venezuela is virtually free of malaria, typhoid, and yellow fever. To maintain this status, the Department of Health and Social Welfare continues its drainage and mosquito control programs. It also builds aqueducts and sewers in towns of fewer than 5,000 persons. In 1995, 79% of the population had access to safe water.

30 HOUSING

During 1977–81, the public sector built 167,325 housing units, and private business built 71,922. In 1981, the government introduced new low-interest housing loans, but that policy did not prevent a housing slump that persisted from 1982 through 1986 as a result of the general recession; housing units built by the public sector in 1986 totaled 91,666. The total number of housing units in 1992 was 3.4 million.

31 EDUCATION

Venezuela has made considerable progress in education in recent years. The illiteracy rate was approximately 7% in 2000. Public education from kindergarten through university is free, and education is compulsory for children aged 7 through 15. Approximately 20% of the national budget is assigned to education.

After nine years of elementary school, children attend two to three years of secondary school. In 1997, there were more than 4.3 million students enrolled in elementary schools; 377,984 in secondary schools; and more than 300,000 in colleges and universities.

There are 17 universities, both national and private, including the University of Venezuela, Los Andes University, Simón Bolívar University, and the Open University. More than 74 institutes of higher learning, colleges, and polytechnic institutes exist where students pursue at least 180 different fields or professions.

32 MEDIA

Venezuela is covered by a network of telephone, telegraph, and radiotelephone services and also is served by international

Photo credit: Anne Kalosh.

A roadside shrine to revered Venezuelan Dr. José Gregorio Hernandez. The Vatican is considering sainthood for Hernandez, who dedicated his life to providing medical care for the impoverished people of Caracas.

cable and radiotelephone systems. In 1995 there were 2.1 million telephones in use. There were 247 radio stations in 1999 and 66 television stations, and an estimated 471 radios and 185 television sets per 1,000 population.

Leading Venezuelan newspapers (all published in Caracas) with their 1999 circulations include *Diario Ultimas Noticias*

(285,000), *Meridiano* (300,000), *El Nacional* (200,000), *El Mundo* (270,000), *Diario 2001* (120,000), and *El Universal* (180,000).

33 TOURISM AND RECREATION

Since the early 1970s, Venezuela has sought foreign investors for the construction, rehabilitation, and management of top-ranking hotels. The number of foreign visitors in 1998 was an estimated 837,061. Tourism receipts totaled $1.1 billion in 1997.

Tourist attractions include Angel Falls, the world's highest waterfall; the many memorials to Simón Bolívar; numerous beach resorts; and the duty-free shopping and superb water sports facilities of the Isla de Margarita. Cultural life in the national capital offers, among other attractions, the Ballet Nuevo Mundo de Caracas. The most popular sports are baseball, soccer (called football), bullfighting, cockfighting, horse racing, and water-related activities.

34 FAMOUS VENEZUELANS

No one in Venezuelan history is as well known, both nationally and internationally, as the great "Liberator" of the South American revolution, Simón Bolívar (1783–1830), renowned for his military genius and his ability to lead and to inspire. Simón Rodríguez (1771–1854), called the "American Rousseau," was the leading liberal scholar of the prerevolutionary period.

Teresa Carreño (1853–1917) won world fame as a concert pianist. The first painter of note in Venezuela was Juan Llovera (1785–1840). Important Venezuelan painters of the nineteenth century were Martín Tovar y Tovar (1828–1902) and Arturo Michelena (1863–98).

The outstanding pioneer of Venezuelan science was José María Vargas (1786–1854).

35 BIBLIOGRAPHY

Fox, Geoffrey. *The Land and People of Venezuela.* New York: HarperCollins, 1991.

George, Uwe. "Venezuela's Islands in Time." *National Geographic,* May 1989, 526–562.

Haggerty, Richard A., ed. *Venezuela: A Country Study.* 4th ed. Washington, D.C.: Library of Congress, 1993.

Heinrichs, Ann. *Venezuela.* New York: Children's Press, 1997.

Jones, Helga. *Venezuela.* Minneapolis: Carolrhoda Books, 2000.

Morrison, Marion. *Venezuela.* Philadelphia: Chelsea House, 1999.

Nagel, Rob, and Anne Commire. "Simon Bolivar." In *World Leaders, People Who Shaped the World.* Volume III: North and South America. Detroit: U*X*L, 1994.

Venezuela in Pictures. Minneapolis: Lerner, 1987.

Waddell, D. A. G. *Venezuela.* Oxford, England, and Santa Barbara, Calif.: Clio Press, 1990.

VIETNAM

Socialist Republic of Vietnam

Cong Hoa Chu Nghia Viet Nam

CAPITAL: Hanoi.

FLAG: The flag is red with a five-pointed gold star in the center.

ANTHEM: *Tien Quan Ça (Forward, Soldiers!).*

MONETARY UNIT: The dong (D) is a paper currency of 10 hao and 100 xu. There are coins of 1, 2, and 5 xu, and notes of 5 xu, 1, 2, and 5 hao, and 1, 2, 5, and 10 dong. D1 = $0.00007 (or $1 = D 14,020.00).

WEIGHTS AND MEASURES: The metric system is the legal standard, but some traditional measures are still used.

HOLIDAYS: Liberation of Saigon, 30 April; May Day, 1 May; Independence Day, 2 September. Movable holidays include the Vietnamese New Year (Tet).

TIME: 7 PM = noon GMT.

1 LOCATION AND SIZE

Situated on the eastern coast of mainland Southeast Asia, the Socialist Republic of Vietnam (SRV) has an area of 329,560 square kilometers (127,244 square miles), slightly larger than the state of New Mexico, and a total boundary length of 7,262 kilometers (4,512 miles).

Vietnam's capital city, Hanoi, is located in the northern part of the country.

2 TOPOGRAPHY

A single mountain chain, the Annam Cordillera (in Vietnamese, Truong Son), extends along Vietnam's western border from north to south, connecting two "rice baskets," which are formed by the densely populated Red River Delta of the Tonkin region in the north and the rich Mekong River Delta in the south. The two low-lying delta regions are both composed of rich soils brought down from the mountainous regions of southern China and mainland Southeast Asia. The highest mountain peak is Fan Si Pan (3,143 meters/10,312 feet).

3 CLIMATE

Mean annual rainfall in the north varies from 172 centimeters (68 inches) for the city of Hanoi to more than 406 centimeters (160 inches) in the mountains. Daily temperatures in the Red River Delta region can fluctuate from as low as 5°C (41°F) in the dry season to about 30°C (86°F) during the rainy season.

The south is more tropical; temperatures in Ho Chi Minh City vary only between 18°C (64°F) and 33°C (91°F) throughout the year. Temperatures in the

Geographic Profile

Geographic Features

Size ranking: 64 of 192
Highest elevation: 3,143 meters (10,312 feet) at Fan Si Pan
Lowest elevation: Sea level at the South China Sea

Land Use†

Arable land:	17%
Permanent crops:	4%
Permanent pastures:	1%
Forests:	30%
Other:	48%

Weather††

Average annual precipitation: 180.8 centimeters (71.2 inches)
Average temperature in January: 25.8°C (78.4°F)
Average temperature in July: 27.1°C (80.8°F)

†*Arable land:* Land used for temporary crops, like meadows for mowing or pasture, gardens, and greenhouses. *Permanent crops:* Land cultivated with crops that occupy its use for long periods, such as cocoa, coffee, rubber, fruit and nut orchards, and vineyards. *Permanent pastures:* Land used permanently for forage crops. *Forests:* Land containing stands of trees. *Other:* Any land not specified, including built-on areas, roads, and barren land.

††The measurements for precipitation and average temperature were taken at weather stations closest to the country's largest city. Precipitation and average temperature can vary significantly within a country, due to factors such as latitude, altitude, coastal proximity, and wind patterns.

terized by tropical rainforest broken by large areas of monsoon forest. In the higher altitudes of the far northwest there are pine forests. Tropical grasses are widespread, and there are mangrove forests fringing parts of the Red River Delta and in the Ca Mau peninsula, which juts into the Gulf of Thailand. Tropical evergreen forests predominate in the south.

Deer and wild oxen are found in the more mountainous areas. There are many species of tropical birds and insects.

5 ENVIRONMENT

During the war of the 1960s and early 1970s, massive bombing raids and defoliation campaigns caused severe destruction of Vietnam's natural plant life, especially in the Central Highlands of the south. More than 50% of the nation's forests have been eliminated, and dioxin, a toxic residue of the herbicide known as Agent Orange, had leached into the country's water supply.

Environmental damage also has been caused by slash-and-burn agriculture, practiced by nomadic tribal peoples in the Central Highlands and in the mountainous regions in the north. Air and water pollution result from the uncontrolled dumping of industrial and domestic contaminants. The nation has 375.8 cubic kilometers (90.2 cubic miles) of water; 78% is used for farming activity and 9% is used for industrial purposes. Excessive use of pesticides and fertilizers also has damaged the nation's soils.

In 1994, 28 of Vietnam's mammal species and 34 bird species were endangered.

Central Highlands range from a mean of about 17°C (63°F) in winter to 20°C (68°F) in summer. Annual rainfall averages about 200 centimeters (79 inches) in lowland regions. The typhoon season lasts from July through November, with the most severe storms occurring along the central coast.

4 PLANTS AND ANIMALS

The mountainous regions in the north, as well as the Annam Cordillera, are charac-

In addition, 338 types of plants were endangered.

6 POPULATION

Rapid population growth is a serious problem in Vietnam. In 1998, the population was estimated at 76.2 million, making Vietnam the fourteenth most populous nation in the world. Population density was estimated at 238 persons per square kilometer (616 per square mile).

The annual population growth rate declined from an average of 2.1% a year during the 1980s to 1.7% during the 1990s. The population estimate for 2000 was 78.3 million, and the projection for the year 2005 is 83.4 million.

The two largest cities in 2000 were Ho Chi Minh City (3.67 million), and Hanoi, the capital (1.3 million).

7 MIGRATION

The war in Vietnam caused severe disruption of living patterns in both the north and the south. At the end of the war in 1975, many inhabitants were living in refugee camps on the edges of major cities. After seizing control of the south in 1975, the Hanoi regime (communists) moved nearly 1.5 million Vietnamese to New Economic Zones in the Central Highlands or along the Cambodian border as part of their plan for development of an advanced socialist economy. Since 1981 another 2.1 million have been resettled.

In addition to this migration within the country, since the war there has been a heavy outflow of Vietnamese fleeing to other countries. About 150,000 were

LOCATION: 102°10′ to 109°30′E; 8°30′ to 23°22′N.
BOUNDARY LENGTHS: China, 1,281 kilometers (796 miles); Cambodia, 982 kilometers (610 miles); Laos, 1,555 kilometers (966 miles). **COASTLINE:** 3,444 kilometers (2,140 miles). **TERRITORIAL SEA LIMIT:** 12 miles.

evacuated from the south in the final weeks of the war with many eventually settling in the United States. During 1978–

Photo credit: Corel Corporation.

A group of Vietnamese children eye the photographer with curiosity and excitement.

87, an estimated one million Vietnamese fled by sea to other countries in Southeast Asia or overland to China. Many, known as "boat people," emigrated illegally.

In 1979 the government instituted the Orderly Departure Program (ODP) allowing legal emigration to the United States. From 1979–84, 59,730 persons emigrated legally through this program, which was suspended by the Vietnamese government in 1986 but later resumed, with 57,000 emigrating to the United States in 1993 alone. In 1984, the United States started a program that offered asylum to Vietnamese political prisoners and all Amerasian children (children of Asian mothers and American fathers).

The major refugee community is in China and Hong Kong. There were 593,213 people of Vietnamese ancestry in the United States in 1990.

8 ETHNIC GROUPS

About 87% of the population of Vietnam (SRV) is composed of ethnic Vietnamese. In addition to the ethnic Vietnamese, there are 53 other ethnic groups living in Vietnam. Many are nomadic tribal peoples living in mountainous areas. The Vietnamese Chinese (Hoa) are descendants of peoples who migrated into the area in recent centuries. The Cham and the Khmer are remnants of past civilizations that controlled the southern parts of the country.

Until recently, the largest ethnic minority in the country was the Chinese, numbering more than two million. Many have fled the country for economic or political reasons in recent years, however, and the total number remaining in 1999 was estimated at just 3% of the population. Other sizable minority groups are the Tay, Montagnards, Khmer, Muong, Thai, and Nung.

9 LANGUAGES

The national language is Vietnamese (*Quoc ngu*). It bears similarities to Khmer, Thai, and Chinese, and at least one-third of the vocabulary is derived from Chinese. Formerly, Vietnamese was written in Chinese characters, but under French rule a

Photo credit: Corel Corporation.

A seaside village located along the Vietnamese coast.

romanized alphabet originally developed by Roman Catholic missionaries in the seventeenth century was adopted as the standard written form of the language. Most of the minority groups have their own spoken languages, and some have their own writing systems, but all Vietnamese children today receive instruction in the national language.

10 RELIGIONS

It was under Chinese rule that the three major religions and philosophical systems of traditional Vietnam—Mahayana Buddhism, Taoism, and Confucianism—all entered the country.

Under French rule, Christianity prospered, and when Vietnam restored its independence in 1954 there were more than two million Catholics in the country, a population that increased to seven million in 1998. Most of the remainder of the population is Buddhist (the majority), although two unorthodox religious sects, the Cao Dai and the Hoa Hao, became popular among peasants and townspeople in the Mekong Delta. In 1978, the Hoa Hao sect claimed 1.3 million members, but no recent statistics are available.

Since reunification of North and South Vietnam in 1975, religious activities have been restricted, although freedom of religion is formally guaranteed in the 1980 constitution.

11 TRANSPORTATION

The war severely damaged Vietnam's transportation network, especially its railways, roads, and bridges. Most goods move by small barges or sampans along the countless waterways. Major ports, such as Haiphong in the north and Da Nang in the south, are frequently clogged with goods because many dockworkers—often Vietnamese Chinese—have fled abroad.

In 1998, Vietnam had 123 oceangoing freighters totaling 527,920 gross registered tons.

The railroads had 2,835 kilometers (1,762 miles) of track in 1998. There are 36 airports with permanent-surface runways. The nation's air fleet remains primitive, as the national airline (Hang Khong Viet Nam) uses Soviet-built passenger planes from the 1950s. There are 93,300 kilometers (57,977 miles) of roads in the country, but only 25% are paved. Vietnam had an estimated 330,000 cars and four million motorcycles in 1995.

12 HISTORY

During the first millennium (thousand years) BC, the Lac peoples, the ancestors of the modern-day Vietnamese, formed a Bronze Age civilization in the vicinity of the Red River Delta in northern Vietnam. In the third century BC, the Red River Delta was incorporated into a kingdom in southern China. A century later, Vietnam was integrated into the expanding Chinese empire. During 1,000 years of Chinese rule, Vietnamese society changed significantly as it was introduced to Chinese political and social institutions; Chinese architecture, art, and literature; and the Chinese written language. In AD 939, during a period of anarchy in China, Vietnamese rebels restored national independence.

During the next several hundred years, the Vietnamese Empire, then known as Dai Viet (Great Viet), gradually developed its own institutions and expanded steadily to the south. The entire Mekong River Delta came under Vietnamese rule during the seventeenth century, but the ruling Le dynasty slipped into civil war between two princely families, and the country was divided between the Trinh in the north and the Nguyen in the south.

The division of Vietnam into two separate political entities came at a time when European adventurers were beginning to expand their commercial and missionary activities into East and Southeast Asia. The country was briefly reunited under a new Nguyen Dynasty (1802–45), but when a new emperor refused to continue the commercial and missionary privileges granted by his predecessor to the French, French forces attacked near Saigon in 1858. In 1884, France completed its conquest of the country, establishing a protectorate over central and northern Vietnam. In 1895, the three sections of Vietnam were included with the protectorates of Laos and Cambodia in a French-ruled Indochinese Union.

Vietnam under Ho Chi Minh

Western-style nationalist movements began to form after World War I (1914–18), and an Indochinese Communist Party, under the leadership of the veteran revolutionary Ho Chi Minh, was formed in 1930. After the collapse of France in World War II (1939–45), Japan occupied Indochina. Shortly after Japan surrendered to Allied forces (the United States, the United Kingdom, and the Soviet Union) in August 1945, Viet-Minh forces, led by the Indochinese Communist Party, launched the nationwide August Revolution to restore Vietnamese independence.

On 2 September, President Ho Chi Minh declared the formation of an independent Democratic Republic of Vietnam (DRV) in Hanoi. Under the Potsdam agreements, Nationalist Chinese troops occupied all of Indochina north of the sixteenth parallel, while British troops occupied the remainder of the old Indochinese Union. Chinese commanders permitted the Viet-Minh to remain in political control of the north, and the British helped the French to restore their authority in the south.

During the summer of 1946, French and Vietnamese negotiators attempted to complete an agreement on the future of Vietnam, but military clashes between Vietnamese and French troops in the north led to the outbreak of war in December 1946. The Franco–Viet-Minh war lasted nearly eight years, ending in July 1954 after a successful series of attacks on the French at Dien Bien Phu (Dien Bien) by Viet-Minh forces.

Vietnam was temporarily partitioned along the seventeenth parallel, pending general elections to bring about national reunification. North of the parallel, the Vietnamese began to build a socialist society, while in the south, an anticommunist government under the Roman Catholic politician Ngo Dinh Diem attempted with American aid to build a viable and independent state.

On 26 October 1955, Diem proclaimed the Republic of Vietnam (RVN), with its capital at Saigon. Vietnamese guerrillas, supported by the Democratic Republic of Vietnam (DRV), initiated low-level political and military activities to weaken the Saigon regime. In 1960, revolutionary forces in the south formed a National Liberation Front (NLF) to coordinate political activities against the Diem regime.

Despite increasing economic and military assistance from the United States, the Diem regime continued to decline, and in November 1963, Diem was overthrown by a military coup. A Military Revolutionary Council, led by the popular southern general Duong Van (Big) Minh, was formed in Saigon but replaced early in 1964 by another military government. During the next 15 months, a number of governments succeeded each other, while the influence of the NLF steadily increased in the countryside. By early 1965, American intelligence was warning that without American intervention, South Vietnam could collapse within six months.

The Vietnam War

Beginning in February 1965, American combat troops were introduced in growing numbers into the south, while a campaign of heavy bombing raids was launched on military and industrial targets in the north. In Saigon, a new military regime seized power in 1967 led by Nguyen Van Thieu and Nguyen Cao Ky, and General Thieu was elected president of the country. By 1967, American troop strength in South Vietnam had reached more than 500,000, while American air strikes over DRV territory were averaging about 100 sorties (missions) a day.

On 30 January 1968, Hanoi launched the Tet Offensive, a massive effort to seize towns and villages throughout the south. The attempt to force the collapse of the Saigon regime failed, but the secondary aim of undermining support for the war in the United States succeeded. President Lyndon B. Johnson agreed to pursue a political settlement. A complete bombing halt was ordered on 1 November, just before the presidential election in the United States that brought Richard M. Nixon to office as the new Republican president.

President Nixon announced a policy of "Vietnamization," according to which American forces would be gradually withdrawn and the bulk of the fighting in the south would be taken over by RVN forces. Following the divisive 1970 American invasion of neutral Cambodia to destroy enemy sanctuaries, and the DRV's 1972 "Easter Offensive" across the seventeenth parallel, both sides were willing to compromise to bring the war to an end.

The Paris Agreement was formally signed on 27 January 1973. However, clashes between revolutionary forces and South Vietnamese units continued in the south, while provisions for a political settlement quickly collapsed. In January 1975, North Vietnamese forces in the south launched a major military offensive, and by 30 April they had occupied the capital of the RVN, Saigon.

Reunification of North and South

During the next 15 months, the DRV moved to complete national reunification of north and south. Nationwide elections for a new National Assembly were held on 25 April 1976. On 2 July, the Socialist Republic of Vietnam (SRV) was established, with its capital remaining at Hanoi. Saigon was renamed Ho Chi Minh City.

Economic reconstruction proved more difficult than reunification. When the regime attempted to destroy the remnants of capitalism and private farming in the south in 1978, thousands fled, and the economy entered a period of severe crisis. Its problems were magnified by the outbreak of war with China over Vietnamese military intervention in Cambodia that had toppled the pro-Chinese Pol Pot government. After a short but bitter battle that caused severe casualties on both sides, the Chinese forces withdrew across the border, but China continued to support guerrilla operations against the current pro-Vietnamese government in Cambodia.

In January 1989, the first direct talks between Vietnam and China since 1979 resulted in Vietnam's agreement to withdraw its troops from Cambodia by the end of September 1989 and China's agreement to end aid to the Khmer Rouge guerrillas once the Vietnamese withdrawal had been achieved. On 23 October 1991, a Cambodian peace agreement was signed.

Vietnam also has stepped up its efforts to attract foreign capital from the West and regularize relations with the world financial system. Issues that affect these processes are the status and treatment of Vietnamese refugees; border and troop withdrawal disputes with Cambodia, Thailand, and the People's Republic of China; conflicts over the Spratly and Paracel Islands in the South China Sea; and conflicts with the United States over the recovery of the remains of American soldiers missing in action (MIA). In 1996, however, the government banned foreign-language advertisement in an attempt to limit the influence of Western culture. The move angered foreign investors. In 1995, Vietnam began to rewrite its trade laws and statutes in order to increase international trade opportunities.

On 3 February 1994, President Bill Clinton lifted the American trade embargo against Vietnam. After the dissolution of the Soviet Union, the government of the newly independent Russia assured the Vietnamese government that close economic relations would be maintained.

That same year, a possible solution to the contested claims over the Spratly and Paracel archipelagos (island chains) off the coast of Vietnam was proposed. It would create a Spratly Development Authority with China and Taiwan sharing 51% of shares and the remainder divided among Brunei, Vietnam, Malaysia, and the Philippines.

In 1996, the Communist Party held its Eighth Congress. The leadership issued decrees in favor of more economic reform and international investment. However, it hesitated to support the kinds of market-oriented reforms international investors believe need to happen to really create a healthy market economy. The Asian financial crisis in 1997 reduced investment in the economy.

13 GOVERNMENT

Under the constitution of 1980, the Socialist Republic of Vietnam (SRV) is a "proletarian dictatorship" led by the Communist Party. The highest state authority is the National Assembly. Members are elected for five-year terms by universal adult suffrage at age 18. The assembly appoints the Council of Ministers (a cabinet of 33 ministers), the chairman of which ranks as premier. The Council of State (12 members in 1987) formerly served as the collective presidency of Vietnam, elected by the National Assembly from among its own members and accountable to it.

Under a new constitution adopted in 1992, the newly created position of president replaced the Council of State; the president has the right to appoint a prime minister subject to the approval of the National Assembly. The National Assembly, with a maximum of 400 members, retained legislative power.

Vietnam is divided into 50 provinces, one special zone (*Vung Tau-Con Dao*), and three municipalities (Hanoi, Haiphong, and Ho Chi Minh City), all administered by the national government.

14 POLITICAL PARTIES

The government of the SRV is a one-party state ruled by the Vietnamese Communist Party (VCP). In theory, two other political parties, the Democratic Party and the Socialist Party, are granted legal existence.

15 JUDICIAL SYSTEM

The highest court in Vietnam is the Supreme People's Court, whose members are appointed for five-year terms by the National Assembly. In addition, there are local people's courts at each administrative level; military courts; and "special courts" established by the National Assembly in certain cases.

16 ARMED FORCES

Since reunification in 1975, Vietnam has emerged as one of the world's leading military powers. As of 2000, the People's Army of Vietnam was estimated at 484,000. Of that figure, the regular army had about 412,000 personnel, the air force 15,000, the air defense force 15,000, and the navy 42,000. Reserves numbered 3–4 million. Military service is required for two or three years.

Military expenditures were estimated to be $650 million or 9.3% of GDP (1997).

Photo credit: EPD/Government of Vietnam.

Name:	Le Kha Phieu
Position:	Secretary general of a communist state
Took office:	1998
Birthplace:	Dong Khe, central Vietnam
Birth date:	27 December 1931
Education:	Vietnamese Military Academy, studied Marxist-Leninist ideology and military strategy

17 ECONOMY

Wet-rice agriculture is an important segment of the Vietnamese economy, and approximately 25% of the population was engaged in agriculture in 1998. The most diversified area in Southeast Asia in terms of mineral resources, Vietnam is well endowed with coal, tin, tungsten, gold, iron, manganese, chromium, and antimony. Cement, textiles, silk, matches, and paper are the main industrial products.

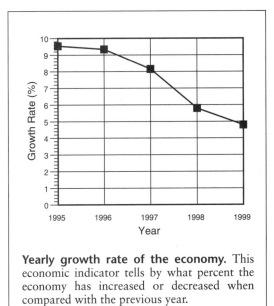

Yearly growth rate of the economy. This economic indicator tells by what percent the economy has increased or decreased when compared with the previous year.

Vietnam's attempts to change from a state-controlled economy to a free-market economy have been slowed by the government's fear of changes that promote increased democracy. Policy changes have been introduced cautiously. Still, Vietnam's economy has grown by an average of 8% each year since 1990. On 3 February 1994, American President Bill Clinton lifted the 30-year-old trade embargo against Vietnam.

Massive improvements to transport and communications networks, combined with industrial development and expansion of exports, are needed. Party leadership, moreover, is concerned about growing unemployment (estimated to be more than 25% in 1995), the widening gap between rich and poor, bankruptcy, and corruption. However, the labor force, with its low wage base, good skill levels, and high motivation, is an excellent resource for growth in manufacturing.

18 INCOME

Vietnam's estimated gross domestic product (GDP) was $135 billion, or about $1,770 per person in 1998. In 1999, the average annual growth in the GDP was nearly 5%, while the annual average inflation rate was 9%.

19 INDUSTRY

Most heavy and medium industry is concentrated in the north, including the state-owned coal, tin, chrome, and other mining enterprises; an engineering works at Hanoi; power stations; and modern tobacco, tea, and canning factories.

The south typically has light industry and consumer goods industries, including pharmaceuticals, textiles, and food processing, although there are some large utilities and cement works. Much of the industrial sector in the north was badly damaged by American bombing raids during the war.

The government now permits the existence of a small amount of private business, mainly in the area of consumer goods and other light industry. The results have been generally favorable; industrial production increased at an average annual rate of 9.5% in the 1980s, and by about 12% per year during the 1990s.

Output by major industries in 1995 (in metric tons) was as follows: cement, 5.7 million; chemical fertilizers, 918,000; steel, 320,000; and cigarettes, 39.8 mil-

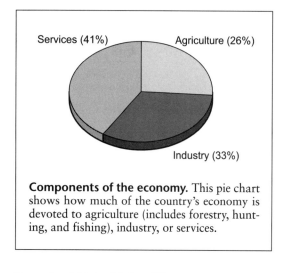

Components of the economy. This pie chart shows how much of the country's economy is devoted to agriculture (includes forestry, hunting, and fishing), industry, or services.

lion. In 1994, 226 million square meters (270 million square yards) of textiles and 145,000 tons of paper were produced.

State-run industries account for about 36% of the domestic economy. The industrial sector still has problems with inefficiency and low productivity. Many Communist Party officials do not want to reduce the state's control over industry, because it would challenge the party's power. Vietnam's assets include low wages, good skill levels, and a motivated work force.

20 LABOR

The total employed labor force in Vietnam was estimated at about 40 million persons by 1998. In 1996, 71% worked in agriculture (26% of economy), about 10% in industry (33%), and 19% in services (41%).

Unemployment has recently become a problem and is worsened by the army's planned demobilization of more than 500,000 troops in the near future. However, a more prominent role given to private enterprise has the potential to lead to more job opportunities. The unemployment estimate for 1995 was 25%.

As of 1992, Vietnamese workers were not free to form or join unions. The government-controlled Confederation of Vietnamese Workers is the sole labor organization, and all workers automatically become members of the union of their workplace. Strikes are prohibited at enterprises that serve the public or are important to the national economy or defense. As of 1996, the prime minister had decided that 54 different sectors fit that definition.

21 AGRICULTURE

About 71% of the total population derives its livelihood from agriculture. Agriculture in the north is concentrated in the lowland areas of the Red River Delta and along the central coast to the south. The Mekong Delta, among the great rice-producing regions of the world, is the dominant agricultural region of the south. Excess grain from the area is shipped to the northern parts of the country. Annual food-grain production averaged 20 million tons in the early 1990s, reaching 30.7 million tons in 1998.

Rice, the main staple of the Vietnamese diet, occupies 94% of all cropland. In 1998, 29.1 million tons of paddy rice were produced. Other crops include corn, sorghum, cassava, sweet potatoes, beans, fruits, and vegetables. In 1998, estimated production (in thousands of tons) was:

sugarcane, 13,421; corn, 1,612; peanuts, 3,887; and soybeans, 141.

Rubber production was given high priority by the Hanoi regime and increased from 40,000 tons in 1975 to 200,000 tons in 1998. Other industrial and export crops produced in Vietnam include coffee, tea, tobacco, pepper, and jute. In 1998, 392,000 tons of coffee, 47,000 tons of tea, 19,000 tons of jute, 32,000 tons of tobacco, and 53,000 tons of cashews were harvested.

The regime announced in mid-1986 that collectivization at a low level had been "basically completed" in the south, with 86.4% of the rural population enrolled in some form of collective organization. As of 1985, there were more than 15,600 agricultural cooperatives nationwide.

22 DOMESTICATED ANIMALS

The most important aspect of animal farming remains the raising of pack animals, mainly water buffalo. Lack of feed, shelter, and technical guidance and an inability to control disease, combined with war damage, hinder growth in this area. Increasing the livestock population is now a major priority of the Hanoi regime. The sizes of herds in 1998 was as follows (in millions): hogs, 18; buffalo, 3; cattle, 4; chickens, 126; and ducks, 50. Meat production in 1998 was 1.6 million tons, of which 74% was pork.

23 FISHING

Fresh and dried fish and fish sauce (known as *nuoc mam*) are major ingredients of the Vietnamese diet, and fishing is an important occupation. Shrimp, lobster, and more than 50 commercial species of fish are found in Vietnamese waters. Ha Long Bay, the major fishing area of the north, is particularly rich in shrimp and crayfish. Fish also abound in Vietnam's rivers and canals.

The fishing industry was severely depleted after the Vietnam War, when many fishermen (often ethnic Chinese) fled the country. In 1997, ocean production was estimated at 1.1 million tons, and inland production was estimated at 451,000 tons.

24 FORESTRY

In 2000, forests covered about 30% of the total land area of Vietnam. Important forestry products include bamboo, resins, lacquer, quinine, turpentine, and pitch. Depletion of forests, however, has been serious, not only through American use of chemicals leading to defoliation in the south during the war, but also because of native farming and grazing practices.

According to scientists who have visited Vietnam in recent years, the damaged areas are recovering faster than anticipated, although reforestation has been slow and some regions are faced with sterility and erosion. Official policy currently emphasizes the replacement of natural forests with export crops such as cinnamon, aniseed, rubber, coffee, and bamboo. Roundwood production was estimated at 35.9 million cubic meters in 1997, with 87% burned as fuel.

25 MINING

Vietnam has some important mineral resources. The principal reserves, located mainly in the north, are anthracite coal, antimony, tin, chrome, apatite, phosphate, manganese, titanium, bauxite, copper, zinc, lead, nickel, graphite, mica, and some gold. Iron reserves are estimated at 520 million tons and apatite reserves at more than 1.7 billion tons. Coal production dominates the country's mining. Anthracite coal production was 7.6 million tons in 1997. Metal production that year included zinc, 15,000 tons; tin, 4,700 tons; and gold, 10,000 kilograms.

26 FOREIGN TRADE

Since reunification, Vietnam has attempted with little success to address the chronic trade imbalance between imports and exports. In 1999, exports totaled $11.5 billion, while imports amounted to $11.6 billion. In 1998, Japan, Germany, the United States, and France were Vietnam's leading export markets. Singapore, South Korea, China, and Japan were the main sources for Vietnam's imports. Major exports were crude oil, rice, sea products, clothing and textiles, coffee, coal, rubber, and nuts. Import commodities included petroleum and steel products, motor vehicles, tires, foods, raw cotton, textiles, sugar, and grain.

27 ENERGY AND POWER

Lack of energy is one of Vietnam's major obstacles to economic development. While coal output is substantial, most of it has been reserved for export. Hydroelectric

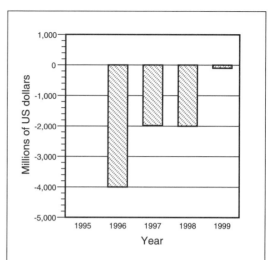

Yearly balance of trade measured in millions of US dollars. The balance of trade is the difference between what a country sells to other countries (its exports) and what it buys (its imports). If a country imports more than it exports, it has a negative balance of trade (a trade deficit). If exports exceed imports, there is a positive balance of trade (a trade surplus).

power accounts for about 84% of the electrical output in 1996. In 1998, 20,620 million kilowatt hours of electricity were generated.

Proven oil reserves as of 1 January 1999 totaled 600 million barrels; production in 1998 amounted to 246,000 barrels per day. In 1999, exports of petroleum accounted for 22% of total exports ($2 billion). Natural gas is believed to exist throughout much of northern Vietnam; proven reserves in 1999 were at 193 billion cubic meters (about 6.8 trillion cubic feet).

28 SOCIAL DEVELOPMENT

Since the end of the war in 1975, Vietnam has been attempting to lay the foundations

Selected Social Indicators

The statistics below are estimates for the period 1996 to 2000. For comparison purposes, data for the United States and averages for low-income countries and high-income countries are also given.

Indicator	Vietnam	Low-income countries	High-income countries	United States
Per capita gross national product (GNP)†	$1,860	$1,870	$25,690	$31,910
Population growth rate	1.8%	2.1%	0.7%	1.1%
People per square kilometer of land	238	73	29	30
Life expectancy in years	69	59	78	77
Number of physicians per 1,000 people	3.5	1.0	2.5	2.5
Number of pupils per teacher (primary school)	35	41	17	14
Illiteracy rate (15 years and older)	6.7%	34%	<5%	3%
Television sets per 1,000 people	184	85	693	844
Energy consumed per capita (kg of oil equivalent)	440	550	5,366	7,937

† The GNP is the total dollar value of all goods and services produced by a country in a year. The per capita GNP is calculated by dividing a country's GNP by its population and adjusting for relative purchasing power. About 15% of the world's 6.1 billion people live in high-income countries, while 40% live in low-income countries.

n.a. = data not available   > = greater than   < = less than

Sources: World Bank. *World Development Indicators.* Washington, D.C.: The World Bank, 2001; Central Intelligence Agency. *The World Factbook.* Washington, D.C.: Government Printing Office, 2000.

of an advanced socialist society. However, attempts to improve social services have been hampered by the poor performance of the economy. In 1992, a social security system was passed into law.

There are continuing restrictions on freedom of the press, religion, and assembly. However, free speech and travel restrictions have eased.

29 HEALTH

Wars in Vietnam since 1946 have undermined much of the progress made in the health field. Especially severe was the damage to urban hospitals in the north. The three decades of intermittent war also had a devastating effect on health conditions in the south. At the war's end in 1975, many infectious diseases were observed to be on the increase.

The World Health Organization (WHO) reported in 1976 that malaria had been both widespread and increasing in the south in 1975. During 1965–74, 5,000 cases of bubonic plague were occurring annually, with a mortality rate of 5%. Saigon was said to have had a tuberculosis rate two-to-three times that of neighboring countries, while leprosy (involving an estimated 80,000–160,000 cases) was increasing. Venereal diseases were said to have afflicted one million persons in the south (about 5% of the total population) and, WHO claimed, 80% of RVN sol-

Vietnamese schoolchildren are seen heaped onto cyclos as they are peddled to a school early one Monday morning. The cyclo is a cheap mode of transportation still used in Vietnam.

diers. Opiate addiction, it was said, affected about 500,000 persons.

Since reunification in 1975, some progress in health care has been made. Tuberculosis has been largely controlled, and the incidence of many contagious diseases has been reduced. In 1990–95, 38% of the population had access to safe water, and 21% had adequate sanitation. Life expectancy was 69 years in 2000.

In 2000, there were 3.5 physicians per 1,000 people. In 1990, there were 3.3 hospital beds per 1,000 inhabitants. About 97% of the population had access to health care services in 1993.

30 HOUSING

Housing is a serious problem in Vietnam, particularly in urban areas of the north where war damage caused problems of overcrowding. By 1986, housing had become a critical problem in Hanoi, particularly in the central sections of the city, where per person living space was reduced to four square meters (43 square feet). Large flats are gradually being erected in the suburbs to ease the problem. In the meantime, many families live in temporary quarters built directly on the sidewalk or attached to other buildings.

Housing is less a problem in the countryside, where many farm families have begun to take advantage of a rising standard of living to build new houses of brick and stone. Similarly, in the rural south, housing is available to meet the requirements of the population because building construction continued at a relatively high level during the war years. In 1989, the majority of housing units were semipermanent (structures with brick walls and tile roofs lasting about 20 years).

31 EDUCATION

In 2000, the adult illiteracy rate for Vietnam was 6.7% (males, 4.3%; females, 9%). After 1975, the educational system in the south was restructured to conform to the socialist guidelines that had been used in the north. The 12-year school cycle was reduced to 10 years, and the more than 20,000 teachers in the south were among those subjected to "reeducation." Today, education is state-controlled at all levels, and five years of primary education is required.

In 1998, primary schools had 324,431 teachers and 10.4 million students. The same year, general secondary schools had 226,491 teachers and 6.6 million students. There are 90 colleges and three universities. The major university is in Hanoi. There were 509,300 students enrolled in higher education institutions during 1997.

32 MEDIA

There were 800,000 telephones in 1995. Hanoi has a strong central broadcasting station, the Voice of Vietnam, boosted by local relay transmitters. Since 1975, almost the entire country has been blanketed by a wired loudspeaker system.

Radio programs beamed abroad include broadcasts in Chinese, English, French, Japanese, Spanish, Thai, Bahasa Indonesia, Russian, Khmer, and Lao, and there are special broadcasts to mountain tribes.

Television was introduced into Vietnam in 1966, and an extensive service, reaching some 80% of the population, was in operation by the early 1970s. Many of the major cities now have television stations. In 2000, there were 106 radios and 184 television sets per 1,000 population.

All press is strictly controlled by the Ministry of Culture and Information. Principal Vietnamese dailies (with their estimated 1999 circulations) are *Nhan Dan* (200,000); *Quan Doi Nhan Dan* (70,000); *Hanoi Moi* (35,000); and *Gai Phong* (100,000).

33 TOURISM AND RECREATION

Vietnam possesses a number of historic and scenic areas of interest to tourists. In the north, the beauty of Ha Long Bay, with its countless grottoes and rock spits jutting vertically into the sea, is well known. Hanoi itself, with its historical monuments, its lakes and pagodas, and its extensive French colonial architecture, is extremely picturesque, but hotel facilities are both inadequate and expensive.

The tourism industry is growing rapidly: there were 1.7 million visitors in 1997. In Hanoi, the increased presence of a foreign community is spurring the availability of Western-style restaurants and bars, hotel and airport renovation and upgrading, accessible public telephones, and advertising of consumer goods.

34 FAMOUS VIETNAMESE

Important figures in Vietnamese history include the sisters Trung Trac and Trung Nhi, national heroines who led a revolt (AD 40–43) against China when that nation was imperial master of Tonkin and North Annam; Ngo Quyen, who regained Vietnamese independence from China in 938; Tran Hung Dao, who defeated the forces of Kublai Khan in 1288; Emperor Le Loi, national hero and brilliant administrator, in whose reign the Vietnamese legal code was promulgated in 1407; and Emperor Gia Long (d.1820), who reunified Vietnam in the early nineteenth century.

The thirteenth-century writer Nguyen Si Co is regarded as one of the first truly Vietnamese authors; he is best known for his collection titled *Chieu Quan Cong Ho.* Other leading literary figures are two fifteenth-century poets, Ho Huyen Qui and Nguyen Binh Khien, whose collection, *Bach Van Thi Tap,* is a classic of Vietnamese literature. Nguyen Du (1765–1820) wrote a famous novel in verse, *Kim Van Kieu.* Hoang Ngoc Phach, who wrote the romantic novel *To Tam* (1925), is credited with the introduction of Western literary standards into Vietnamese literature.

Phan Boi Chau (1875–1940) was Vietnam's first modern nationalist and, like China's Sun Yat-sen, is claimed by Vietnamese Communists and nationalists alike as their spiritual leader. Ho Chi Minh ("The Enlightener") was born Nguyen That Thanh (1890–1969). Often referred to as "Uncle Ho," he was president of the DRV from 1945 until his death. General Vo Nguyen Giap (1912–75), a professor of history turned strategist, organized the first anti-French guerrilla groups in 1944, led the Viet-Minh in its eight-year struggle against France, and defeated the French at Dien Bien Phu.

Le Duan (1907–86), first secretary of the Communist Party, presided over Vietnam's reunification and the formation of the SRV. Le Duc Tho (1911–90), a member of the Communist Party Politburo but with no post in the government, was the DRV's chief negotiator in talks that led to the 1973 Paris Peace Agreement; for his role, Le shared with United States Secretary of State Henry Kissinger the 1973 Nobel Peace Prize.

35 BIBLIOGRAPHY

Cole, Wendy M. *Vietnam.* Philadelphia: Chelsea House, 1999.

Dahlby, Tracy. "The New Saigon." *National Geographic,* April 1995, 60–87.

Merrick, Patrick. *Vietnam.* Chanhassen, MN: Child's World, 2001.

Nagel, Rob, and Anne Commire. "Ho Chi Minh." In *World Leaders, People Who Shaped the World.* Volume I: Africa and Asia. Detroit: U*X*L, 1994.

Park, Ted. *Vietnam.* Austin, Tex.: Raintree Steck-Vaughn, 2001.

Pimlott, John. *Vietnam, the Decisive Battles.* New York: Macmillan, 1990.

Short, Anthony. *The Origins of the Vietnam War.* New York: Longman, 1989.

Truong Nhu Tang. *Vietcong Memoir.* San Diego: Harcourt Brace Jovanovich, 1986.

White, Peter T. "Hanoi: The Capital Today." *National Geographic,* November 1989, 561–594.

Williams, Michael C. *Vietnam at the Crossroads.* New York: Council on Foreign Relations Press, 1992.

Wills, Karen. *Vietnam.* San Diego, Calf.: Lucent Books, 2000.

YEMEN

Republic of Yemen
Al-Jumhuriyah al-Yamaniyah

CAPITAL: Sana (Şanʻā).

FLAG: The national flag is a tricolor of red, white, and black horizontal stripes.

ANTHEM: *Al-Watani (Peace to the Land).*

MONETARY UNIT: The Yemeni riyal (YR) is a paper currency of 100 fils. There are coins of 1, 5, 10, 25, and 50 fils and notes of 1, 5, 10, 20, 50, and 100 riyals. YR1 = $0.00626 (or $1 = YR159.70).

WEIGHTS AND MEASURES: The metric system is being introduced, but local measures remain in common use.

HOLIDAYS: Labor Day, 1 May; Day of National Unity, 22 May; National Day, 14 October; Independence Day, 30 November. Movable Muslim holidays include Laylat al-Miraj, ʻId al-Fitr, ʻId al-ʻAdhaʼ, Milad an-Nabi, and 1st of Muharram.

TIME: 3 PM = noon GMT.

1 LOCATION AND SIZE

Yemen, located in the southern part of the Arabian Peninsula, is slightly larger than twice the size of the state of Wyoming with a total area of 527,970 square kilometers (203,850 square miles). Yemen has a total boundary length of 3,652 kilometers (2,269 miles).

Sana, the capital, is in the western part of the country.

2 TOPOGRAPHY

The topography of Yemen features a narrow coastal plain backed by flat-topped hills and rugged mountains. The interior of the country is desert. The highest known point rises 3,760 meters (12,337 feet) above the Red Sea coast. The western part of the country contains fertile soil on highland plateaus.

3 CLIMATE

Extreme humidity combines with high temperatures—as high as 54°C (129°F) in the shade—to produce a stiflingly hot climate in parts of the country. The climate of the highlands is generally considered the best in Arabia, with temperatures between 22°C (72°F) in June, the hottest month, to 14°C (57°F) in January. Rainfall in the highlands ranges from 41 centimeters (16 inches) to 81 centimeters (32 inches).

4 PLANTS AND ANIMALS

Vegetation is scarce along the coast, but in the highlands and stream beds it is plentiful. Acacia, date palm, and many fruit trees are common. Many varieties of grapes are cultivated.

Geographic Profile

Geographic Features

Size ranking: 48 of 192
Highest elevation: 3,760 meters (12,337 feet) at Jabal
    Hadhur (Jabal an Nabi Shu'ayb)
Lowest elevation: Sea level at the Arabian Sea

Land Use†

Arable land:	3%
Permanent crops:	0%
Permanent pastures:	30%
Forests:	4%
Other:	63%

Weather††

Average annual precipitation: 41 centimeters (16
    inches)
Average temperature in January: 25.5°C (77.9°F)
Average temperature in July: 32.2°C (90.0°F)

†*Arable land:* Land used for temporary crops, like
meadows for mowing or pasture, gardens, and greenhouses. *Permanent crops:* Land cultivated with crops
that occupy its use for long periods, such as cocoa,
coffee, rubber, fruit and nut orchards, and vineyards.
Permanent pastures: Land used permanently for forage crops. *Forests:* Land containing stands of trees.
Other: Any land not specified, including built-on
areas, roads, and barren land.

††The measurements for precipitation and average
temperature were taken at weather stations closest to
the country's largest city. Precipitation and average
temperature can vary significantly within a country,
due to factors such as latitude, altitude, coastal proximity, and wind patterns.

Wild mammals include the baboon, gazelle, leopard, and mountain hare. Scorpions and millipedes are common, but snakes are more rare. Many varieties of birds are found, as well as more than 27,000 varieties of insects and more than 600 species of flowering plants.

5 ENVIRONMENT

Yemen's main environmental problems have long been scarcity of water, soil ero-sion, and expansion of the desert. Water pollution is a problem due to contaminants from the oil industry and untreated sewage. The nation uses 93.4% of its available water for farming activity and 2% for industrial purposes. Natural forests in mountainous areas have been destroyed by agricultural clearing and livestock overgrazing. As of 1987, endangered species included the northern bald ibis, the South Arabian leopard, and two species of turtle.

6 POPULATION

The population of Yemen was officially estimated at 17.5 million in 2000, and a projected population of 20.8 million for the year 2005. During the 1990s, the population increased by an average of 2.3% a year. Recent estimates place the population density at 32 persons per square kilometer (83 per square mile). The largest metropolitan areas in 2000 were Ta'izz (Taiz), with 2.2 million people, and Al Hudaydah (Hodeida), with nearly 1.8 million residents. Sana, the capital, had a population of 629,000 in 2000. Aden ('Adan), the chief port and capital of the former People's Democratic Republic of Yemen (PDRY or South Yemen), had a population of 562,000 in 2000.

7 MIGRATION

There were 1.2 million citizens of Yemen working abroad in 1986, mostly in Sa'udi Arabia and other Gulf states. Yemen took Iraq's side in the Persian Gulf War (1991), which followed Iraq's 1990 annexation of Kuwait. As a result, Sa'udi Arabia expelled an estimated 800,000 to 1 million

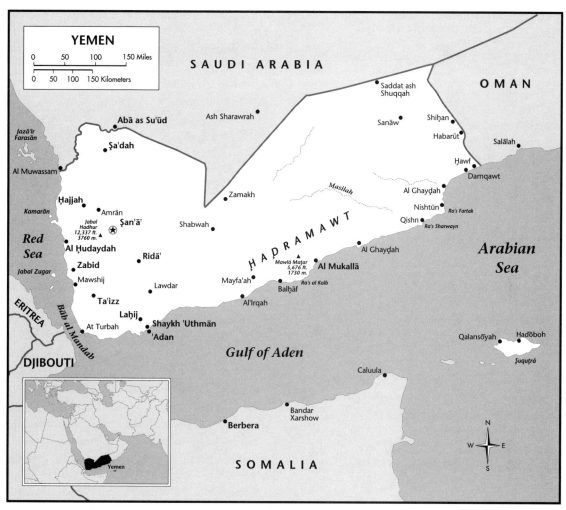

LOCATION 12°41′ to 17°32′N; 42°32′ to 53°5′E. **BOUNDARY LENGTHS:** Oman, 288 kilometers (179 miles); Sa'udi Arabia, 1,458 kilometers (907 miles); coastline, 1,906 kilometers, (1,183 miles).

Yemeni workers by revoking their work privileges.

In 1969, following the establishment of a socialist government in the People's Democratic Republic of Yemen (PDRY or South Yemen), more than 300,000 people fled to the north to the Yemen Arab Republic (YAR), and virtually all minority groups left the country.

In 1992 more than 60,000 Yemenis returned from the Horn of Africa (region of Africa south of Yemen), chiefly because of turmoil in Somalia. Yemen was harboring 57,000 Somali refugees in 1999, in addition to others from Ethiopia and Eritrea.

8 ETHNIC GROUPS

Since independence, the population has been almost entirely Arab. Many ethnologists contend that the purest "Arab" stock is to be found in Yemen. There is a small minority of Akhdam.

9 LANGUAGES

Arabic, the national language, is spoken in a variety of dialects. Mahri, a rare and relatively unstudied language of unknown origins, is spoken in the east. English is widely understood.

10 RELIGIONS

The Republic of Yemen is a Muslim country. Almost all of the inhabitants are Sunni Muslims of the Shafi'i school. Most of those remaining are Shi'ite Muslims of the Zaydi sect. In addition, there is a small minority of Isma'ilis, members of another Shi'ite Muslim sect. Of the 45,000 Jews who lived in the country in 1949, about 500 remained in 2000. In remote areas there is still evidence of shamanism, spirit worship, and other native forms of religion.

11 TRANSPORTATION

In 1996, Yemen had about 64,725 kilometers (40,220 miles) of roadway, with only 8% paved. Passenger cars numbered 227,800 in 1995, and there were 281,800 commercial vehicles. The main port is Al-Hudaydah. Yemen Airways (Alyemda), the national airline, operates services between Sana, Ta'izz, and Al Hudaydah and also schedules flights to Egypt, Ethiopia, Kuwait, Sa'udi Arabia, and the United Arab Emirates (UAE). The airline carried 707,000 passengers in 1997. The principal airfield is Ar-Rahba International Airport, north of Sana.

12 HISTORY

For thousands of years before the Christian era, present-day Yemen was the site of a series of wealthy kingdoms that dominated world trade. The kingdom of Sheba (tenth to second centuries BC) is the best known of these. Ethiopian Christians invaded in AD 525, followed by Persians 50 years later. Islam was accepted in the next century, and Yemen became the battleground of Muslim religious factions.

In the ninth century, a Zaydi ruler, Yahya al-Hadi ila'l Haqq, founded a line of *imams* (leaders) that survived until the second half of the twentieth century. The Ottoman Turks overran the country in 1517 and maintained varying degrees of control over it for the next 400 years. By the twentieth century they controlled only the northwestern part, which they evacuated at the close of World War I (1914–18), leaving the current Zaydi imam in power. This area, although only part of present-day Yemen, was called Yemen at the time.

British Influence

Meanwhile, the British had established a presence in the southern part of the region in the nineteenth century, first occupying Aden in 1839. The port was used as a refueling station on the route to India and then became a major trading center after the opening of the Suez Canal in 1869.

To protect its foothold in Aden, the United Kingdom had signed agreements with rulers of the surrounding tribes and states, grouping them into two separate protectorates. In 1959, the United Kingdom formed the six states of the western protectorate into the Federation of Arab Emirates of the South. In 1963, Aden was merged into the federation, which later became known as the Federation of South Arabia. The dispute over the future form and direction of this new political unit, as well as over which other states would join it, resulted in several years of violence, as various political parties and other groups struggled for power.

On 30 November 1967, all the states of the protectorates were combined, the last British soldiers withdrew, and the National Liberation Front (NLF) took control, declaring the independence of the People's Republic of South Yemen. On 22 June 1969, the head of the NLF was ousted by a group of young leftists within the organization. The new regime, headed by a five-man council, renamed the country the People's Democratic Republic of Yemen (PDRY), developed close ties with the Soviet Union, and secured economic aid from it and China.

Meanwhile, in the north, Yemen (the formerly Turkish-controlled area) joined the League of Arab States in 1945, and, in 1958, formed a federation with the newly established United Arab Republic (UAR), comprised of Egypt and Syria. In December 1961, however, this union was dissolved.

Period of Civil Strife

In September 1962, Yemen's royal government was overthrown by revolutionary forces that established the Yemen Arab Republic (YAR). A civil war between the royalists (defenders of the imamate) and the republican government lasted until 1970, and drew intervention by other Arab states in the area. Sa'udi Arabia supported the royalist cause, and Egypt came to the assistance of the republic, dispatching up to 70,000 troops to the YAR. The republican government remained in control.

Following its formation in 1969, the PDRY in the north was involved in conflicts with all three of its neighbors. A separatist movement was supported in Oman; there were border skirmishes with Sa'udi forces in 1969 and 1973; and the PDRY fought a brief war with the YAR in February–March 1979. The war with YAR ended with a truce, mediated by the Arab League, and an agreement in principle to seek unification of the two Yemens.

Movement toward unification proceeded, although with numerous delays, throughout the 1980s. It was slowed by internal problems in each country, including a 1986 civil war in the PDRY that set back relations between the two countries, especially since 50,000 refugees fled the YAR. Both governments later confirmed their commitment to unity.

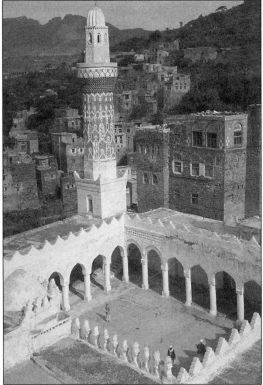

Photo credit: Paty Lam Kim, Gif sur Yvette, France.

A mosque decorated in Persian style, Jibla.

Unification

On 22 May 1990, the unified Republic of Yemen was proclaimed. A 30-month transition period was set for unifying the different political and economic systems. The army, police, and civil service were never integrated as planned, however. Meanwhile, the economy was hard hit by the consequences of Yemen's support for Iraq after that country invaded Kuwait. It is estimated that Sa'udi Arabia expelled between 800,000 and 1,000,000 Yemeni workers, thus depriving Yemen of some $3 billion in foreign exchange. In addi-

tion, Sa'udi Arabia and the other Persian Gulf states ended $2 billion in foreign aid. Unemployment in Yemen reached 30%.

Free and fair parliamentary elections were held in April 1992 with President Saleh's General People's Congress just missing a majority victory. A three-party coalition was formed, but started to come apart in late 1993. Although the quarrel appeared to be patched up with an agreement in February 1994, fighting broke out in May of that year.

In a few months, thousands of casualties had been suffered; tribes, clans, and militias were engaged in seeking their own conflicting goals, and the city of Aden was under siege. Some observers attributed the civil conflict to the recent discovery of massive oil reserves in the south and to Sa'udi Arabia's interest in weakening Yemen by promoting the breakup of the union. By July 1994, the north had beaten the rebellious south and began restoring order. The economy had severely declined. The International Monetary Fund and the World Bank stepped in after the war and began programs that helped bring inflation down from 70–90% to under 10%.

In July 1998 there was a military skirmish with Sa'udi Arabia because of an ongoing border dispute. Both countries claim Duwaima Island and two other small but strategic islands in the Red Sea. Sa'udi ships shelled the island but Yemeni forces later regained control.

13 GOVERNMENT

The 1990 unity constitution established a political system based on free, multiparty

Photo credit: EPD/Office of the President.

Name:	Ali Abdulla
Position:	President of a republic
Took office:	22 May 1990
Birthplace:	Bayt al-Ahmar, Yemen
Birth date:	1942 (est.)
Religion:	Islam
Children:	Five children

The unified government established 17 governorates, subdivided into districts.

14 POLITICAL PARTIES

The Yemen Social Party (YSP)—originally the National Liberation Front—was the PDRY's only political party, and survived to represent southern interests in the unified Yemen. Before unification, political parties played no role in North Yemen. Tribal allegiances were more important political factors.

After unity, the northern leader, General Saleh, formed the General People's Congress (GPC) which became the country's largest party. The second-largest bloc in the parliament is held by the Islaah Party, a fusion of tribal and Islamic interests that opposed the unity constitution because it did not sufficiently adhere to Islamic principles. At least five smaller parties have been active in the politics of unified Yemen.

In the 1993 election, the northern GPC won the majority again, with 124 seats. Islaah won 61 seats. The southern YSP took 55 seats; independents, 47; and other parties, 13. After the 1994 civil war, the GPC and Islaah formed a unity government.

15 JUDICIAL SYSTEM

Under a 1991 decree, the separate judicial systems of the former YAR and the former PDRY have been unified at the Supreme Court level. The separate lower courts systems continue to function in their respective halves of the country.

elections. During the transitional period a presidential council was created with five members, three from the North and two from the South, to oversee executive operations. In 1998, the council appointed a prime minister (Dr. Abd al-Karim Ali al-Iryani) who picked a 38-member cabinet. A 301-member parliament also was formed, with 159 members chosen from the north, 111 from the south, and 31 at large. In 2001, the prime minister was Abdul-Qader Bagammal; the president was Ali Abdulla.

16 ARMED FORCES

In 2000, the consolidated armed forces numbered 66,300, based on two years of required service. The army of 61,000 is supplied primarily with weapons from Russia. The navy of 1,800 mans 13 patrol and coast combatants and nine other ships. The air force, with 3,500 members, has 49 combat aircraft. The paramilitary security forces number 50,000.

17 ECONOMY

The unification in 1990 of North and South Yemen posed the immediate challenge of merging two different economies. When Yemen aligned itself with Iraq during the Persian Gulf War (1991), Sa'udi Arabia and the Gulf states, Yemen's main aid donors and hosts to large numbers of Yemeni workers and their families, ended the Yemenis' privileged status.

After the Gulf crisis, Yemen was confronted with high unemployment (perhaps as high as 25–30%), lost income, halving of US military aid, a sharp cutback in US foreign aid programs, and other canceled foreign assistance. Yemen also faced the cost of food imports and social services for the returnees totaling about $500 million. In addition, the civil conflict in 1994 between the north and south increased the need for external aid.

In 1995, the government began a five-year program that removed all controls on the exchange rate. Trade policy reform, privatization, and elimination of price controls also began. The domestic economy grew by 6.2% in 1995, 3.2% in 1996, and an estimated 6.6% in 1997.

18 INCOME

In 1998, Yemen's gross domestic product (GDP) was reported to be more than $12.1 billion, or about $740 per person.

19 INDUSTRY

In northern Yemen, industry has been based on food processing, but there is a heavy reliance on imported raw materials. Southern industries include clothing, processed food, metal products, soap, and perfumes.

The refinery at Aden processed 60,000 barrels of oil per day in 1994 after being damaged in the civil war. After repairs, output reached 100,000 barrels per day in 1995.

20 LABOR

In 1998, Yemen's work force was estimated at 5 million. According to 1992 estimates, 64% of the labor force is employed in agriculture and fishing, 25% in services, and 11% in commerce and industry. The unemployment rate was estimated at 25% in 1995.

The labor codes of the former YAR and PDRY remained in effect as of 1995 (and were amended in 1997). The labor federations of the two countries merged in 1990, creating the singular Yemeni Confederation of Labor Unions. In 1999, it had 350,000 members in 15 unions.

21 AGRICULTURE

As of July 1993, Yemen imported 70% of its food requirements, including 1.8 million tons of wheat annually. Traditionally,

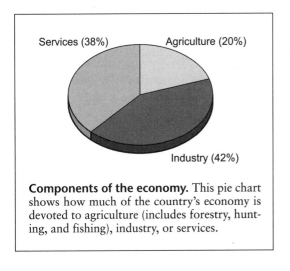

Services (38%) Agriculture (20%)

Industry (42%)

Components of the economy. This pie chart shows how much of the country's economy is devoted to agriculture (includes forestry, hunting, and fishing), industry, or services.

Yemen was famous for its coffee, shipped from the port of Mukallā (Al Mukhah), from which the English word "mocha" derives. The main cash crop is qat *(Catha edulis)*, a mild stimulant chewed by many Yemenis on a daily basis.

Agricultural output in 1998 (in tons) included sorghum, 474,000; tomatoes, 231,000; wheat, 167,000; grapes, 155,000; bananas, 85,000; seed cotton, 24,000; sesame seed, 17,000; coffee, 11,000; and cotton, 5,000.

22 DOMESTICATED ANIMALS

Animal farming is an important part of the economy. In 1998, the livestock population was estimated at 4.5 million sheep, 4.1 million goats, 1.1 million head of cattle, 500,000 donkeys, and 180,000 camels. About 56 million broilers (young chickens raised for meat) and 26,000 eggs were marketed in 1998.

23 FISHING

The annual fish catch in 1997 was about 115,654 tons. Principal species included Indian and Spanish mackerel, cuttlefish, lobster, and scavengers. Exports of fish and fish products were valued at $24 million in 1997.

24 FORESTRY

Grazing by goats and the cutting of timber for fuel and construction have almost completely eliminated Yemen's forests. Roundwood production totaled 324,000 cubic meters (424,000 cubic yards) in 1997, all of it used for fuel. Lumber is imported.

25 MINING

Until the recent discovery of petroleum, the mineral industry had been limited to the production of cement, dimension stone, gypsum, and salt. In 1996, production of cement amounted to one million tons; dimension stone, 410,000 cubic meters (14.5 million cubic feet); gypsum, 80,000 tons; and salt, 110,000 tons.

26 FOREIGN TRADE

Oil accounts for 85% of Yemen's exports. Yemen also exports fish products. The Yemeni government estimated 1999 total exports at $2 billion and imports at $2.3 billion. In 1998, China, South Korea, Singapore, and Thailand were the leading export markets. The United Arab Emirates, Sa'udi Arabia, the United States, and France were the main sources of Yemen's imports.

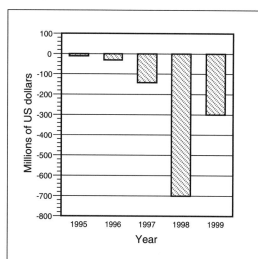

Yearly balance of trade measured in millions of US dollars. The balance of trade is the difference between what a country sells to other countries (its exports) and what it buys (its imports). If a country imports more than it exports, it has a negative balance of trade (a trade deficit). If exports exceed imports, there is a positive balance of trade (a trade surplus).

27 ENERGY AND POWER

In 1999, crude oil production amounted to 409,000 barrels per day. Proven oil reserves as of 1 January 2000 were four billion barrels. Yemen also had natural gas reserves estimated at 478 billion cubic meters (16.9 trillion cubic feet). As of 1996, Yemen had two operating refineries. Total electricity production was 2.2 billion kilowatt hours in 1998.

28 SOCIAL DEVELOPMENT

While the government has expanded its role in providing assistance, traditional means still prevail. Families and tribes care for their sick, handicapped, unemployed, and widows and orphans. Those without family or tribal ties beg or have recourse to Islamic pious foundations (*waqfs*).

The state operates orphanages and finances other welfare measures. Effective in 1988, a provident fund system provides old age, disability, survivor, and workers' compensation benefits. The Yemen Family Planning Association provides contraceptives and advisory services through local clinics and health centers.

Women have limited access to education, although women in the south typically have a higher level of education than those in the north. Females are required to get permission from a male family member before traveling, and are rarely allowed to travel unescorted. Social customs discourage most women from becoming politically active.

29 HEALTH

Malaria, typhus, tuberculosis, dysentery, whooping cough, measles, hepatitis, schistosomiasis, and typhoid fever are widespread, and inadequate sewage disposal is a general health hazard. Life expectancy was 56 years in 2000.

In 2000, Yemen averaged 0.2 doctors per 1,000 people, and 1 hospital bed per 1,196 people. Only 1% of Yemen's gross domestic product went to health expenditures in 1997.

30 HOUSING

About one-fourth of urban housing units are huts, tents, or other makeshift structures. In the hot coastal region, most dwellings are straw huts. In the highlands,

Selected Social Indicators

The statistics below are estimates for the period 1996 to 2000. For comparison purposes, data for the United States and averages for low-income countries and high-income countries are also given.

Indicator	Yemen	Low-income countries	High-income countries	United States
Per capita gross national product (GNP)†	**$730**	$1,870	$25,690	$31,910
Population growth rate	**3.7%**	2.1%	0.7%	1.1%
People per square kilometer of land	**32**	73	29	30
Life expectancy in years	**56**	59	78	77
Number of physicians per 1,000 people	**0.2**	1.0	2.5	2.5
Number of pupils per teacher (primary school)	**n.a.**	41	17	14
Illiteracy rate (15 years and older)	**53%**	34%	<5%	3%
Television sets per 1,000 people	**286**	85	693	844
Energy consumed per capita (kg of oil equivalent)	**201**	550	5,366	7,937

† The GNP is the total dollar value of all goods and services produced by a country in a year. The per capita GNP is calculated by dividing a country's GNP by its population and adjusting for relative purchasing power. About 15% of the world's 6.1 billion people live in high-income countries, while 40% live in low-income countries.

n.a. = data not available   > = greater than   < = less than

Sources: World Bank. *World Development Indicators.* Washington, D.C.: The World Bank, 2001; Central Intelligence Agency. *The World Factbook.* Washington, D.C.: Government Printing Office, 2000.

the poorer people live in huts of stone or baked brick. Wealthier Yemenis live in large houses whose upper parts, which may rise from two to eight stories, are usually of baked brick with windows outlined in decorative designs.

31 EDUCATION

In the unified Republic of Yemen, the literacy rate was estimated to be just under 40% in 2000. The country has about 11,000 primary schools with 2.7 million pupils. At the secondary level, there were 354,288 students in 1997.

There are two universities: San'a University and the University of Aden. Total university enrollment in 1997 was 65,675.

32 MEDIA

There were about 162,100 telephones in 1995. The government operates several radio stations and two television networks, one of them partly commercial. There were about 64 radios and 286 television sets per 1,000 population in 1997. In the same year there were three daily newspapers including *Al-Thawrah* with a circulation of 110,000.

33 TOURISM AND RECREATION

Tourists can visit historic and religious sites (such as the Ghumdau Palace and the Great Mosque in Sana) and exotic markets, and enjoy scenic areas including the Red Sea coast. In 1997, there were 81,000

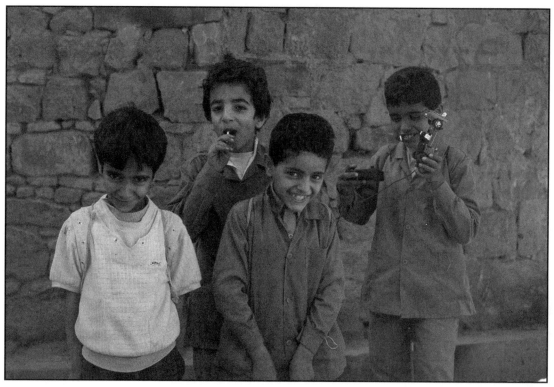

Schoolboys in Sana, Yemen's capital city.

tourist arrivals in hotels and receipts totaled $69 million.

34 FAMOUS YEMENIS

Imam Yahya ibn Muhammad Hamid ad-Din (1869?–1948) ruled during the period when Yemen established its independence. Ali Abdulla (b.1942) became president of the YAR in 1978, ending a period of upheaval in which his two immediate predecessors were assassinated.

35 BIBLIOGRAPHY

Crouch, Michael. *An Element of Luck: To South Arabia and Beyond.* New York: Radcliffe Press, 1993.

Dresch, Paul. *Tribes, Government, and History in Yemen.* New York: Oxford University Press, 1989.

Hestler, Anna. *Yemen.* New York: Marshall Cavendish, 1999.

Mackintosh-Smith, Tim. *Yemen: The Unknown Arabia.* Woodstock, NY: Overlook Press, 2000.

Wenner, Manfred W. *The Yemen Arab Republic: Development and Change in an Ancient Land.* Boulder, Colo.: Westview Press, 1991.

YUGOSLAVIA

Federal Republic of Yugoslavia
Federativna Republika Jugoslavijá

CAPITAL: Belgrade.

FLAG: The flag is a tricolor of blue, white, and red horizontal stripes.

MONETARY UNIT: The new dinar (JD) replaced the dinar on 24 January 1994. The new dinar is fixed on par with the German mark. US$1 = JD5.05. As of December 1998, JD1 = $0.1 (or $1 = JD10).

WEIGHTS AND MEASURES: The metric system is in force.

HOLIDAYS: New Year's Day, 1 and 2 January; Orthodox Christmas, 7 January; Orthodox New Year, 13 January; Unification of Serbia, 28 March; FR Yugoslavia Day, 27 April; Labor Day, 1 May; Victory Day, 9 May; St. Vitus Day, 28 June; Serbian Uprising, 7 July.

TIME: 1 PM = noon GMT.

1 LOCATION AND SIZE

Yugoslavia consists of the states of Serbia and Montenegro and is located in southern Europe between Bosnia and Herzegovina and Bulgaria. It borders on the Adriatic Sea. Its total area is 102,350 square kilometers (39,500 square miles), slightly larger than the state of Kentucky, and a total boundary length of 2,445 kilometers (1,519 miles).

2 TOPOGRAPHY

In the north, Serbia and Montenegro consists of rich, fertile plains. The east and southeast feature mountains and hills, while the southwest is the high shoreline of the Adriatic Sea, with no islands. The highest mountain in Yugoslavia is Daravica, in the Prokletija range, at 2,656 meters (8,714 feet).

3 CLIMATE

In the north, the climate features hot, humid summers and cold winters, with well distributed rainfall. To the south, the summers are hot and dry. Inland areas experience heavy snowfall.

4 PLANTS AND ANIMALS

Large animals found in Yugoslavia include types of hare, pheasant, deer, stag, wild boar, chamois, mouflon, crane, duck, and goose.

5 ENVIRONMENT

Coastal waters are polluted from sewage outlets, especially in tourist areas. Around Belgrade and other cities, air pollution is a problem. However, Belgrade's air pollution decreased from 605 to 132 micrograms per cubic meter (0.9 to 0.2 grains

Geographic Profile

Geographic Features

Size ranking: 106 of 192
Highest elevation: 2,656 meters (8,714 feet) at
  Daravica
Lowest elevation: Sea level at the Adriatic Sea

Land Use†

Arable land:	30%
Permanent crops:	5%
Permanent pastures:	20%
Forests:	25%
Other:	20%

Weather††

Average annual precipitation: 70.1 centimeters (27.6
  inches)
Average temperature in January: –0.2°C (31.6°F)
Average temperature in July: 22.6°C (72.7°F)

†*Arable land:* Land used for temporary crops, like
meadows for mowing or pasture, gardens, and greenhouses. *Permanent crops:* Land cultivated with crops
that occupy its use for long periods, such as cocoa,
coffee, rubber, fruit and nut orchards, and vineyards.
Permanent pastures: Land used permanently for forage crops. *Forests:* Land containing stands of trees.
Other: Any land not specified, including built-on
areas, roads, and barren land.

††The measurements for precipitation and average
temperature were taken at weather stations closest to
the country's largest city. Precipitation and average
temperature can vary significantly within a country,
due to factors such as latitude, altitude, coastal proximity, and wind patterns.

per 100 cubic feet) during 1990–95. Yugoslavia is vulnerable to destructive earthquakes. In 1994, Yugoslavia had 118
nature reserves and 19 protected areas.

6 POPULATION

The total population was officially estimated at 11.2 million in 2000, with Serbia
accounting for 93% and Montenegro for
7%; estimated population for 2005 is 11.3
million. The average annual population
growth rate during the 1990s was 0.8%.

Population density for Yugoslavia was
about 104 persons per square kilometer
(269 per square mile). About 60% of the
population lived in urban areas. In 2000,
the estimated metropolitan population of
Belgrade was 1.2 million.

7 MIGRATION

The breakup of the Socialist Federal
Republic of Yugoslavia (Yugoslav SFR) in
1991 and the ethnic violence that followed
resulted in large migrations to and from its
various republics. In early 1999, the
United Nations reported that there were
more than two million refugees in Yugoslavia. About 508,600 were from Bosnia
and Herzegovina, and Croatia, 220,000
were from Slovenia, and more than
1,000,000 internally displaced.

8 ETHNIC GROUPS

The population is comprised of 63% ethnic Serbs, 14% Albanians, 6% Montenegrins, and 4% Hungarians. Of the
remaining 13%, various East European
ethnicities are represented.

9 LANGUAGES

About 95% of the population speaks the
Serbian language; the remaining 5%
speaks Albanian. The Serbian language,
like Russian, uses the Cyrillic alphabet,
but the Latin alphabet also is frequently
used.

10 RELIGIONS

An estimated 65% of the population is
Eastern Orthodox (a form of Christianity); 19% Muslim; 4% Roman Catholic;
1% Protestant; 11% others.

YUGOSLAVIA

BOUNDARY LENGTHS: Romania, 476 kilometers (296 miles); Bulgaria, 318 kilometers (198 miles); Macedonia, 221 kilometers, (137 miles); Albania, 287 kilometers (178 miles); Croatia (south), 25 kilometers (16 miles); Bosnia and Herzegovina, 527 kilometers (327 miles); Croatia (north), 241 kilometers (150 miles); Hungary, 151 kilometers (94 miles); Adriatic Sea coastline, 199 kilometers, (124 miles).

11 TRANSPORTATION

Yugoslavia controls one of the major land routes from western Europe to Turkey, occupying a strategic location on the Adriatic Coast. As of 1997, there were 50,414 kilometers (31,327 miles) of roads. With an extensive river system, Serbia's river fleet had the second-largest transport capacity in Europe. Due to the trade sanctions, Serbia's merchant marine fleet in 1995 operated under the flags of Malta, Panama, Cyprus, and Saint Vincent and the Grenadines. Montenegro had one merchant ship in 1998. There are 48 airports, five with runways long enough to handle large jets in 1998.

12 HISTORY

SERBIA

Origins and Middles Ages

Around the seventh century, the Serbs began settling in the areas now known as Bosnia and Montenegro, straddling the line that divided the eastern and western halves of the Roman Empire since 395. The Serbs organized several principalities made up of a number of clans. Between the ninth and twelfth centuries, several Serbian principalities evolved, among them Raška in the mountainous north of Montenegro and southern Serbia, and Zeta (southern Montenegro along the Adriatic coast).

In 863, the two Greek scholars Constantine (Cyril) and Methodius learned the area's Slavic language and translated the Holy Scriptures into Slavic using an original alphabet of their own invention. These texts were to be used by missionaries to convert people to Christianity. Thus, the liturgy in the Slavic language was introduced in Bulgaria, Macedonia, and Serbia in competition with the usual liturgy in Greek.

The medieval Serbian empire, under Stephen Dušan the Mighty (r.1331–55) controlled—aside from the central Serbian lands—Macedonia, parts of present-day Greece, and Albania. Dušan, who was crowned tsar of "the Serbs and Greeks" in 1346, gave Serbia its first code of laws based on a combination of Serbian customs and Byzantine law. His attempt to conquer the throne of Byzantium failed, however, when the Byzantines called on the advancing Ottoman Turks for help in 1345.

Under Ottoman Rule

Dušan's heirs could not hold his empire together against the Turks of the Ottoman Empire. Following a series of wars between the Turks and the Serbs, Hungarians, Albanians, Venetians, and other Europeans, the Turks succeeded in overtaking Constantinople in 1453 and all of Serbia by 1459. For the next three-and-a-half centuries, Serbs and others had to learn how to survive under Ottoman rule. Non-Turks had to pay a tax for defense support, and were subjected to the practice of forceful wrenching of Christian boys between the age of 8 and 20 from their families to be converted to Islam and trained as government administrators. Over the two centuries after 1459 many Serbs left their lands and settled north of the Sava and Danube Rivers in Hungary and Austria.

In 1805, the Serbs defeated the Turks and gained control of the Belgrade region. The Turks reoccupied Serbia by 1813 and revenged themselves with a terrible reign of terror. Turk retaliation included pillaging, looting, and enslaving women and children, while killing all males over age 15 and torturing any captured leader who was not able to escape.

By 1830, Serbia had gained its autonomy and was accepted internationally as a virtually independent state. Through the rest of the 19th century, Serbians continued to strive for increased territory and autonomy. Late in the century, there was a period of stable political and economic development, interrupted by the 1908 Austrian annexation of Bosnia and Herzegovina, the 1912 and 1913 Balkan Wars, and World War I (1914–18).

The War Decades

With the backing of Russia, the Balkan countries (Serbia, Bulgaria, Montenegro, and Greece) formed the Balkan League, agreed provisionally among themselves on territorial divisions, and attacked Turkey in 1912. The league quickly defeated the Turks. The second Balkan War in 1913 ended with the defeat of Bulgaria by Serbia, Montenegro, Greece, Romania, and Turkey itself, which gained back Adrianople and Thrace.

Austria viewed Serbian expansion with great alarm. Naturally, the large Serbian population in Bosnia and Herzegovina looked at Serbia with great hopes for their liberation. In Serbia and Bosnia, secret organizations were operating in support of pro-Serbian and terrorist acts. The Austro-Hungarian political and military leadership, bent on war against Serbia, needed only a spark to ignite a conflagration. The spark was provided by the 28 June 1914 assassination of Austria's Archduke Ferdinand and his wife in Sarajevo. Austria presented an ultimatum to Serbia on 23 July with ten requests that were accepted by Serbia in a desperate effort to avoid a war. Austria, however, declared war on Serbia on 28 July 1914. They began bombing Belgrade the same day, and sent armies across the Danube and Sava Rivers to invade Serbia on 11 August 1914, taking the Serbs by total surprise. The Serbian army twice repelled the Austrian forces in 1914, with tremendous losses in men and materials and civilian refugees. Eventually, they were successful in driving the Austrian forces out of Serbia in October 1918.

The Corfu Declaration of 20 July 1917 consisted of 14 points delineating the future joint state of Yugoslavia, comprised of Serbs, Croats, and Slovenes while treating both Macedonians and Montenegrins as Serbs. But this first Yugoslavia, born out of the distress of World War I, had no time to consolidate and work out its problems. On 6 April 1941, Yugoslavia was attacked by Germany, Italy, Hungary, Romania, and Bulgaria, resulting in its occupation and division among Germany and its allies. Southeast Serbia was taken by Bulgaria, while Hungary occupied the Vojvodina area. Germans controlled the rest of Serbia. In the fall of 1941 Josip Broz Tito was leading the communist partisan movement to conquer Yugoslavia for communism.

After the end of World War II (1939–45), the communist-led forces took control of Serbia and Yugoslavia and instituted a violent dictatorship that committed systematic crimes and human rights violations on an unexpectedly large scale. Thousands upon thousands sent back to Yugoslavia from Austria were tortured and massacred.

Communist Yugoslavia

The second Yugoslavia was formed as a Federative People's Republic of five nations (Slovenes, Croats, Serbs, Macedonians, and Montenegrins) with their individual republics and Bosnia and Herzegovina as a buffer area with its mix of Serb, Muslim, and Croat populations. Tito attempted a balancing act to satisfy most of the nationality issues that were carried over, unresolved, from the first Yugoslavia. However, he failed to satisfy anyone. The official position of the Marxist Yugoslav regime was that national rivalries and conflicting interests would gradually diminish through their absorption into a new socialist order. Without capitalism, nationalism was supposed to fade away.

The elections of 11 November 1945—boycotted by the noncommunist coalition parties—gave the communist-led People's Front 90% of the vote. A Constituent Assembly met on 29 November, abolished the monarchy and established the Federative People's Republic of Yugoslavia. In January 1946, a new constitution was adopted based on the 1936 constitution of the Soviet Union. Tito quickly nationalized the economy through a policy of forced industrialization, supported by the collectivization of the agriculture. Yugoslavia began to develop a foreign policy independent of the Soviet Union.

The nonaligned position served Tito's Yugoslavia well by allowing Tito to draw on economic and political support from the Western powers while neutralizing any aggression from the Soviet bloc. Overall, in the 1970s and 1980s, Yugoslavia maintained fairly good relations with its neighboring states by solving disputes and developing cooperative projects and trade.

Meanwhile, Slobodan Milošević had become the head of the Communist Party in Serbia in early 1987. He was able to take control of the leadership in Montenegro and to impose Serbian control over the region of Kosovo. The League of Communists of Yugoslavia convened in January 1990 to review proposed reforms such as free multiparty elections and freedom of speech. In April 1990 the first free elections since before World War II were held in Slovenia.

Yugoslavia's Dissolution

The collapse of communist regimes in Eastern Europe in 1989 had a deep impact in Yugoslavia. In Slovenia, the Communist Party agreed to shed its monopoly of power and lost in the first multiparty elections in April 1990. In Serbia and Montenegro, the communists won on 9 December 1990 on the basis of their strong Serbian nationalism. The Serbian determination to maintain a unitary Yugo- slavia hardened, while the determination of the Slovenes and Croats to gain their independence grew stronger.

The new constitution proclaimed by Serbia in September 1990 provided for a unicameral legislature of 250 seats and the elimination of autonomy for Vojvodina and Kosovo. The first elections were held on 9 December 1990. More than 50 par- ties and 32 presidential candidates partici- pated. Slobodan Milošević's Socialist Party of Serbia received two-thirds of the votes and 194 out of the 250 seats. Having gained control of Serbia, Montenegro, Kosovo, and Vojvodina, Milošević con- trolled four of the eight votes in the collec- tive presidency of Yugoslavia.

Slovenia and Croatia proceeded with their declarations of independence on 25 June 1991. Increased fighting from July 1991 caused tremendous destruction of entire cities (Vukovar), and large-scale damage to the medieval city of Dubrovnik.

On 27 April 1992, Serbia and Mon- tenegro formed their own Federal Repub- lic of Yugoslavia. The United Nations, convinced that Serbia and Montenegro was supporting the aggression against Bosnia and Herzegovina, imposed eco- nomic sanctions. In spite of the sanctions, Milošević's Socialist Party won the elec- tions of 22 December 1992. The desperate economic situation of Serbia caused by its assistance to the Bosnian Serbs and the UN-imposed sanctions finally forced Milošević to disassociate Serbia from the Bosnian Serbs and to close the borders with Bosnia in September 1994.

In 1995, Bosnian Serbs took over the "safe areas" of Srebenica and Zepa (near the Croatian border) that were under United Nations protection. On 30 August 1995, leaders of NATO countries ordered air raids on the new Bosnian Serb posi- tions. Two weeks later, the Serbs ended their siege of Sarajevo and agreed to start negotiating over the future of Bosnia. Pres- sured by the air strikes and diplomacy, Serb officials joined leaders from Bosnia and Croatia on 31 October 1995 in Day- ton, Ohio, for a round of peace talks. On 21 November 1995, the presidents of Bos- nia, Croatia, and Serbia finally agreed to terms that would end the fighting in Bos- nia after four years and an estimated 250,000 casualties. The agreement called for 60,000 United Nations peacekeepers.

Meanwhile, the International War Crimes Tribunal set out to find and prose- cute Serbian soldiers accused of atrocities. The tribunal filed its first charges in March 1996.

Serbia's President Milošević originally promised to privatize the economy and bring about market reforms. By early 1996, however, he was reversing himself by reasserting state control over major industries and silencing political opposi- tion. In March 1996, a demonstration in Belgrade brought out 20,000 protesters against Milošević's administration. The protesters blamed the government for starting the conflict with Bosnia and ruin- ing the Serbian economy. More demon- strations came later in 1996 when Milošević voided the results of local elec- tions because opposition parties won majorities in 14 of Serbia's 19 largest cities. Miloševic lost much of his popular support. By February 1997, he agreed to recognize the results of the elections. In July 1997, Miloševic was appointed to the presidency of Yugoslavia by the federal parliament, allowing him to maintain control for four more years.

In March 1998, armed violence between ethnic Albanians and Yugoslav troops killed 80 people in the region of Kosovo. About 90% of Kosovo consists of ethnic Albanians. There was international concern that a conflict in Kosovo could spill over into Macedonia or other parts of the Balkans. The Serbian government launched a crackdown against the Kosovo Liberation Army, a makeshift guerilla force that wants to separate Kosovo from Serbia.

MONTENEGRO

Montenegro's name came from the Venetian meaning "Black Mountain." Living in a very harsh mountain territory, the Montenegrins were natural and fierce fighters and not even the large Turkish armies could conquer them. In 1516, Montenegro became a theocracy, and for the next three centuries, until 1851, Montenegro was ruled by its bishops. The Montenegro area was an almost impregnable mountain fortress with some limited access from the Adriatic coast where the Turks had taken hold. The population was comprised of Slav and Albanian Muslims.

Following the 1913 Balkan War, Montenegro and Serbia became neighbor states, both primarily populated by Serbs. Montenegro also gained access to the Adriatic Sea south of Lake Scutari (Skadarsko Jezerol), which was divided in 1913 between Montenegro and the newly formed Albanian state.

Between 1880 and 1912, Montenegro took advantage of an era of relative peace to develop roads, education, agriculture, postal services, and banks, mostly with foreign investment especially from Italy. For higher education, most Montenegrins studied at the University of Belgrade and came back home with progressive and democratic ideas, along with deep and personal ties and commitment to the Serbian goals of national unification.

The first Montenegrin parliament met in 1905, with 62 elected and 14 ex-officio members. By 1914, Serbia and Montenegro proposed a union in which they would share their armed forces, foreign policy, and customs while maintaining their separate royal dynasties. World War I (1914–18) interrupted this process. Montenegro's poor defense against Austrian attacks led to Austrian occupation for the better part of the war. Thus Montenegro ceased to officially participate in the war as an ally of Serbia and the Western powers against Austria.

Montenegro became part of the first Yugoslavia on 1 December 1918, not as Montenegro, but as part of the Kingdom of Serbia. Montenegrins participated very actively in Yugoslavia's political life, mostly supporting the centralist Serbian positions. During World War II (1939–45), Italy controlled Montenegro. In the post-World War II Socialist Federative Yugoslavia, Josip Broz Tito reestablished

Montenegro as a separate republic to balance the influence of Serbs in general. Most Montenegrins took the side of the Serbian centralists and, in the late 1980s and early 1990s, supported Slobodan Milošević. With the demise of Yugoslavia, Montenegro joined Serbia in forming the Federal Republic of Yugoslavia. Being a less-developed area, Montenegro depends heavily on Serbian assistance—difficult to obtain under the impact of economic sanctions. It is in the interest of Serbia to avoid any direct clash with Hungary. Serbia and Montenegro are isolated and facing adversary states.

In May 1998, Milo Djukanovic was elected Montenegro's president. Montenegro stopped recognizing the Yugoslav federal government that month because Milošević had replaced Montenegro's prime minister with his own choice, Momir Bulatovic. The move was seen as part of a growing confrontation between Montenegro and Yugoslav governments.

Vojislav Koštunica defeated Milošević in the 2000 presidential elections.

13 GOVERNMENT

The government of Serbia and Montenegro was established when the state declared its independence on 11 April 1992. The constitution was enacted on 27 April 1992. A bicameral (two-house) Federal Assembly consists of a 40-seat (20 Serbian, 20 Montenegrin) Chamber of Republics (upper house) and a 138-seat (108 Serbian, 30 Montenegrin) Chamber of Deputies or Citizens (lower house). The federal president, elected by the Federal Assembly, serves a term of four years (with a two-term limit). The federal president nominates the prime minister, who serves as the head of government. The republics of Serbia and Montenegro each elect their own president. The president of Serbia carries significant power throughout Yugoslavia.

14 POLITICAL PARTIES

The main political party operating in Yugoslavia is the Serbian Socialist Party (SPS—formerly the Communist Party), led by Slobodan Milošević. After the parliamentary elections of November 1996, other representation included the Zajedno Coalition, the Democratic Party of Socialists of Montenegro, the Serbian Radical Party, the People's Party of Montenegro, the Union of Vojvodina Hungarians, and the Vojvodina Coalition. Serbia has nearly 120 registered political parties.

15 JUDICIAL SYSTEM

The judiciary is independent according to the constitution, but in reality it is influenced by the government. The court system consists of local, district, and supreme courts at the republic level for Serbia and Montenegro. Yugoslavia has a Federal Supreme Court, a Federal Constitutional Court, and a military court system. Defendants have the right to be present at the trial and to have an attorney.

16 ARMED FORCES

Serbia and Montenegro maintains a People's Army—Ground Forces (for internal and border patrols of 85,000); Naval Forces (7,000); Air and Air Defense Forces (17,000); Frontier Guard; Territorial

Defense Force; and Civil Defense. As of 2000, some 34,000 international peace-keeping troops are stationed in Yugoslavia as part of the Kosovo Peace Implementation Force. Yugoslavia spent about 6.5% ($911 million) of its gross domestic product (GDP) on defense in 1999.

17 ECONOMY

The United Nations imposed trade sanctions against Yugoslavia from 1992 until 1995. By 1994, hyperinflation had brought the cash economy to a virtual halt. In 1996, the gross domestic product (GDP) was only half of what it had been in 1990.

18 INCOME

In 1998, Yugoslavia had an estimated gross domestic product (GDP) of $2,300 per person. The inflation rate in that same year was 48%. That year, average monthly wages fell from about $800 to under $80.

19 INDUSTRY

Industrial output fell by an estimated 60% between 1989 and 1996. Industries include machine building, metallurgy, mining, and production of consumer goods, electronics, petroleum products, chemicals, and pharmaceuticals.

20 LABOR

The government reported that there were nearly 23 million employed persons in 1999 and 819,000 unemployed persons, for an unemployment rate of 25.8%. Unemployment varies from city to city. There are no independent labor unions, and strikes are often ended with brutal police force.

21 AGRICULTURE

Yugoslavia had 3.7 million hectares (9.1 million acres) of farmland in 1995. Vojvodina, in Serbia, is Yugoslavia's main agricultural region. Between 1991 and 1996, total agricultural production declined by 10%. Major crops in 1996 included 5 million tons of corn, 2.3 million tons of sugar beets, 1.5 million tons of wheat, and 976,000 tons of potatoes. Fodder (animal feed) crops to support intensive beef and dairy production are grown; the central regions produce fruit, grapes, and livestock, due to the long growing season. Along the Adriatic Sea, small amounts of olives, citrus fruit, and rice are cultivated.

22 DOMESTICATED ANIMALS

In 1998, Yugoslavia had 4.1 million pigs and hogs, 2.4 million sheep, 1.9 million head of cattle, 86,000 horses, and 24 million poultry. Total meat production that year was 1.04 million tons; milk, 2 million tons. Total livestock production declined by 11% between 1990 and 1996, made worse by an outbreak of foot and mouth disease in 1997, which adversely affected exports.

23 FISHING

The total catch in 1997 was 7,368 tons, 95% from inland waters. Common carp accounted for 24% of the catch.

24 FORESTRY

Estimated forest coverage was 1.7 million hectares (4.3 million acres) in 1995. Total

---

Selected Social Indicators

The statistics below are estimates for the period 1996 to 2000. For comparison purposes, data for the United States and averages for low-income countries and high-income countries are also given.

Indicator	Yugoslavia	Low-income countries	High-income countries	United States
Per capita gross national product (GNP)†	**$1,800**	$1,870	$25,690	$31,910
Population growth rate	**0.5%**	2.1%	0.7%	1.1%
People per square kilometer of land	**104**	73	29	30
Life expectancy in years	**72**	59	78	77
Number of physicians per 1,000 people	**n.a.**	1.0	2.5	2.5
Number of pupils per teacher (primary school)	**n.a.**	41	17	14
Illiteracy rate (15 years and older)	**n.a.**	34%	<5%	3%
Television sets per 1,000 people	**273**	85	693	844
Energy consumed per capita (kg of oil equivalent)	**n.a.**	550	5,366	7,937

† The GNP is the total dollar value of all goods and services produced by a country in a year. The per capita GNP is calculated by dividing a country's GNP by its population and adjusting for relative purchasing power. About 15% of the world's 6.1 billion people live in high-income countries, while 40% live in low-income countries.

n.a. = data not available   > = greater than   < = less than

Sources: World Bank. *World Development Indicators.* Washington, D.C.: The World Bank, 2001; Central Intelligence Agency. *The World Factbook.* Washington, D.C.: Government Printing Office, 2000.

---

roundwood production in 1997 was 1.3 million cubic meters (1.7 million cubic yards) of which 3.8% was used for fuel.

25 MINING

Yugoslavia's mineral resources include oil, gas, coal, antimony, copper, lead, zinc, nickel, gold, pyrite, and chromium. Mine output of metals in 1996 included (in tons): lead-zinc, 894,000; bauxite, 323,000; iron ore, 110,000; copper, 20,206; magnesium, 2,500; nickel, 2,556; silver, 68,805 kilograms; and gold, 3,000 kilograms.

26 FOREIGN TRADE

The United Nations imposed sanctions on Yugoslavia in May 1992 and lifted them in December 1995. During the war and while sanctions were in force, senior Serbian officials set up dozens of companies in Cyprus to carry out millions of dollars in illegal trade. In 1996, Yugoslavia's government reported exports at $1.8 billion and imports at $4.1 billion.

27 ENERGY AND POWER

Yugoslavia has hydroelectric potential, but there are frequent electrical breakdowns during the peak winter months. In 1998, electric capacity was 11.8 million kilowatts; energy generation was about 33.8 billion kilowatt hours.

In 1995, Yugoslavia produced 38,620 tons of coal, 890 million cubic meters

(31.4 billion cubic feet) of natural gas, and 1.1 million tons of crude oil.

28 SOCIAL DEVELOPMENT

Yugoslavia started its current social welfare system in 1992. Veterans and disabled veterans have a separate system. Child welfare includes family assistance dealing with areas such as reproduction, protection, training, and preschool education.

29 HEALTH

The government provides obligatory health care to citizens. In 1995, there was one doctor for every 495 people. That year, there were 228 health institutions and about 3,000 other (mostly private) clinics. Hospital and clinic beds numbered 56,107 in 1995, for a ratio of one bed per 188 persons.

30 HOUSING

At the beginning of 1996, Yugoslavia had 3.1 million dwellings, with an average of 3.4 people per dwelling. There were 14,337 new housing units completed in 1995.

31 EDUCATION

Education is compulsory for eight years, between the ages of 7 and 15. In 1997, Yugoslavia had 437,780 students in primary schools and 815,029 students in secondary schools. In 1997, there were 172,313 university students. Serbia has universities at Belgrade, Novi Sad, Pristina, Niš, and Kragujevac.

32 MEDIA

There were nearly 2.6 million telephones in Yugoslavia in 1995. That year, there were 109 radio stations, and 24 television stations.

The first Serbian-language newspaper was printed in Vienna, Austria, in 1791. Yugoslavia's 590 newspapers had a total circulation of 301.5 million in 1995. There are 13 dailies. Seven of them are privately owned and are not always favorable of the government. There also are about 50 Albanian-language newspapers.

33 TOURISM AND RECREATION

During the political instability and economic sanctions of 1992–95, tourism was not a factor in the economy of Serbia and Montenegro. In 1998, Yugoslavia had 282,639 tourist arrivals, down 5% from the previous year. Serbia has dozens of spa resorts such as Vrnjacka Banja, Mataruska Banja, Niska Banja, Banja Kovilaca, and Bukovicka Banja.

34 FAMOUS SERBS AND MONTENEGRINS

Stephen Dušan (r.1331–55) was ruler of the medieval Nemanjid dynasty empire. Prince Lazar (d.1389) was beheaded after losing the Battle of Kosovo against the Turks. Djordje Petrovic Karadjordje ("Black George," 1762–1817) was the leader of a Serbian revolt against the Turks. Zivojin Misic (1855–1921) was a distinguished military leader during World War I. Prince Paul of Yugoslavia (1893–1976) ruled as a regent for Peter II (1923–70) from 1934 to 1941 as a tool of the Nazi government. Marshal Josip Broz Tito

(1892–1980) was president of the Yugoslav SFR from 1953 until his death. Slobodan Miloševic (b.1941) was elected president of Serbia in 1990 and 1992 before being elected president of Yugoslavia in 1997.

35 BIBLIOGRAPHY

Andryszewski, Tricia. *Kosovo: The Splintering of Yugoslavia*. Brookfield, Conn.: Millbrook Press, 2000.

Banac, Ivo. *The Nationality Question in Yugoslavia*. Ithaca, NY: Cornell University Press, 1984.

Glenny, Michael. *The Fall of Yugoslavia: The Third Balkan War*. New York: Penguin, 1992.

Ramet, Sabrina P. *Balkan Babel: The Disintegration of Yugoslavia from the Death of Tito to Ethnic War*. Boulder, Colo.: Westview, 1996.

Ramet, Sabrina P. *Beyond Yugoslavia: Politics, Economics, and Culture in a Shattered Community*. Boulder, Colo.: Westview, 1995.

West, Richard. *Tito: And the Rise and Fall of Yugoslavia*. New York: Carroll & Graf, 1995.

ZAMBIA

Republic of Zambia

CAPITAL: Lusaka.

FLAG: The flag is green, with a tricolor of dark red, black, and orange vertical stripes at the lower corner of the fly, topped by a golden flying eagle.

ANTHEM: *Stand and Sing for Zambia.*

MONETARY UNIT: The kwacha (κ) of 100 ngwee replaced the Zambian pound (z£) on 15 January 1968. There are coins of 1, 2, 5, 10, 20, and 50 ngwee, and notes of 1, 2, 5, 10, 20, 50, 100, and 500 kwacha. κ1 = $0.00037 (or $1 = κ2,661.82).

WEIGHTS AND MEASURES: The metric system is used.

HOLIDAYS: New Year's Day, 1 January; Youth Day, 11 March; Labor Day, 1 May; African Freedom Day, 24 May; Heroes' Day, 1st Monday after 1st weekend in July; Unity Day, Tuesday after Heroes' Day; Farmers' Day, 5 August; Independence Day, 24 October; Christmas, 25 December. Movable religious holidays include Good Friday and Easter Monday.

TIME: 2 PM = noon GMT.

1 LOCATION AND SIZE

A landlocked country in southcentral Africa, Zambia has an area of 752,610 square kilometers (290,584 square miles), slightly larger than the state of Texas, with a total boundary length of 5,664 kilometers (3,519 miles). Zambia's capital city, Lusaka, is located in the southcentral part of the country.

2 TOPOGRAPHY

Most of the landmass in Zambia is a high plateau. In the northeast, the Muchinga Mountains exceed 1,800 meters (5,900 feet) in height. Lower elevations are encountered in the valleys of the major river systems. The Luangwa and Kafue Rivers are both tributaries of the upper Zambezi. There are three large natural lakes (Bangweulu, Mweru, and Tangany-ika) and one of the world's largest man-made lakes, Lake Kariba.

3 CLIMATE

Although Zambia lies within the tropics, much of it has a pleasant climate because of the altitude. There are wide seasonal variations in temperature and rainfall. The northern and northwestern provinces have an annual rainfall of about 125 centimeters (50 inches), while areas in the far south have as little as 75 centimeters (30 inches). Daytime temperatures may range from 23° to 31°C (73–88°F), dropping at night to as low as 5°C (41°F) in June and July.

4 PLANTS AND ANIMALS

Most of the territory is plateau, and the prevailing type of vegetation is open

Geographic Profile

Geographic Features

Size ranking: 38 of 192
Highest elevation: 2,301 meters (7,550 feet) at Mafinga Hills
Lowest elevation: 329 meters (1079 feet) at the Zambezi River

Land Use†

Arable land:	7%
Permanent crops:	0%
Permanent pastures:	40%
Forests:	39%
Other:	14%

Weather††

Average annual precipitation: 92.3 centimeters (36.3 inches)
Average temperature in January: 20.9°C (69.6°F)
Average temperature in July: 17.8°C (64.0°F)

†*Arable land:* Land used for temporary crops, like meadows for mowing or pasture, gardens, and greenhouses. *Permanent crops:* Land cultivated with crops that occupy its use for long periods, such as cocoa, coffee, rubber, fruit and nut orchards, and vineyards. *Permanent pastures:* Land used permanently for forage crops. *Forests:* Land containing stands of trees. *Other:* Any land not specified, including built-on areas, roads, and barren land.

††The measurements for precipitation and average temperature were taken at weather stations closest to the country's largest city. Precipitation and average temperature can vary significantly within a country, due to factors such as latitude, altitude, coastal proximity, and wind patterns.

woodland. Acacia and baobab trees, thorn trees and bushes, and tall perennial grasses are widespread, becoming coarser and sparser in the drier areas to the south. To the north and east grows a thin forest. The southwest has forests of Zambian teak.

The national parks and game reserves, such as the Kafue National Park, conserve the wildlife threatened by settlement. In the Luangwa River valley can be found giraffe, zebra, rhinoceros, elephant, baboon, monkey, hyena, wolf, and lion.

Zambia has a wealth of bird life, including the eagle, gull, kingfisher, lark, babbler, sunbird, stork, and bee-eater. There are more than 150 recorded species of reptiles, including 78 species of snakes and 66 of lizards. The range of species of fish also is wide.

5 ENVIRONMENT

Both traditional and modern farming methods in Zambia involve clearing large areas of forest. As of 1985, the nation had lost 700 square kilometers (270 square miles) of forestland, mainly to slash-and-burn agriculture but also to firewood gathering and charcoal production. Water pollution is a problem due to contamination by sewage and toxic industrial chemicals. The nation uses 26% of its available water supply for farming and 11% for industry. Roughly 36% of Zambia's city dwellers and 73% of the people living in rural areas do not have pure water. Air pollution is created by the use of oil products for cars and coal in industrial activity.

Wildlife is endangered in some areas by hunting; the National Parks and Wildlife Act (1982) requires automatic imprisonment for trading illegally in elephant tusks and rhinoceros horns. In 1994, 10 of the nation's mammal species, including the black rhinoceros, and 10 bird species were threatened, as well as one type of plant.

6 POPULATION

In 2000, the population was estimated at 9.9 million. The projected population for 2005 is 11 million. Lusaka, the capital, had 1.7 million inhabitants in 2000. Overall, population density is 13 persons per

LOCATION: 9° to 18°s; 23° to 34°E. **BOUNDARY LENGTHS:** Tanzania, 338 kilometers (210 miles); Malawi, 837 kilometers (523 miles); Mozambique, 419 kilometers (260 miles); Zimbabwe, 797 kilometers (498 miles); Namibia (Caprivi Strip), 233 kilometers (145 miles); Angola, 1,110 kilometers (690 miles); Democratic Republic of the Congo (DROC), 1,930 kilometers (1,193 miles).

square kilometer (34 per square mile) in 1998.

7 MIGRATION

In 1999, Zambia had 200,000 Angolan, Mozambican, Rwandan, Congonese, and Zairian refugees.

8 ETHNIC GROUPS

The African community, 98.7% of Zambia's total population, belongs to various Bantu groups, including the Bemba (37% of Zambia's African population), Tonga (19%), Lunda (12%), and Nyanja (11%). In all, there are at least 73 different African societal classifications. Europeans,

Photo credit: © Corel Corporation.

Giraffe can be found in the Luangwa River valley.

cational and administrative purposes, seven main languages are recognized: Bemba, Lozi, Lunda, Kaonde, Luvale, Tonga, and Nyanja. English is the official language.

10 RELIGIONS

An amendment to the 1996 constitution declares the country a Christian nation, but allows for freedom of practice. An estimated 5% of the population follows African tribal religions, while 85% profess some form of Christianity, more than one-third being Roman Catholics.

11 TRANSPORTATION

The Zambia Railways system consists of 2,164 kilometers (1,344 miles) of track. Zambia had 39,700 kilometers (24,670 miles) of roadway in 1999, of which 18% was paved. In 1995, there were 164,000 registered motor vehicles, including 96,000 passenger cars. Zambia Airways provides international service from Lusaka to several African and European countries, as well as domestic service to 17 Zambian centers. In 1997, 318,000 passengers were carried on scheduled domestic and international flights. Mpulungu on Lake Tanganyika is Zambia's only port.

12 HISTORY

Iron working and agriculture were practiced in some parts of Zambia by about AD 100. By AD 900, mining and trading were present in southern Zambia. Between the fifteenth and the eighteenth centuries, various groups of Bantu migrants from the southern Congo (formerly Zaire, now the

accounting for 1.1% of the population, are mainly of British origin. Asians, mainly migrants from the Indian subcontinent, and people of mixed race, account for 0.2% of the population.

9 LANGUAGES

Some 80 different languages have been identified, most of them of the Bantu family (of south and central Africa). For edu-

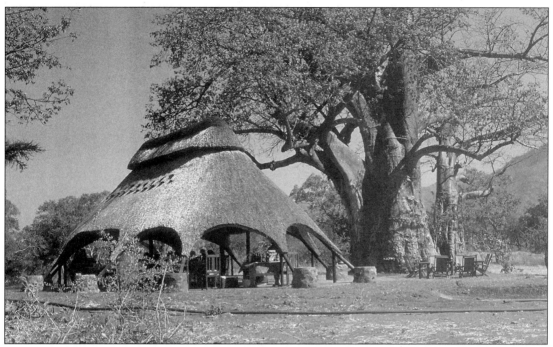

Photo credit: Edson P. Tembo of the Zambia National Tourist Board.

Kayila Lodge under the shade of a baobab tree in the lower Zambezi National Park.

Democratic Republic of the Congo) settled in Zambia. By the beginning of the nineteenth century, three large-scale political units existed in Zambia: the Bemba system of chieftainships; the Lunda kingdom of Kazembe; and the kingdom of the Lozi. Zambia was affected by two "invasions" in the mid-nineteenth century. There were a series of migrations, commonly referred to as the *mfecane*, by groups fleeing across the Zambezi River to avoid raids by Shaka's Zulu empire in South Africa. The other invasion came in the form of traders from the north—Nyamwezi, Arabs, and Swahili—drawing Zambia into long-distance trading systems.

The first significant European contact was through Christian missionaries. In 1884, François Coillard, a French Protestant missionary, settled in Barotseland (now the Western Province). In the 1890s, Cecil Rhodes's British South Africa Company extended its charter north of the Zambezi River. From 1891 to the end of 1923, the territory of Zambia—then known as Northern Rhodesia—was ruled by this private company. In the 1920s, new methods of exploiting the extensive mineral deposits in the "copperbelt" region transformed the economic life of the territory. Northern Rhodesia now was seen for the first time as a source of wealth, and European settlements multiplied rapidly.

In 1953, Northern Rhodesia became a member of the Federation of Rhodesia and Nyasaland, an arrangement opposed by an overwhelming majority of Africans in the territory. However, the federation continued through the 1950s. In 1960, despite clear economic benefits, the majority of Africans in both Northern Rhodesia and Nyasaland opposed the continuance of the federation in its present form.

The Republic of Zambia Is Born

On 31 December 1963, the Federation of Rhodesia and Nyasaland was formally dissolved. On 24 October 1964, Northern Rhodesia became an independent republic, and its name was changed to Zambia. Kenneth Kaunda, the leader of the ruling United National Independence Party (UNIP), became the nation's first president. Kaunda was reelected in 1969, 1973, 1978, and 1983, surviving a series of coup (overthrow) attempts during 1980–81. During the 1970s, Zambia played a key role in the movement toward black majority rule in Rhodesia, providing a base from which Patriotic Front guerrillas infiltrated Rhodesia. A drastic decline of world copper prices in the early 1980s, coupled with a severe drought, left Zambia in a perilous economic position. The continuing civil war in Angola also had repercussions in Zambia, bringing disruption of Zambian trade routes and casualties among Zambians along the border.

By 1990, a growing opposition to UNIP's monopoly of power had coalesced

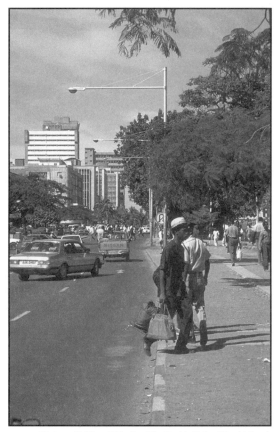

Photo credit: Edson P. Tembo of the Zambia National Tourist Board.

Busy Cairo Road in Lusaka, capital of Zambia.

in the Movement for Multiparty Democracy (MMD). In December 1990, after a tumultuous year that included riots in Lusaka and a coup attempt, Kaunda signed legislation ending UNIP's legal monopoly of power. After difficult negotiations between the government and opposition groups, Zambia enacted a new constitution in August 1991. It enlarged the National Assembly, established an electoral commission, and allowed for more than one presidential candidate. Candidates no longer are required to be UNIP members.

In September, Kaunda announced the date for Zambia's first multiparty parliamentary and presidential elections in 19 years. Frederick J. T. Chiluba (MMD) defeated Kaunda, 81% to 15%. Once in power, Chiluba's MMD became tyrannical and corrupt. The press began to criticize Chiluba's government and Chiluba lashed back. On 4 March 1993, the government declared a three-month state of emergency and detained 26 UNIP members, including three of Kaunda's sons. Chiluba lifted the state of emergency on May 25 and released all but eight of the detainees, whom he charged with offenses from treason to possession of seditious documents. President Chiluba and the MMD won huge victories in the November 1996 election but only by committing widespread vote fraud. Foreign donors suspended aid briefly in early 1997, but have since started to lend money.

Photo credit: EPD/Embassy of the Republic of Zambia.

Name:	Frederick Jacob Titus Chiluba
Position:	President of a republic
Took office:	2 November 1991
Birthplace:	Kitwe, Zambia
Birth date:	30 April 1943
Religion:	Born-again Christian
Children:	Nine children
Of interest:	Chiluba stands just under five feet tall in height.

13 GOVERNMENT

In August 1991, a new constitution was adopted. The president is now elected directly by universal suffrage and may serve a maximum of two five-year terms. The National Assembly has 150 directly elected members and up to eight appointed by the president, also for five-year terms. Candidates for office no longer are required to be members of the ruling party (UNIP).

14 POLITICAL PARTIES

With the proclamation of a one-party state in December 1972, Kenneth Kaunda's United National Independence Party (UNIP) became the only legal party in Zambia. With growing unrest in the late 1980s, a Movement for Multiparty Democracy (MMD) was formed. Finally, in December 1990, Kaunda signed into law a bill legalizing opposition political parties.

Multiparty presidential and parliamentary elections were held on 31 October and 1 November 1991, the first in 19 years. The MMD's leader, Frederick Chiluba, easily won the presidency, 81% to 15% for Kaunda. The MMD got 125 seats to 15 for UNIP in the National Assembly. Since then, new opposition parties have been formed: the Multi-Racial Party (MRP), the National Democratic Alliance (NADA), the United Democratic Party, and the United Democratic Congress Party. With the exception of the UNIP, more than 30 opposition parties operate without government interference.

Elections held on 20 November 1996 gave landslide victories to President Chiluba and the MMD. However, independent observers condemned the elections as being rigged by the MMD.

15 JUDICIAL SYSTEM

The law is administered by several High Courts that hear criminal and civil cases and appeals from lower courts. Resident magistrate courts also are established at various centers. The local courts deal mainly with customary law, especially cases relating to marriage, property, and inheritance. Under the constitution of 1991, the Supreme Court is the highest court in Zambia and serves as the final court of appeal. The chief justice and other judges are appointed by the president.

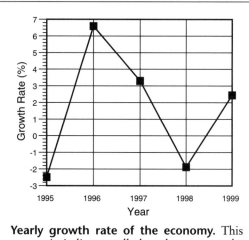

Yearly growth rate of the economy. This economic indicator tells by what percent the economy has increased or decreased when compared with the previous year.

16 ARMED FORCES

As of 2000, the strength of the armed forces was 21,600; paramilitary forces, consisting of two police battalions, totaled 1,400. The army numbered 20,000; the air force had 1,600 members and 63 combat aircraft. Military service is voluntary.

17 ECONOMY

As of 1995, the Zambian economy is in an unstable condition. High inflation, severe drought, declining export prices, and failed economic policies have all taken their toll. In 1992, Zambia was classified as a least developed country by the United Nations. The impact of inflation on the poor, the middle class, and business has eroded public support for the government's reform policies, and the expected recovery of the early 1990s has been slow to appear.

18 INCOME

In 1998, Zambia's gross domestic product (GDP) was $8.3 billion, and per capita was $880. That year, the inflation rate for consumer prices was 64%.

19 INDUSTRY

In 1998 manufacturing output accounted for 13% of the gross domestic product (GDP). The manufacturing sector declined by an average of 1% each year during 1990–95, after growing by an average of 4% per year during the 1980s. Apart from copper refining, the most important industries are those connected with the manufacture of sulfuric acid, fertilizer, glass, batteries, cigarettes, textiles, yarn, vehicle and tractor assembling, sawmilling, tire retreading, processing of food and drink, and the manufacture of cement and cement products.

20 LABOR

In 1998, recorded employment in Zambia totaled four million, the majority in subsistence agriculture. Of the remainder, some 9% were in transport and services, and 6% in mining, manufacturing, and construction. Unemployment is estimated at more than one-third of the potential labor force.

About 60% of the nation's 300,000 wage earners were unionized in 1999. There were at least 19 labor unions, most

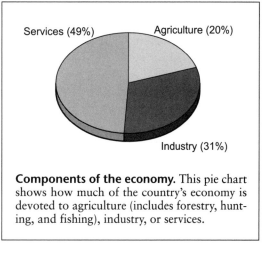

Components of the economy. This pie chart shows how much of the country's economy is devoted to agriculture (includes forestry, hunting, and fishing), industry, or services.

of them affiliated with the Zambia Congress of Trade Unions (ZCTU).

21 AGRICULTURE

The majority of Zambia's population engages in farming. The principal crops for domestic consumption are corn, sorghum, and cassava, while the main export crops are tobacco, corn, sugarcane, peanuts, and cotton. Production of tobacco, the most important export crop, was estimated at 10,000 tons in 1998, double the 1989–91 harvest. In 1994 and 1995, tobacco production was 7,000 tons each year. Marketed corn production in 1998 was 650,000 tons (down from 1.1 million tons in 1991). Cotton production reached 17,000 tons of fiber. Also marketed in 1998 were 1.65 million tons of sugarcane, 7,000 tons of sunflowers, 57,000 tons of peanuts, and 7,000 tons of wheat.

22 DOMESTICATED ANIMALS

The estimated livestock population in 1998 included 3.1 million head of cattle,

600,000 goats, 285,000 hogs, and 65,000 sheep. Cattle production in certain regions is limited by sleeping sickness, carried by the tsetse fly. During 1998, cattle slaughterings totaled 265,000 head.

23 FISHING

The fishing industry plays an important part in the rural economy. Large quantities of fish are transported by rail to processing centers, where they are frozen or dried. The catch in 1997 was 70,702 tons.

24 FORESTRY

About 39% of Zambia is covered by woodland. Roundwood production was about 14.6 million cubic meters (19.1 million cubic yards) in 1997, 92% of it for fuel needs.

25 MINING

Mining is central to Zambia's economy, accounting for 80% of foreign exchange earnings in 1996. Zambia is among the world's top six producers of copper ore, refined copper, and refined cobalt. It also is reported to be the world's leading producer of emeralds. In 1996, copper content of concentrates mined amounted to 333,700 tons.

In 1996, 100,000 tons of coal and 3,710 tons of cobalt from concentrates were mined. In 1993, zinc output was 7,900 tons. Minor quantities of silver, gold, selenium, iron ore, feldspar, and tin are produced. Amethysts also are mined.

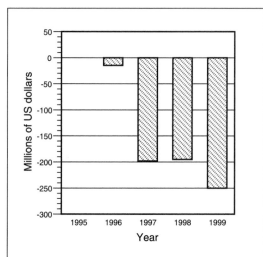

Yearly balance of trade measured in millions of US dollars. The balance of trade is the difference between what a country sells to other countries (its exports) and what it buys (its imports). If a country imports more than it exports, it has a negative balance of trade (a trade deficit). If exports exceed imports, there is a positive balance of trade (a trade surplus).

26 FOREIGN TRADE

Minerals are the leading export items, mainly copper (80%) and cobalt (10%). Other leading export commodities were zinc, lead, and tobacco. Crude oil, manufactured goods machinery, transport equipment, and foodstuffs are the main imports.

Zambia's leading export partner in 1998 was Sa'udi Arabia ($113 million), followed by Japan ($110 million), the United Kingdom ($110 million), and France ($70 million). Imports (in millions) arrived from South Africa ($591), the

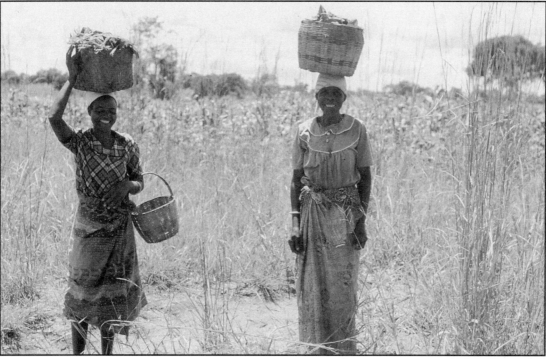

Photo credit: Cory Langley.

Although women in Zambia have full legal rights under the law, there is still discrimination in matters of inheritance, property ownership, marriage, education, and employment.

United Kingdom ($72), Zimbabwe ($89), and Japan ($39).

27 ENERGY AND POWER

The mining industry is the largest consumer of energy, accounting for about half of the total commercial energy demand. The main source of electricity was hydropower (70%), followed by petroleum products (20%), and coal (10%). A total of 8.16 billion kilowatt hours of electricity was produced in 1998. Crude oil is imported by means of a leaking pipeline from Tanzania.

28 SOCIAL DEVELOPMENT

Social welfare services are provided by the government in association with local authorities and voluntary agencies. Statutory and remedial welfare services include emergency relief, care for the aged, protection of children, adoption, and probation. Employers and employees are required to make contributions toward a worker's retirement at age 55. The Zambia Youth Service operates specially constructed camps that provide vocational training for unemployed and unskilled youth.

Women have full legal rights under the law, but discrimination happens in matters

Selected Social Indicators

The statistics below are estimates for the period 1996 to 2000. For comparison purposes, data for the United States and averages for low-income countries and high-income countries are also given.

Indicator	Zambia	Low-income countries	High-income countries	United States
Per capita gross national product (GNP)†	$720	$1,870	$25,690	$31,910
Population growth rate	2.5%	2.1%	0.7%	1.1%
People per square kilometer of land	13	73	29	30
Life expectancy in years	38	59	78	77
Number of physicians per 1,000 people	<0.1	1.0	2.5	2.5
Number of pupils per teacher (primary school)	41	41	17	14
Illiteracy rate (15 years and older)	22%	34%	<5%	3%
Television sets per 1,000 people	145	85	693	844
Energy consumed per capita (kg of oil equivalent)	630	550	5,366	7,937

† The GNP is the total dollar value of all goods and services produced by a country in a year. The per capita GNP is calculated by dividing a country's GNP by its population and adjusting for relative purchasing power. About 15% of the world's 6.1 billion people live in high-income countries, while 40% live in low-income countries.

n.a. = data not available   > = greater than   < = less than

Sources: World Bank. World Development Indicators. Washington, D.C.: The World Bank, 2001; Central Intelligence Agency. The World Factbook. Washington, D.C.: Government Printing Office, 2000.

of inheritance, property ownership, marriage, education, and employment.

29 HEALTH

As of 1992, government records indicate nine hospitals and a few small outpatient clinics. Medical personnel in 1995 included one doctor for every 13,403 population. In 1994, an estimated 47% of the population had access to safe water and 42% to adequate sanitation.

Malaria and tuberculosis are major health problems, and hookworm and schistosomiasis afflict a large proportion of the population. Average life expectancy was estimated at 38 years in 2000. In 1997, blood surveys indicated that 19% of the adult population was infected with HIV (the virus that causes AIDS).

30 HOUSING

Widespread instances of overcrowding and slum growth have for many years focused government attention on urban housing problems. Mining companies have constructed townships for the families of African workers.

31 EDUCATION

Primary education lasts for seven years and is compulsory. Secondary education is for five years. In 1995, 1.5 million pupils

Victoria Falls, on the border with Zimbabwe, is a favorite tourist attraction.

were in 3,883 primary schools, and 199,154 students attended secondary schools. Adult illiteracy was estimated at 22% (14.8% for men and 28.8% for women) in 2000. The University of Zambia was established in 1965. Other institutions of higher learning include technical colleges and a two-year college of agriculture. All higher level institutions had 15,343 pupils in 1990.

32 MEDIA

The central government is responsible for postal and telecommunication services. About 98,000 telephones were in use in 1995. The Zambia Broadcasting Service, which provides radio programs in English and seven local languages, and Zambian Television are government owned and operated. In 2000 there were 145 television receivers per 1,000 population.

Zambia has three daily newspapers: owned by the United National Independence Party (UNIP) is *Times of Zambia*, founded in 1943, with an estimated 1999 circulation of 32,000; and the government-owned *Zambia Daily Mail*, published in Lusaka, with a circulation of 40,000.

33 TOURISM AND RECREATION

One of the most impressive tourist attractions in Zambia is Victoria Falls on the border with Zimbabwe. In 1972, a new national park system created 17 parks covering 8% of the entire country. The Kafue National Park, one of the largest in Africa, with 22,500 square kilometers (8,700 square miles) of bush, forest, and plain, is well-served with tourist facilities. South Luangwa National Park is another outstanding wildlife area. In 1998, Zambia received 362,000 foreign visitors, the majority from Africa. In 1998, there were 4,239 hotel rooms with 7,162 beds and a 50% occupancy rate.

34 FAMOUS ZAMBIANS

Kenneth David Kaunda (b.1924) was Zambia's president from independence in 1964 until 1991. Frederick J. T. Chiluba (b.1943) ousted Kaunda in 1991 in Zambia's first free elections and was reelected in 1996. Nalumino Mundia (1927–88), long prominent in Zambian political affairs, was prime minister 1981–85, when he became ambassador to the United States.

35 BIBLIOGRAPHY

Burdette, Marcia M. *Zambia: Between Two Worlds.* Boulder, Colo.: Westview Press, 1988.

Grotpeter, John J. *Historical Dictionary of Zambia.* Metuchen, N.J.: Scarecrow, 1979.

Hansen, Karen Tranberg. *Distant Companions: Servants and Employers in Zambia, 1900–1985.* Ithaca: Cornell University Press, 1989.

Holmes, Timothy. *Zambia.* New York: Benchmark Books, 1998.

Lauré. Jason. *Zambia.* Chicago: Children's Press, 1994.

Rotberg, Robert I. *The Rise of Nationalism in Central Africa: The Making of Malawi and Zambia, 1873–1964.* Cambridge, Mass.: Harvard University Press, 1965.

ZIMBABWE

Republic of Zimbabwe

CAPITAL: Harare.

FLAG: The flag has seven equal horizontal stripes of green, yellow, red, black, red, yellow, and green. At the hoist is a white triangle, which contains a representation in yellow of the bird of Zimbabwe superimposed on a red star.

ANTHEM: *God Bless Africa.*

MONETARY UNIT: The Zimbabwe dollar (z$) is a paper currency of 100 cents. There are coins of 1, 5, 10, 20, and 50 cents and 1 dollar, and notes of 2, 5, 10, and 20 dollars. z$1 = us$0.0262 (or us$1 = z$38.17).

WEIGHTS AND MEASURES: The metric system is used.

HOLIDAYS: New Year's Day, 1 January; Independence Day, 18 April; Workers' Day, 1 May; Africa Day, 25 May; Heroes' Days, 11–13 August; Christmas Day, 25 December; Boxing Day, 26 December. Movable holidays are Good Friday, Holy Saturday, Easter Monday, and Whitmonday.

TIME: 2 PM = noon GMT.

1 LOCATION AND SIZE

A landlocked country of south-central Africa, Zimbabwe (formerly Rhodesia) lies between the Zambezi River on the north and the Limpopo River on the south. It has an area of 390,580 square kilometers (150,804 square miles), slightly larger than the state of Montana. Zimbabwe's total boundary length is 3,066 kilometers (1,905 miles). The capital city, Harare, is located in the northeast part of the country.

2 TOPOGRAPHY

Most of Zimbabwe is rolling plateau. The highveld (or high plateau) stretches southwest to northeast, ending in the Inyanga mountains. On either side of the highveld is the middleveld. The lowveld is made up of wide, grassy plains in the basins of the Zambezi and the Limpopo rivers. Streams flow southeast from the watershed of the highveld to the Limpopo and Sabi Rivers and northwest into the Zambezi.

3 CLIMATE

Temperatures on the highveld vary from 12–13°C (54–55°F) in winter to 24°C (75°F) in summer. On the lowveld the temperatures are usually 6°C (11°F) higher, and summer temperatures in the Zambezi and Limpopo valleys average between 32° and 38°C (90–100°F).

Rainfall decreases from east to west. The eastern mountains receive more than 100 centimeters (40 inches) annually, while Harare has 81 centimeters (32 inches) and Bulawayo 61 centimeters (24

Geographic Profile

Geographic Features

Size ranking: 59 of 192
Highest elevation: 2,592 meters (8,504 feet) at Mount Inyangani
Lowest elevation: 162 meters (532 feet) at the junction of the Lundi and Save Rivers

Land Use†

Arable land:	7%
Permanent crops:	0%
Permanent pastures:	13%
Forests:	23%
Other:	57%

Weather††

Average annual precipitation: 86.3 centimeters (34.0 inches)
Average temperature in January: 20°C (68.0°F)
Average temperature in July: 13.6°C (56.5°F)

†*Arable land:* Land used for temporary crops, like meadows for mowing or pasture, gardens, and greenhouses. *Permanent crops:* Land cultivated with crops that occupy its use for long periods, such as cocoa, coffee, rubber, fruit and nut orchards, and vineyards. *Permanent pastures:* Land used permanently for forage crops. *Forests:* Land containing stands of trees. *Other:* Any land not specified, including built-on areas, roads, and barren land.

††The measurements for precipitation and average temperature were taken at weather stations closest to the country's largest city. Precipitation and average temperature can vary significantly within a country, due to factors such as latitude, altitude, coastal proximity, and wind patterns.

inches). The south and southwest receive little rainfall.

4 PLANTS AND ANIMALS

The country is mostly grassland, although the moist and mountainous east supports tropical evergreen and hardwood forests. Trees include teak and mahogany, knobthorn, msasa, and baobab. Among the numerous flowers and shrubs are hibiscus, spider lily, leonotus, cassia, tree wisteria, and dombeya.

Mammals include elephant, lion, buffalo, hippopotamus, rhinoceros, gorilla, chimpanzee, baboon, giraffe, eland, gemsbok, waterbuck, zebra, warthog, lynx, aardvark, porcupine, fox, badger, otter, hare, bat, shrew, and scaly anteater. Snakes and lizards abound. About 500 species of birds include the ant-thrush, bee-eater, bishop bird, bush-warbler, emerald cuckoo, grouse, and pheasant.

5 ENVIRONMENT

Among the most serious of Zimbabwe's environmental problems is erosion of its agricultural lands and expansion of the desert. Air and water pollution result from the combined effects of transportation vehicles, mining, fertilizers, and the cement industry. Zimbabwe's cities produce 500,000 tons of solid waste per year. In 1994, nine of the nation's mammal species and six bird species were endangered, as well as 96 types of plants. Zimbabwe has about half of the world's population of black rhinoceroses, an endangered species.

6 POPULATION

The population was estimated at 11.2 million in 2000 and projected to be 11.7 million in 2005. Population density in 1998 was about 31 persons per square kilometer (80 per square mile). In 2000, Harare, the capital, had a population of 1.8 million.

7 MIGRATION

By early 1987, 110,000 whites were estimated to have remained in Zimbabwe, about half the number on independence in

LOCATION: 15°37′ to 22°25′s; 25°14′ to 33°4′E. **BOUNDARY LENGTHS:** Mozambique, 1,231 kilometers (762 miles); South Africa, 225 kilometers (140 miles); Botswana, 813 kilometers (505 miles); Zambia, 797 kilometers (498 miles).

1980. There also were about 25,000 persons of mixed race and 10,000 Asians. By the end of 1992, famine and civil war in Mozambique had driven an estimated 136,600 Mozambicans into Zimbabwe. Between 1992 and 1996, 241,000 Mozambican refugees in Zimbabwe returned to Mozambique. There is a small but steady flow of Zimbabweans into South Africa in search of better paid employment.

8 ETHNIC GROUPS

Africans in Zimbabwe are mainly related to the two major Bantu-speaking groups, the Shona (about 71% of the population) and the Ndebele (about 16%). Europeans are almost entirely either immigrants from

Elephant crossing, Hwange National Park.

the United Kingdom or South Africa or their descendants.

9 LANGUAGES

Six major dialects of the same Bantu language, Shona, are spoken. The Ndebele speak modified versions of Ndebele (or Sindebele). English, the official language, is spoken by most Europeans and by an increasing number of Africans.

10 RELIGIONS

About 60% of the total population was Christian as of 1999. Traditional religious practices are still followed by at least 40% of the population. Of professing Chris-tians, Protestants constitute some 17%, followers of African native churches, 14%, and Roman Catholics, 8.7%. There are small populations of Jews and Muslims, as well as some Baha'is and Hindus.

11 TRANSPORTATION

In 1995, the National Railways of Zimbabwe, a public corporation, operated 2,759 kilometers (1,714 miles) of rail lines. In 1999, there were 18,338 kilometers (11,395 miles) of road, with 62% paved. In 1995, there were 270,000 motor vehicles, including 180,000 passenger cars. Harare and Bulawayo are the principal airports.

12 HISTORY

The remains of ironworking cultures that date back to AD 300 have been discovered in what is now Zimbabwe. Bantu-speaking Shona arrived from the north between the tenth and eleventh centuries AD. They gradually developed gold and ivory trade with the coast, and by the mid-fifteenth century had established a strong empire, with its capital at the ancient city of Zimbabwe.

By the time the British began arriving in the mid-nineteenth century, the Shona people had long been subjected to slave raids and their empire destroyed by the Ndebele, fleeing the Zulus in South Africa. David Livingstone, a Scottish missionary and explorer, was chiefly responsible for opening Central Africa to the Europeans.

To prevent Portuguese and Boer (Dutch) expansion into the area, both the British government and Cecil Rhodes actively sought to acquire territory. In 1888, Lobengula, king of the Ndebele, accepted a treaty with Great Britain and granted Rhodes exclusive mineral rights to the lands he controlled. Rhodes was then able to obtain a royal charter for his British South Africa Company (BSAC) in 1889. The BSAC sent a group of settlers into Mashonaland, where they founded the town of Salisbury (now Harare). With the defeat of the Ndebele and the Shona between 1893 and 1897, Europeans were guaranteed unlimited settlement. The name Rhodesia was commonly used by 1895.

In 1923, Southern Rhodesia was annexed to the British government; its African inhabitants thereby became British subjects, and the colony received its basic constitution. In 1953, the Central African Federation was formed, consisting of the three British territories of Northern Rhodesia (now Zambia), Nyasaland (now Malawi), and Southern Rhodesia, with each territory retaining its original constitution. In 1962, Nyasaland and Northern Rhodesia withdrew from the federation, which disbanded in 1963, and Southern Rhodesia sought independence under the name of Rhodesia.

The white-settler government demanded independence under the existing political framework. The African nationalists also demanded independence, but under conditions of universal franchise and African majority rule. Negotiations repeatedly broke down, and on 11 November 1965, the government of Rhodesian Prime Minister Ian Smith issued a unilateral declaration of independence (since known as UDI). In December, the United Nations Security Council passed a resolution calling for selective mandatory sanctions against Rhodesia. Further attempts at a negotiated settlement ended in failure. In a referendum held on 20 June 1969, Rhodesia's voters—92% white—approved the establishment of a republic.

Rhodesia declared itself a republic on 2 March 1970. The United Kingdom called the declaration illegal, and 11 countries closed their consulates in Rhodesia. The United Nations Security Council called on member states not to recognize any acts by the illegal regime and condemned Portugal and South Africa for maintaining relations with Rhodesia. Problems in Rhodesia deepened after UDI, largely as a result of regional and international political pres-

Life in the countryside.

sure, African nationalist demands, and African guerrilla activities. A meeting took place in Geneva in October 1976 between the British and Smith governments and four African nationalist groups. On 3 March 1978, the Smith regime signed an internal agreement with Bishop Abel Muzorewa, Ndabaningi Sithole, and other leaders, providing for qualified majority rule and universal suffrage. Bishop Muzorewa, whose party won a majority in the elections of April 1979, became the first black prime minister of the country (now renamed Zimbabwe-Rhodesia).

However, fighting between the different factions continued, and further negotiations in England later that year resulted in an agreement, by 21 December, on a new, democratic constitution, democratic elections, and independence. Following elections held in February, Robert Mugabe became prime minister and formed a coalition government that included Joshua Nkomo. The independent nation of Zimbabwe was proclaimed on 18 April 1980, and the new parliament opened on 14 May 1980.

Independence and Factionalism

Following independence, Zimbabwe initially made significant economic and social progress, but internal dissent was a growing problem. A long-simmering rivalry erupted between Mugabe's dominant Zimbabwe African National Union (ZANU)-

Patriotic Front Party, which represented the majority Shona tribes, and Nkomo's Zimbabwe African People's Union (ZAPU), which had the support of the minority Ndebele. Mugabe ousted Nkomo from the cabinet in February 1982. On 8 March 1983, Nkomo went into exile, but returned to Parliament in August.

Armed rebels continued to operate in Matabeleland until 1987, when the two largest political parties, ZANU and ZAPU, agreed to merge. By this point, however, the political instability of Zimbabwe's neighbors to the south and east was threatening the country. In 1986, South African forces raided the premises of the South African black-liberation African National Congress in Harare, and 10,000 Zimbabwean troops were deployed in Mozambique. They were seeking to keep antigovernment forces in that country from severing Zimbabwe's rail, road, and oil-pipeline links with the port of Beira in Mozambique.

In the meantime dissatisfaction with the economic situation at home led to growing opposition to Mugabe. In January 1992, Sithole returned from seven years of self-imposed exile in the United States. In July, Ian Smith chaired a meeting of Rhodesian-era parties seeking to form a coalition in opposition to Mugabe. In May 1992 a new pressure group, the Forum for Democratic Reform, was launched in preparation for the 1995 elections. It evolved into the Forum Party, which advocates free enterprise, clean government, respect for human rights, and a drastic reduction of state control of the economy.

In the March 1990 elections, Mugabe was reelected with 78.3% of the vote. There was a sharp drop in voter participation, and the election was marred by restrictions on opposition activity and open intimidation of opposition voters. With a slumping economy, worsened by an extensive drought in 1991 and 1992, the Mugabe government lost support. It responded by restricting human and political rights, placing checks on the formerly independent judiciary, and tampering with the election process.

In September 1995, the International Monetary Fund suspended economic aid because the government had not made any serious move at reducing its spending. Zimbabwe's Finance Ministry reduced expenditures for social programs and education, but increased civil service wages and pension benefits for veterans offset any savings.

In January 1998, riots and looting broke out in Harare for two days due to sharp price increases for food (the value of Zimbabwe's currency had declined by 70% in one year). The government set up a program of price controls for basic food items as a stopgap (temporary solution). Like most African nations, Zimbabwe continues to struggle with the issues of economic growth and political liberalization.

13 GOVERNMENT

Under the constitution that took effect on 18 April 1980, independent Zimbabwe has a two-chamber Parliament. The lower house, the House of Assembly, had 100 members, and the upper house, or Senate,

Photo credit: EPD/Office of the President.

Name: Robert Gabriel Mugabe
Position: Executive president of a parliamentary democracy
Took office: 31 December 1987
Birthplace: Kutama, Zimbabwe
Birth date: 21 February 1924
Education: Fort Hare University, South Africa, bachelor's degree in English and history, 1951; bachelor's degree in education
Spouse: Grace Marufu
Of interest: Mugabe's wedding to Grace Marufu in August 1996 was called "wedding of the century." About 40,000 guests attended the ceremony.

prime minister. The president (Robert Mugabe in 2001) is directly elected for a six-year term and may be reelected. There is universal suffrage (voting) beginning at age 18.

[14] POLITICAL PARTIES

The principal black parties in Zimbabwean politics originated in the struggle for independence on a tribal basis, although in 2000 it appeared to still be a one party state. The Zimbabwe African People's Union (ZAPU) was formed in December 1961 and led by Joshua Nkomo. It was split in July 1963 by the creation of the Zimbabwe African National Union (ZANU), led by the Reverend Ndabaningi Sithole, and later by Robert Mugabe. Both ZAPU and ZANU took up arms against the government and in 1976 allied themselves in the Patriotic Front (PF).

After much hostility and bitterness during most of the 1980s, ZAPU and ZANU finally agreed in late 1987 to merge under the name of ZANU. New parties began to emerge in the late 1980s and early 1990s in preparation for the expected elections in 1995, including Tekere's Zimbabwe Unity Movement (ZUM). In January, long-time Mugabe rival Sithole returned from exile and created his own party, also using the ZANU name as ZANU-Ndonga or sometimes ZANU-Sithole.

President Mugabe's ZANU-PF has undisputed control over the executive and legislative branches of government. The party controls most of the large newspapers, radio stations, and television sta-

had 40 members. In August 1987, as soon as the constitution allowed, the separate representation for whites in Parliament was abolished. The two houses of Parliament were merged after the 1990 elections into a chamber of 150 members. Another constitutional change created an executive presidency and abolished the office of tions, and gets its funding from the government.

15 JUDICIAL SYSTEM

A four-member Supreme Court, headed by the chief justice, hears cases involving violations of fundamental rights guaranteed in the constitution and hears appeals of other cases. There is a High Court consisting of general and appeals divisions. Below the High Court are regional courts with civil jurisdiction and courts with both civil and criminal jurisdiction.

16 ARMED FORCES

Regular armed forces numbered 39,000 in 2000. The army had 35,000 members organized into 15 infantry battalions, one artillery regiment, one armored regiment, one engineer regiment, and supporting units. The air force had 4,000 personnel and 58 combat aircraft. The national police force has 19,500 members, with 2,300 support personnel. Estimated defense expenditures for 1997–98 were $427 million, or 4.6% of the gross domestic product (GDP).

17 ECONOMY

Zimbabwe has developed one of the most varied economies in Africa. It has abundant agricultural and mineral resources and well-developed industry. However, problems abound. Although Zimbabwe began to recover from the effects of the devastating 1991–92 drought, the unemployment rate is above 50% (1999) and thousands remain chronically dependent on food support. Together with the International Monetary Fund (IMF), Zimbabwe drew up a 1991–95 economic reform plan.

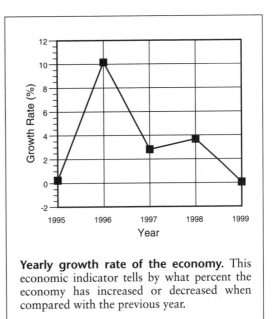

Yearly growth rate of the economy. This economic indicator tells by what percent the economy has increased or decreased when compared with the previous year.

18 INCOME

In 1998, Zimbabwe's gross domestic product (GDP) was $26.2 billion, or about $2,400 per person. In 1999, the average inflation rate was 32%, resulting in a growth rate in GDP of nearly zero.

19 INDUSTRY

Zimbabwe has a substantial cotton and textile industry and a sizable metal and engineering sector. Manufacturing accounted for 17% of the domestic economy in 1998. Other leading industries are food processing, sugar refining, tobacco, clothing, chemicals, beverages, industrial coke, cement, pig iron and crude steel, nitrogenous and phosphate fertilizers,

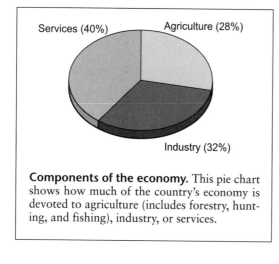

Services (40%) Agriculture (28%)

Industry (32%)

Components of the economy. This pie chart shows how much of the country's economy is devoted to agriculture (includes forestry, hunting, and fishing), industry, or services.

potatoes, tea, and pyrethrum also are grown.

22 DOMESTICATED ANIMALS

In 1998, some 4.5 million head of cattle, 2.75 million goats, 520,000 sheep, 270,000 hogs, and 107,000 donkeys were held. Chickens numbered about 16 million. In 1998, cattle slaughterings totaled 370,000 head; pigs, 230,000 head; and goats, 100,000 head. Fresh milk production from cows totaled 570,000 tons from 350 dairy suppliers in 1998.

23 FISHING

There is some commercial fishing on Lake Kariba. The total catch in 1997 was estimated at 18,241 tons.

24 FORESTRY

In 1994, 23% of Zimbabwe's land area was classified as forested, but this estimate included scattered tree savanna. About 100,000 tons of teak, mahogany, and mukwa (kiaat) are cut annually. Roundwood production totaled 7.9 million cubic meters in 1997 (78% burned as fuel); sawn wood production was 207,000 cubic meters.

unwrought nickel and tin, wood pulp, and furniture.

20 LABOR

In 1998, there were more than 4.9 million employed civilians in Zimbabwe, or 42% of the total population. The monthly minimum wage in 1999 was $17 in the agricultural sector to $52 in the manufacturing sector. The unemployment rate in 1993 was about 45%.

21 AGRICULTURE

In 1992, drought severely affected the output of every crop except tobacco. Tobacco production in 1998 exceeded 260,000 tons. Corn production in 1998 totaled only 1.4 million tons, down from 2.4 million tons in 1994. In 1998, cotton production totaled 95,000 tons. Marketed production figures for other crops in 1998 were wheat, 280,000 tons; sorghum, 72,000 tons; soybeans, 110,000 tons; peanuts, 60,000 tons; coffee, 10,000 tons; and sunflower seeds, 29,000 tons. Rice,

25 MINING

Zimbabwe is a world leader in the production of lithium and asbestos, and has more than half of the world's known reserves of chromium. In 1996, Zimbabwe produced more than 50 different types of minerals from more than 400 mines. In order of value, the most important minerals are gold, asbestos, nickel, coal, copper, chromite, tin, and silver. Mineral output in

Yearly balance of trade measured in millions of US dollars. The balance of trade is the difference between what a country sells to other countries (its exports) and what it buys (its imports). If a country imports more than it exports, it has a negative balance of trade (a trade deficit). If exports exceed imports there is a positive balance of trade (a trade surplus).

1996 included coal, 5.1 million tons; chromium ore, 697,000 tons; asbestos, 165,000 tons; nickel, 11,561 tons; copper, 7,600 tons; and gold, 24,699 kilograms.

26 FOREIGN TRADE

Tobacco typically accounts for 30% of exports; gold, 14%; ferrochrome, 8.5%; and sugar, 4.5%. Other exports include crude inedible nonfood materials, nickel, asbestos, copper, sugar, cotton, and tobacco. The leading imports in 1999 were machinery and transport equipment, chemicals, and fuel.

During 1998, South Africa took $334 million of Zimbabwe's exports; the United Kingdom, $184 million; and Germany,

$131 million. Imports came mainly from South Africa, $1.4 billion; the United Kingdom, $129 million; and the United States, $93 million.

27 ENERGY AND POWER

Zimbabwe relies heavily on hydroelectricity and coal for its energy needs. Wood also is still important. Petroleum accounts for only 9% of Zimbabwe's total energy consumption, but provides most motor fuels. Coal production in 1994 totaled six million tons, with much of that amount going to the coal-fired Hwange plant for electricity production. In 1982, a plant producing ethanol from sugarcane opened and now produces some 20% of motor fuel requirements. The use of solar energy is increasing. In 1998, Zimbabwe produced 6.9 billion kilowatt hours of electricity. That year, Zimbabwe imported about 20% of its electricity from Zambia.

28 SOCIAL DEVELOPMENT

The Ministry of Labour, Manpower Planning, and Social Welfare deals with child welfare, delinquency, adoption, family problems, refugees, the aged, and public assistance. Voluntary welfare organizations providing facilities for the aged, the handicapped, and care of children receive some government assistance. Workers' compensation is provided to those Africans whose earnings fall below a set minimum yearly wage. In 1993, a social security system was introduced.

The Law and Order Maintenance Act, now more than 30 years old, gives police extensive powers to prosecute political opponents. Although it is rarely used, the

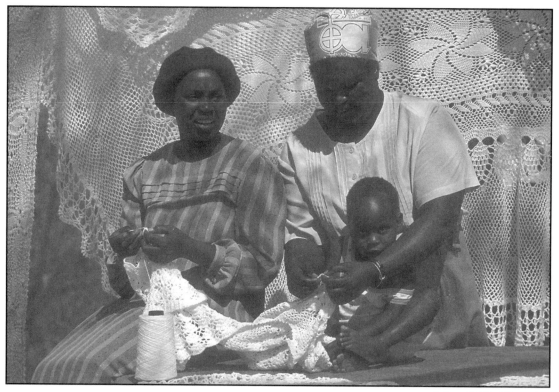

Photo credit: © Corel Corporation.

Women doing crochet work.

policy severely restricts the rights of defendants.

29 HEALTH

About 85% of the population had access to health care services in 1992. There were four levels of health care delivery in Zimbabwe as of 1992: (1) 56 rural hospitals and 927 health centers; (2) 55 district hospitals; (3) eight provincial and four general hospitals; and (4) five central hospitals located in major cities. For the period 1990 to 1997 there were 10 doctors per 10,000 people. Average life expectancy was 40 years in 2000.

Tuberculosis has been a major health problem. Malaria and measles are commonly reported. Local campaigns are underway to control schistosomiasis, which affects a large percentage of the African population. In 1997, 25.8% of all adults in Zimbabwe were infected with HIV, the virus that leads to AIDS.

30 HOUSING

In rural areas, Africans live in villages and on farms in housing that is mainly of brick or mud and stick construction with thatch or metal roofs. Urban housing is generally of brick.

Selected Social Indicators

The statistics below are estimates for the period 1996 to 2000. For comparison purposes, data for the United States and averages for low-income countries and high-income countries are also given.

Indicator	Zimbabwe	Low-income countries	High-income countries	United States
Per capita gross national product (GNP)†	$2,690	$1,870	$25,690	$31,910
Population growth rate	2.1%	2.1%	0.7%	1.1%
People per square kilometer of land	31	73	29	30
Life expectancy in years	40	59	78	77
Number of physicians per 1,000 people	<0.2	1.0	2.5	2.5
Number of pupils per teacher (primary school)	45	41	17	14
Illiteracy rate (15 years and older)	7.3%	34%	<5%	3%
Television sets per 1,000 people	180	85	693	844
Energy consumed per capita (kg of oil equivalent)	861	550	5,366	7,937

† The GNP is the total dollar value of all goods and services produced by a country in a year. The per capita GNP is calculated by dividing a country's GNP by its population and adjusting for relative purchasing power. About 15% of the world's 6.1 billion people live in high-income countries, while 40% live in low-income countries.

n.a. = data not available   > = greater than   < = less than

Sources: World Bank. *World Development Indicators.* Washington, D.C.: The World Bank, 2001; Central Intelligence Agency. *The World Factbook.* Washington, D.C.: Government Printing Office, 2000.

31 EDUCATION

The adult illiteracy rate in 2000 was about 7.3% (4.5% for men and 10% for women). In 1998 there were 2.5 million students in 4,706 primary schools with 64,538 teachers. The same year, general secondary schools had 847,296 students. The University of Zimbabwe provides higher education on a multiracial basis; there were nine colleges in 1987. In 1996, there were 46,673 students in all higher level institutions.

32 MEDIA

In 1995 there were 128 main telephone lines, with about 1.2 telephones per 100 people. Radio Zimbabwe broadcasts over two AM and three FM channels, and government-produced television programs are broadcast from Harare and Bulawayo. In 2000 there were 180 television sets per 1,000 population. There are two daily papers and more than 40 periodicals published in Zimbabwe. The dailies, with their 1999 circulations, are the *Herald* (Harare), 122,000; and the *Chronicle* (Bulawayo), 74,000.

33 TOURISM AND RECREATION

Tourist attractions include Victoria Falls and the Kariba Dam on the Zambezi River; numerous wildlife sanctuaries and game reserves, including Hwange National Park; the eastern highlands; the Matobo Hills; and the Zimbabwe ruins near Masvingo. There are safari areas in the Zambezi Valley below the Kariba Dam.

In 1997, 1.5 million tourists visited Zimbabwe, with total receipts estimated at $230 million.

34 FAMOUS ZIMBABWEANS

The country's former name, Rhodesia, was derived from Cecil John Rhodes (1853–1902), whose company administered the area during the late 19th and early 20th centuries. Lobengula (1833–94), king of the Ndebele, headed an unsuccessful rebellion of his people against the settlers in 1893.

Prominent African nationalist leaders are Joshua Nkomo (1917–99), leader of ZAPU; Bishop Abel Muzorewa (b.1925) of the United Methodist Church, who became the nation's first black prime minister in 1979; and ZANU leader Robert Gabriel Mugabe (b.1924), who became prime minister after independence. Ian Smith (b.1919) was prime minister from 1964 to 1979.

35 BIBLIOGRAPHY

Barnes-Svarney, Patricia L. *Zimbabwe*. Philadelphia: Chelsea House, 1999.
Cheney, Patricia. *The Land and People of Zimbabwe*. New York: Lippincott, 1990.
Halvorsen, Lisa. *Zimbabwe*. Woodbridge, CT: Blackbirch Press, 2000.
Nkomo, Joshua. *The Story of My Life*. London: Mowbrays, 1984.
O'Toole, Thomas. *Zimbabwe in Pictures*. Minneapolis: Lerner Pub. Co., 1988.
Sheehan, Sean. *Zimbabwe*. New York: Marshall Cavendish, 1999.

GLOSSARY

abdicate: To formally give up a claim to a throne; to give up the right to be king or queen.

aboriginal: The first known inhabitants of a country. A species of animals or plants which originated within a given area.

acid rain: Rain (or snow) that has become slightly acid by mixing with industrial air pollution.

adobe: A brick made from sun-dried heavy clay mixed with straw, used in building houses. A house made of adobe bricks.

adult literacy: The ability of adults to read and write.

agrarian economy: An economy where agriculture is the dominant form of economic activity. A society where agriculture dominates the day-to-day activities of the population is called an agrarian society.

air link: Refers to scheduled air service that allows people and goods to travel between two places on a regular basis.

airborne industrial pollutant: Pollution caused by industry that is supported or carried by the air.

allies: Groups or persons who are united in a common purpose. Typically used to describe nations that have joined together to fight a common enemy in war.

In World War I, the term Allies described the nations that fought against Germany and its allies. In World War II, Allies described the United Kingdom, United States, the USSR and their allies, who fought against the Axis Powers of Germany, Italy, and Japan.

aloe: A plant particularly abundant in the southern part of Africa, where leaves of some species are made into ropes, fishing lines, bow strings, and hammocks. It is also a symbolic plant in the Islamic world; anyone who returns from a pilgrimage to Mecca (Mekkah) hangs aloe over his door as a token that he has performed the journey.

Altaic language family: A family of languages spoken in portions of northern and eastern Europe, and nearly the whole of northern and central Asia, together with some other regions. The family is divided into five branches: the Ugrian or Finno-Hungarian, Smoyed, Turkish, Mongolian, and Tunguse.

althing: A legislative assembly.

amendment: A change or addition to a document.

Amerindian: A contraction of the two words, American Indian. It describes native peoples of North, South, or Central America.

amnesty: An act of forgiveness or pardon, usually taken by a government, toward persons for crimes they may have committed.

Anglican: Pertaining to or connected with the Church of England.

animal husbandry: The branch of agriculture that involves raising animals.

animism: The belief that natural objects and phenomena have souls or innate spiritual powers.

annex: To incorporate land from one country into another country.

annual growth rate: The rate at which something grows over a period of 12 months.

annual inflation rate: The rate of inflation in prices over the course of a year.

anthracite coal: Also called hard coal, it is usually 90 to 95 percent carbon, and burns cleanly, almost without a flame.

anti-Semitism: Agitation, persecution, or discrimination (physical, emotional, economic, political, or otherwise) directed against the Jews.

apartheid: The past governmental policy in the Republic of South Africa of separating the races in society.

appeasement: To bring to a state of peace.

appellate: Refers to an appeal of a court decision to a high authority.

aquaculture: The culture or "farming" of aquatic plants or other natural produce, as in the raising of catfish in "farms."

aquatic resources: Resources that come from, grow in, or live in water, including fish and plants.

aquifer: An underground layer of porous rock, sand, or gravel that holds water.

arable land: Land that can be cultivated by plowing and used for growing crops.

arbitration: A process whereby disputes are settled by a designated person, called the arbitrator, instead of by a court of law.

archipelago: Any body of water abounding with islands, or the islands themselves collectively.

archives: A place where records or a collection of important documents are kept.

arctic climate: Cold, frigid weather similar to that experienced at or near the north pole.

aristocracy: A small minority that controls the government of a nation, typically on the basis of inherited wealth.

armistice: An agreement or truce which ends military conflict in anticipation of a peace treaty.

artesian well: A type of well where the water rises to the surface and overflows.

ASEAN *see* Association of Southeast Asian Nations

Association of Southeast Asian Nations: ASEAN was established in 1967 to promote political, economic, and social cooperation among its six member countries: Indonesia, Malaysia, the Philippines, Singapore, Thailand, and Brunei. ASEAN headquarters are in Jakarta, Indonesia. In January

1992, ASEAN agreed to create the ASEAN Free Trade Area (AFTA).

asylum: To give protection, security, or shelter to someone who is threatened by political or religious persecution.

atoll: A coral island, consisting of a strip or ring of coral surrounding a central lagoon.

atomic weapons: Weapons whose extremely violent explosive power comes from the splitting of the nuclei of atoms (usually uranium or plutonium) by neutrons in a rapid chain reaction. These weapons may be referred to as atom bombs, hydrogen bombs, or H-bombs.

austerity measures: Steps taken by a government to conserve money or resources during an economically difficult time, such as cutting back on federally funded programs.

Australoid: Pertains to the type of aborigines, or earliest inhabitants, of Australia.

Austronesian language: A family of languages which includes practically all the languages of the Pacific Islands—Indonesian, Melanesian, Polynesian, and Micronesian sub-families. Does not include Australian or Papuan languages.

authoritarianism: A form of government in which a person or group attempts to rule with absolute authority without the representation of the citizens.

autonomous state: A country which is completely self-governing, as opposed to being a dependency or part of another country.

autonomy: The state of existing as a self-governing entity. For instance, when a country gains its independence from another country, it gains autonomy.

average inflation rate: The average rate at which the general prices of goods and services increase over the period of a year.

average life expectancy: In any given society, the average age attained by persons at the time of death.

Axis Powers: The countries aligned against the Allied Nations in World War II, originally applied to Nazi Germany and Fascist Italy (Rome-Berlin Axis), and later extended to include Japan.

Baha'i: The follower of a religious sect founded by Mirza Husayn Ali in Iran in 1863.

Baltic states. The three formerly communist countries of Estonia, Latvia, and Lithuania that border on the Baltic Sea.

Bantu language group: A name applied to the languages spoken in central and south Africa.

Baptist: A member of a Protestant denomination that practices adult baptism by complete immersion in water.

barren land: Unproductive land, partly or entirely treeless.

barter: Trade practice where merchandise is exchanged directly for other merchandise or services without use of money.

bedrock: Solid rock lying under loose earth.

bicameral legislature: A legislative body consisting of two chambers, such as the U.S. House of Representatives and the U.S. Senate.

bill of rights: A written statement containing the list of privileges and powers to be granted to a body of people, usually introduced when a government or other organization is forming.

bituminous coal: Soft coal; coal which burns with a bright-yellow flame.

black market: A system of trade where goods are sold illegally, often for excessively inflated prices. This type of trade usually develops to avoid paying taxes or tariffs levied by the government, or to get around import or export restrictions on products.

bloodless coup: The sudden takeover of a country's government by hostile means but without killing anyone in the process.

boat people: Used to describe individuals (refugees) who attempt to flee their country by boat.

bog: Wet, soft, and spongy ground where the soil is composed mainly of decayed or decaying vegetable matter.

Bolshevik Revolution. A revolution in 1917 in Russia when a wing of the Russian Social Democratic party seized power. The Bolsheviks advocated the violent overthrow of capitalism.

bonded labor: Workers bound to service without pay; slaves.

border dispute: A disagreement between two countries as to the exact location or length of the dividing line between them.

Brahman: A member (by heredity) of the highest caste among the Hindus, usually assigned to the priesthood.

broadleaf forest: A forest composed mainly of broadleaf (deciduous) trees.

Buddhism: A religious system common in India and eastern Asia. Founded by and based upon the teachings of Siddhartha Gautama, Buddhism asserts that suffering is an inescapable part of life. Deliverance can only be achieved through the practice of charity, temperance, justice, honesty, and truth.

buffer state: A small country that lies between two larger, possibly hostile countries, considered to be a neutralizing force between them.

bureaucracy: A system of government that is characterized by division into bureaus of administration with their own divisional heads. Also refers to the inflexible procedures of such a system that often result in delay.

Byzantine Empire: An empire centered in the city of Byzantium, now Istanbul in present-day Turkey.

CACM *see* Central American Common Market.

canton: A territory or small division or state within a country.

capital punishment: The ultimate act of punishment for a crime, the death penalty.

capitalism: An economic system in which goods and services and the means to produce and sell them are privately owned, and prices and wages are determined by market forces.

Caribbean Community and Common Market (CARICOM): Founded in 1973 and with its headquarters in Georgetown, Guyana, CARICOM seeks the establishment of a common trade policy and increased cooperation in the Caribbean region. Includes 13 English-speaking Caribbean nations: Antigua and Barbuda, the Bahamas, Barbados, Belize, Dominica, Grenada, Guyana, Jamaica, Montserrat, Saint Kitts-Nevis, Saint Lucia, St. Vincent/Grenadines, and Trinidad and Tobago.

CARICOM *see* Caribbean Community and Common Market.

carnivore: Flesh-eating animal or plant.

carob: The common English name for a plant that is similar to and sometimes used as a substitute for chocolate.

cartel: An organization of independent producers formed to regulate the production, pricing, or marketing practices of its members in order to limit competition and maximize their market power.

cash crop: A crop that is grown to be sold rather than kept for private use.

cassation: The reversal or annulling of a final judgment by the supreme authority.

cassava: The name of several species of stout herbs, extensively cultivated for food.

caste system: One of the artificial divisions or social classes into which the Hindus are rigidly separated according to the religious law of Brahmanism. Membership in a caste is hereditary, and the privileges and disabilities of each caste are transmitted by inheritance.

Caucasian or Caucasoid: The white race of human beings, as determined by genealogy and physical features.

cease-fire: An official declaration of the end to the use of military force or active hostilities, even if only temporary.

censorship: The practice of withholding certain items of news that may cast a country in an unfavorable light or give away secrets to the enemy.

census: An official counting of the inhabitants of a state or country with details of sex and age, family, occupation, possessions, etc.

Central American Common Market (CACM): Established in 1962, a trade alliance of five Central American nations. Participating are Costa Rica, El Salvador, Guatemala, Honduras, and Nicaragua.

Central Powers: In World War I, Germany and Austria-Hungary, and their allies, Turkey and Bulgaria.

centrally planned economy: An economic system all aspects of which are supervised and regulated by the government.

centrist position: Refers to opinions held by members of a moderate political group; that is, views that are somewhere in the middle of popular thought between conservative and liberal.

cession: Withdrawal from or yielding to physical force.

chancellor: A high-ranking government official. In some countries it is the prime minister.

cholera: An acute infectious disease characterized by severe diarrhea, vomiting, and, often, death.

Christianity: The religion founded by Jesus Christ, based on the Bible as holy scripture.

Church of England: The national and established church in England. The Church of England claims continuity with the branch of the Catholic Church that existed in England before the Reformation. Under Henry VIII, the spiritual supremacy and jurisdiction of the pope were abolished, and the sovereign (king or queen) was declared head of the church.

circuit court: A court that convenes in two or more locations within its appointed district.

CIS *see* Commonwealth of Independent States

city-state: An independent state consisting of a city and its surrounding territory.

civil court: A court whose proceedings include determinations of rights of individual citizens, in contrast to criminal proceedings regarding individuals or the public.

civil jurisdiction: The authority to enforce the laws in civil matters brought before the court.

civil law: The law developed by a nation or state for the conduct of daily life of its own people.

civil rights: The privileges of all individuals to be treated as equals under the laws of their country; specifically, the rights given by certain amendments to the U.S. Constitution.

civil unrest: The feeling of uneasiness due to an unstable political climate, or actions taken as a result of it.

civil war: A war between groups of citizens of the same country who have different opinions or agendas. The Civil War of the United States was the conflict between the states of the North and South from 1861 to 1865.

climatic belt: A region or zone where a particular type of climate prevails.

Club du Sahel: The Club du Sahel is an informal coalition which seeks to reverse the effects of drought and the desertification in the eight Sahelian zone countries: Burkina Faso, Chad, Gambia, Mali, Mauritania, Niger, Senegal, and the Cape Verde Islands. Headquarters are in Ouagadougou, Burkina Faso.

CMEA *see* Council for Mutual Economic Assistance.

coalition government: A government combining differing factions within a country, usually temporary.

coastal belt: A coastal plain area of lowlands and somewhat higher ridges that run parallel to the coast.

coastal plain: A fairly level area of land along the coast of a land mass.

coca: A shrub native to South America, the leaves of which produce organic compounds that are used in the production of cocaine.

coke: The solid product of the carbonization of coal, bearing the same relation to coal that charcoal does to wood.

cold war: Refers to conflict over ideological differences that is carried on by words and diplomatic actions, not by military action. The term is usually used to refer to the tension that existed between the United States and the USSR from the 1950s until the breakup of the USSR in 1991.

collective bargaining: The negotiations between workers who are members of a union and their employer for the purpose of deciding work rules and policies regarding wages, hours, etc.

collective farm: A large farm formed from many small farms and supervised by the government; usually found in communist countries.

collective farming: The system of farming on a collective where all workers share in the income of the farm.

colloquial: Belonging to ordinary, everyday speech: often especially applied to common words and phrases which are not used in formal speech.

colonial period: The period of time when a country forms colonies in and extends control over a foreign area.

colonist: Any member of a colony or one who helps settle a new colony.

colony: A group of people who settle in a new area far from their original country, but still under the jurisdiction of that country. Also refers to the newly settled area itself.

COMECON *see* Council for Mutual Economic Assistance.

commerce: The trading of goods (buying and selling), especially on a large scale, between cities, states, and countries.

commercial catch: The amount of marketable fish, usually measured in tons, caught in a particular period of time.

commercial crop: Any marketable agricultural crop.

commission: A group of people designated to collectively do a job, including a government agency with certain law-making powers. Also, the power given to an individual or group to perform certain duties.

commodity: Any items, such as goods or services, that are bought or sold, or agricultural products that are traded or marketed.

common law: A legal system based on custom and decisions and opinions of the law courts. The basic system of law of England and the United States.

common market: An economic union among countries that is formed to remove trade barriers (tariffs) among those countries, increasing economic cooperation. The European Community is a notable example of a common market.

commonwealth: A commonwealth is a free association of sovereign independent states that has no charter, treaty, or constitution. The association promotes cooperation, consultation, and mutual assistance among members.

Commonwealth of Independent States: The CIS was established in December 1991 as an association of 11 republics of the former Soviet Union. The members include: Russia, Ukraine, Belarus (formerly Byelorussia), Moldova (formerly Moldavia), Armenia, Azerbaijan, Uzbekistan, Turkmenistan, Tajikistan, Kazakhstan, and Kyrgyzstan (formerly Kirghiziya). The Baltic states—Estonia, Latvia, and Lithuania—did not join. Georgia maintained observer status before joining the CIS in November 1993.

Commonwealth of Nations: Voluntary association of the United Kingdom and its present dependencies and associated states, as well as certain former dependencies and their dependent territories. The term was first used officially in 1926 and is embodied in the Statute of Westminster (1931). Within the Commonwealth, whose secretariat (established in 1965) is located in London, England, are numerous subgroups devoted to economic and technical cooperation.

commune: An organization of people living together in a community who share the ownership and use of property. Also refers to a small governmental district of a country, especially in Europe.

communism: A form of government whose system requires common ownership of property for the use of all citizens. All profits are to be equally distributed and prices on goods and services are usually set by the state. Also, communism refers directly to the official doctrine of the former U.S.S.R.

compulsory: Required by law or other regulation.

compulsory education: The mandatory requirement for children to attend school until they have reached a certain age or grade level.

conciliation: A process of bringing together opposing sides of a disagreement for the purpose of compromise. Or, a way of settling an international dispute in which the disagreement is submitted to an independent committee that will examine the facts and advise the participants of a possible solution.

concordat: An agreement, compact, or convention, especially between church and state.

confederation: An alliance or league formed for the purpose of promoting the common interests of its members.

Confucianism: The system of ethics and politics taught by the Chinese philosopher Confucius.

coniferous forest: A forest consisting mainly of pine, fir, and cypress trees.

conifers: Cone-bearing plants. Mostly evergreen trees and shrubs which produce cones.

conscription: To be required to join the military by law. Also known as the draft. Service personnel who join the military because of the legal requirement are called conscripts or draftees.

conservative party: A political group whose philosophy tends to be based on established traditions and not supportive of rapid change.

constituency: The registered voters in a governmental district, or a group of people that supports a position or a candidate.

constituent assembly: A group of people that has the power to determine the election of a political representative or create a constitution.

constitution: The written laws and basic rights of citizens of a country or members of an organized group.

constitutional monarchy: A system of government in which the hereditary sovereign (king or queen, usually) rules according to a written constitution.

constitutional republic: A system of government with an elected chief of state and elected representation, with a written constitution containing its governing principles. The United States is a constitutional republic.

consumer goods: Items that are bought to satisfy personal needs or wants of individuals.

continental climate: The climate of a part of the continent; the characteristics and peculiarities of the climate are a result of the land itself and its location.

continental shelf: A plain extending from the continental coast and varying in width that typically ends in a steep slope to the ocean floor.

copra: The dried meat of the coconut; it is frequently used as an ingredient of curry, and to produce coconut oil. Also written *cobra, coprah,* and *copperah.*

Coptic Christians: Members of the Coptic Church of Egypt, formerly of Ethiopia.

cordillera: A continuous ridge, range, or chain of mountains.

corvette: A small warship that is often used as an escort ship because it is easier to maneuver than larger ships like destroyers.

Council for Mutual Economic Assistance (CMEA): Also known as COMECON, the alliance of socialist economies was established on 25 January 1949 and abolished 1 January 1991. It included Afghanistan*, Albania, Angola*, Bulgaria, Cuba, Czechoslovakia, Ethiopia*, East Germany, Hungary, Laos*, Mongolia, Mozambique*, Nicaragua*, Poland, Romania, USSR, Vietnam, Yemen*, and Yugoslavia. Nations marked with an asterisk were observers only.

counterinsurgency operations: Organized military activity designed to stop rebellion against an established government.

county: A territorial division or administrative unit within a state or country.

coup d'ètat or coup: A sudden, violent overthrow of a government or its leader.

court of appeal: An appellate court, having the power of review after a case has been decided in a lower court.

court of first appeal: The next highest court to the court which has decided a case, to which that case may be presented for review.

court of last appeal: The highest court, in which a decision is not subject to review by any higher court. In the United States, it could be the Supreme Court of an individual state or the U.S. Supreme Court.

cricket (sport): A game played by two teams with a ball and bat, with two wickets (staked target) being defended by a batsman. Common in the United Kingdom and Commonwealth of Nations countries.

criminal law: The branch of law that deals primarily with crimes and their punishments.

crown colony: A colony established by a commonwealth over which the monarch has some control, as in colonies established by the United Kingdom's Commonwealth of Nations.

Crusades: Military expeditions by European Christian armies in the eleventh, twelfth, and thirteenth centuries to win land controlled by the Muslims in the middle east.

cultivable land: Land that can be prepared for the production of crops.

Cultural Revolution: An extreme reform movement in China from 1966 to 1976; its goal was to combat liberalization by restoring the ideas of Mao Zedong.

Cushitic language group: A group of Hamitic languages that are spoken in Ethiopia and other areas of eastern Africa.

customs union: An agreement between two or more countries to remove trade barriers with each other and to establish common tariff and nontariff policies with respect to imports from countries outside of the agreement.

cyclone: Any atmospheric movement, general or local, in which the wind blows spirally around and in towards a center. In the northern hemisphere, the cyclonic movement is usually counter-clockwise, and in the southern hemisphere, it is clockwise.

Cyrillic alphabet: An alphabet adopted by the Slavic people and invented by Cyril and Methodius in the ninth century as an alphabet that was easier for the copyist to write. The Russian alphabet is a slight modification of it.

decentralization: The redistribution of power in a government from one large central authority to a wider range of smaller local authorities.

deciduous species: Any species that sheds or casts off a part of itself after a definite period of time. More commonly used in reference to plants that shed their leaves on a yearly basis as opposed to those (evergreens) that retain them.

declaration of independence: A formal written document stating the intent of a group of persons to become fully self-governing.

deficit: The amount of money that is in excess between spending and income.

deficit spending: The process in which a government spends money on goods and services in excess of its income.

deforestation: The removal or clearing of a forest.

deity: A being with the attributes, nature, and essence of a god; a divinity.

delta: Triangular-shaped deposits of soil formed at the mouths of large rivers.

demarcate: To mark off from adjoining land or territory; set the limits or boundaries of.

demilitarized zone (DMZ): An area surrounded by a combat zone that has had military troops and weapons removed.

demobilize: To disband or discharge military troops.

democracy: A form of government in which the power lies in the hands of the people, who can govern directly, or can be governed indirectly by representatives elected by its citizens.

denationalize: To remove from government ownership or control.

deportation: To carry away or remove from one country to another, or to a distant place.

depression: A hollow; a surface that has sunken or fallen in.

deregulation: The act of reversing controls and restrictions on prices of goods, bank interest, and the like.

desalinization plant: A facility that produces freshwater by removing the salt from saltwater.

desegregation: The act of removing restrictions on people of a particular race that keep them socially, economically, and, sometimes, physically, separate from other groups.

desertification: The process of becoming a desert as a result of climatic changes, land mismanagement, or both.

détente: The official lessening of tension between countries in conflict.

devaluation: The official lowering of the value of a country's currency in relation to the value of gold or the currencies of other countries.

developed countries: Countries which have a high standard of living and a well-developed industrial base.

development assistance: Government programs intended to finance and promote the growth of new industries.

dialect: One of a number of regional or related modes of speech regarded as descending from a common origin.

dictatorship: A form of government in which all the power is retained by an absolute leader or tyrant. There are no rights granted to the people to elect their own representatives.

dike: An artificial riverbank built up to control the flow of water.

diplomatic relations: The relationship between countries as conducted by representatives of each government.

direct election: The process of selecting a representative to the government by balloting of the voting public, in contrast to selection by an elected representative of the people.

disarmament: The reduction or depletion of the number of weapons or the size of armed forces.

dissident: A person whose political opinions differ from the majority to the point of rejection.

dogma: A principle, maxim, or tenet held as being firmly established.

domain: The area of land governed by a particular ruler or government, sometimes referring to the ultimate control of that territory.

domestic spending: Money spent by a country's government on goods used, investments, running of the government, and exports and imports.

dominion: A self-governing nation that recognizes the British monarch as chief of state.

dormant volcano: A volcano that has not exhibited any signs of activity for an extended period of time.

dowry: The sum of the property or money that a bride brings to her groom at their marriage.

draft constitution: The preliminary written plans for the new constitution of a country forming a new government.

Druze: A member of a Muslim sect based in Syria, living chiefly in the mountain regions of Lebanon.

dual nationality: The status of an individual who can claim citizenship in two or more countries.

duchy: Any territory under the rule of a duke or duchess.

due process: In law, the application of the legal process to which every citizen has a right, which cannot be denied.

durable goods: Goods or products which are expected to last and perform for several years, such as cars and washing machines.

duty: A tax imposed on imports by the customs authority of a country. Duties are generally based on the value of the goods (*ad valorem* duties), some other factors such as weight or quantity (specific duties), or a combination of value and other factors (compound duties).

dyewoods: Any wood from which dye is extracted.

dynasty: A family line of sovereigns who rule in succession, and the time during which they reign.

earned income: The money paid to an individual in wages or salary.

Eastern Orthodox: The outgrowth of the original Eastern Church of the Eastern Roman Empire, consisting of eastern Europe, western Asia, and Egypt.

EC *see* European Community

ecclesiastical: Pertaining or relating to the church.

echidna: A spiny, toothless anteater of Australia, Tasmania, and New Guinea.

ecological balance: The condition of a healthy, well-functioning ecosystem, which includes all the plants and animals in a natural community together with their environment.

ecology: The branch of science that studies organisms in relationship to other organisms and to their environment.

economic depression: A prolonged period in which there is high unemployment, low production, falling prices, and general business failure.

economically active population: That portion of the people who are employed for wages and are consumers of goods and services.

ecotourism: Broad term that encompasses nature, adventure, and ethnic tourism; responsible or wilderness-sensitive tourism; soft-path or small-scale tourism; low-impact tourism; and sustainable tourism. Scientific, educational, or academic tourism (such as biotourism, archetourism, and geotourism) are also forms of ecotourism.

elected assembly: The persons that comprise a legislative body of a government who received their positions by direct election.

electoral system: A system of choosing government officials by votes cast by qualified citizens.

electoral vote: The votes of the members of the electoral college.

electorate: The people who are qualified to vote in an election.

emancipation: The freeing of persons from any kind of bondage or slavery.

embargo: A legal restriction on commercial ships to enter a country's ports, or any legal restriction of trade.

emigration: Moving from one country or region to another for the purpose of residence.

empire: A group of territories ruled by one sovereign or supreme ruler. Also, the period of time under that rule.

enclave: A territory belonging to one nation that is surrounded by that of another nation.

encroachment: The act of intruding, trespassing, or entering on the rights or possessions of another.

endangered species: A plant or animal species whose existence as a whole is threatened with extinction.

endemic: Anything that is peculiar to and characteristic of a locality or region.

Enlightenment: An intellectual movement of the late seventeenth and eighteenth centuries in which scientific thinking gained a strong foothold and old beliefs were challenged. The idea of absolute monarchy was questioned and people were gradually given more individual rights.

enteric disease: An intestinal disease.

epidemic: As applied to disease, any disease that is temporarily prevalent among people in one place at the same time.

Episcopal: Belonging to or vested in bishops or prelates; characteristic of or pertaining to a bishop or bishops.

ethnolinguistic group: A classification of related languages based on common ethnic origin.

EU *see* European Union

European Community: A regional organization created in 1958. Its purpose is to eliminate customs duties and other trade barriers in Europe. It promotes a common external tariff against other countries, a Common Agricultural Policy (CAP), and guarantees of free movement of labor and capital. The original six members were Belgium, France, West Germany, Italy, Luxembourg, and the Netherlands. Denmark, Ireland, and the United Kingdom became members in 1973; Greece joined in 1981;

Spain and Portugal in 1986. Other nations continue to join.

European Union: The EU is an umbrella reference to the European Community (EC) and to two European integration efforts introduced by the Maastricht Treaty: Common Foreign and Security Policy (including defense) and Justice and Home Affairs (principally cooperation between police and other authorities on crime, terrorism, and immigration issues).

exports: Goods sold to foreign buyers.

external migration: The movement of people from their native country to another country, as opposed to internal migration, which is the movement of people from one area of a country to another in the same country.

faction: People with a specific set of interests or goals who form a subgroup within a larger organization.

fallout: The precipitation of particles from the atmosphere, often the result of a ground disturbance by volcanic activity or a nuclear explosion.

family planning: The use of birth control to determine the number of children a married couple will have.

Fascism: A political philosophy that holds the good of the nation as more important than the needs of the individual. Fascism also stands for a dictatorial leader and strong oppression of opposition or dissent.

federal: Pertaining to a union of states whose governments are subordinate to a central government.

federation: A union of states or other groups under the authority of a central government.

fetishism: The practice of worshipping a material object that is believed to have mysterious powers residing in it, or is the representation of a deity to which worship may be paid and from which supernatural aid is expected.

feudal estate: The property owned by a lord in medieval Europe under the feudal system.

feudal society: In medieval times, an economic and social structure in which persons could hold land given to them by a lord (nobleman) in return for service to that lord.

final jurisdiction: The final authority in the decision of a legal matter. In the United States, the Supreme Court would have final jurisdiction.

Finno-Ugric language group: A subfamily of languages spoken in northeastern Europe, including Finnish, Hungarian, Estonian, and Lapp.

fiscal year: The twelve months between the settling of financial accounts, not necessarily corresponding to a calendar year beginning on January 1.

fjord: A deep indentation of the land forming a comparatively narrow arm of the sea with more or less steep slopes or cliffs on each side.

fly: The part of a flag opposite and parallel to the one nearest the flagpole.

fodder: Food for cattle, horses, and sheep, such as hay, straw, and other kinds of vegetables.

folk religion: A religion with origins and traditions among the common people of a nation or region that is relevant to their particular life-style.

foreign exchange: Foreign currency that allows foreign countries to conduct financial transactions or settle debts with one another.

foreign policy: The course of action that one government chooses to adopt in relation to a foreign country.

Former Soviet Union: The FSU is a collective reference to republics comprising the former Soviet Union. The term, which has been used as both including and excluding the Baltic republics (Estonia, Latvia, and Lithuania), includes the other 12 republics: Russia, Ukraine, Belarus, Moldova, Armenia, Azerbaijan, Uzbekistan, Turkmenistan, Tajikistan, Kazakhstan, Kyrgizstan, and Georgia.

fossil fuels: Any mineral or mineral substance formed by the decomposition of organic matter buried beneath the earth's surface and used as a fuel.

free enterprise: The system of economics in which private business may be conducted with minimum interference by the government.

free-market economy: An economic system that relies on the market, as opposed to government planners, to set the prices for wages and products.

frigate. A medium-sized warship.

fundamentalist: A person who holds religious beliefs based on the complete acceptance of the words of the Bible or other holy scripture as the truth. For instance, a fundamentalist would believe the story of creation exactly as it is told in the Bible and would reject the idea of evolution.

game reserve: An area of land reserved for wild animals that are hunted for sport or for food.

GDP *see* gross domestic product.

genocide: Planned and systematic killing of members of a particular ethnic, religious, or cultural group.

Germanic language group: A large branch of the Indo-European family of languages including German itself, the Scandinavian languages, Dutch, Yiddish, Modern English, Modern Scottish, Afrikaans, and others. The group also includes extinct languages such as Gothic, Old High German, Old Saxon, Old English, Middle English, and the like.

glasnost: President Mikhail Gorbachev's frank revelations in the 1980s about the state of the economy and politics in the Soviet Union; his policy of openness.

global greenhouse gas emissions: Gases released into the atmosphere that contribute to the greenhouse effect, a condition in which the earth's excess heat cannot escape.

global warming: Also called the greenhouse effect. The theorized gradual warming of the earth's climate as a result of the burning of fossil fuels, the use of man-made chemicals, deforestation, etc.

GMT *see* Greenwich Mean Time.

GNP *see* gross national product.

grand duchy: A territory ruled by a nobleman, called a grand duke, who ranks just below a king.

Greek Catholic: A person who is a member of an Orthodox Eastern Church.

Greek Orthodox: The official church of Greece, a self-governing branch of the Orthodox Eastern Church.

Greenwich (Mean) Time: Mean solar time of the meridian at Greenwich, England, used as the basis for standard time throughout most of the world. The world is divided into 24 time zones, and all are related to the prime, or Greenwich mean, zone.

gross domestic product: A measure of the market value of all goods and services produced within the boundaries of a nation, regardless of asset ownership. Unlike gross national product, GDP excludes receipts from that nation's business operations in foreign countries.

gross national product: A measure of the market value of goods and services produced by the labor and property of a nation. Includes receipts from that nation's business operation in foreign countries

groundwater: Water located below the earth's surface, the source from which wells and springs draw their water.

guano: The excrement of seabirds and bats found in various areas around the world. Gathered commercially and sold as a fertilizer.

guerrilla: A member of a small radical military organization that uses unconventional tactics to take their enemies by surprise.

gymnasium: A secondary school, primarily in Europe, that prepares students for university.

hardwoods: The name given to deciduous trees, such as cherry, oak, maple, and mahogany.

harem: In a Muslim household, refers to the women (wives, concubines, and servants in ancient times) who live there and also to the area of the home they live in.

harmattan: An intensely dry, dusty wind felt along the coast of Africa between Cape Verde and Cape Lopez. It prevails at intervals during the months of December, January, and February.

heavy industry: Industries that use heavy or large machinery to produce goods, such as automobile manufacturing.

hoist: The part of a flag nearest the flagpole.

Holocaust: The mass slaughter of European civilians, the vast majority Jews, by the Nazis during World War II.

Holy Roman Empire: A kingdom consisting of a loose union of German and Italian territories that existed from around the ninth century until 1806.

home rule: The governing of a territory by the citizens who inhabit it.

homeland: A region or area set aside to be a state for a people of a particular national, cultural, or racial origin.

homogeneous: Of the same kind or nature, often used in reference to a whole.

Horn of Africa: The Horn of Africa comprises Djibouti, Eritrea, Ethiopia, Somalia, and Sudan.

housing starts: The initiation of new housing construction.

human rights activist: A person who vigorously pursues the attainment of basic rights for all people.

human rights issues: Any matters involving people's basic rights which are in question or thought to be abused.

humanist: A person who centers on human needs and values, and stresses dignity of the individual.

humanitarian aid: Money or supplies given to a persecuted group or people of a country at war, or those devastated by a natural disaster, to provide for basic human needs.

hydrocarbon: A compound of hydrogen and carbon, often occurring in organic substances or derivatives of organic substances such as coal, petroleum, natural gas, etc.

hydrocarbon emissions: Organic compounds containing only carbon and hydrogen, often occurring in petroleum, natural gas, coal, and bitumens, and which contribute to the greenhouse effect.

hydroelectric potential: The potential amount of electricity that can be produced hydroelectrically. Usually used in reference to a given area and how many hydroelectric power plants that area can sustain.

hydroelectric power plant: A factory that produces electrical power through the application of water-power.

IBRD *see* World Bank.

illegal alien: Any foreign-born individual who has unlawfully entered another country.

immigration: The act or process of passing or entering into another country for the purpose of permanent residence.

imports: Goods purchased from foreign suppliers.

indigenous: Born or originating in a particular place or country; native to a particular region or area.

Indo-Aryan language group: The group that includes the languages of India; also called Indo-European language group.

Indo-European language family: The group that includes the languages of India and much of Europe and southwestern Asia.

industrialized nation: A nation whose economy is based on industry.

infanticide: The act of murdering a baby.

infidel: One who is without faith or belief; particularly, one who rejects the distinctive doctrines of a particular religion.

inflation: The general rise of prices, as measured by a consumer price index. Results in a fall in value of currency.

installed capacity: The maximum possible output of electric power at any given time.

insurgency: The state or condition in which one rises against lawful authority or established government; rebellion.

insurrectionist: One who participates in an unorganized revolt against an authority.

interim government: A temporary or provisional government.

interim president: One who is appointed to perform temporarily the duties of president during a transitional period in a government.

internal migration: Term used to describe the relocation of individuals from one region to another without leaving the confines of the country or of a specified area.

International Date Line: An arbitrary line at about the 180th meridian that designates where one day begins and another ends.

Islam: The religious system of Mohammed, practiced by Moslims and based on a belief in Allah as the supreme being and Mohammed as his prophet. The spelling variations, Muslim and Muhammad, are also used, primarily by Islamic people. Islam also refers to those nations in which it is the primary religion.

isthmus: A narrow strip of land bordered by water and connecting two larger bodies of land, such as two continents, a continent and a peninsula, or two parts of an island.

Judaism: The religious system of the Jews, based on the Old Testament as revealed to Moses and characterized by a belief in one God and adherence to the laws of scripture and rabbinic traditions.

Judeo-Christian: The dominant traditional religious makeup of the United States and other countries based on the worship of the Old and New Testaments of the Bible.

junta: A small military group in power of a country, especially after a coup.

khan: A sovereign, or ruler, in central Asia.

khanate: A kingdom ruled by a khan, or man of rank.

kwashiorkor: Severe malnutrition in infants and children caused by a diet high in carbohydrates and lacking in protein.

kwh: The abbreviation for kilowatt-hour.

labor force: The number of people in a population available for work, whether actually employed or not.

labor movement: A movement in the early to mid-1800s to organize workers in groups according to profession to give them certain rights as a group, including bargaining power for better wages, working conditions, and benefits.

land reforms: Steps taken to create a fair distribution of farmland, especially by governmental action.

landlocked country: A country that does not have direct access to the sea; it is completely surrounded by other countries.

least developed countries: A subgroup of the United Nations designation of "less developed countries;" these countries generally have no significant economic growth, low literacy rates, and per person gross national product of less than $500. Also known as undeveloped countries.

leeward: The direction identical to that of the wind. For example, a *leeward tide* is a tide that runs in the same direction that the wind blows.

leftist: A person with a liberal or radical political affiliation.

legislative branch: The branch of government which makes or enacts the laws.

leprosy: A disease that can effect the skin and/or the nerves and can cause ulcers of the skin, loss of feeling, or loss of fingers and toes.

less developed countries (LDC): Designated by the United Nations to include countries with low levels of output, living standards, and per person gross national product generally below $5,000.

literacy: The ability to read and write.

Maastricht Treaty: The Maastricht Treaty (named for the Dutch town in which the treaty was signed) is also known as the Treaty of European Union. The treaty creates a European Union by: (a) committing the member states of the European Economic Community to both European Monetary Union (EMU) and political union; (b) introducing a single currency (European Currency Unit, ECU); (c) establishing a European System of Central Banks (ESCB); (d) creating a European Central Bank (ECB); and (e) broadening EC integration by including both a common foreign and security policy (CFSP) and cooperation in justice and home affairs (CJHA). The treaty entered into force on November 1, 1993.

Maghreb states: The Maghreb states include the three nations of Algeria, Morocco, and Tunisia; sometimes includes Libya and Mauritania.

maize: Another name (Spanish or British) for corn or the color of ripe corn.

majority party: The party with the largest number of votes and the controlling political party in a government.

mangrove: A tree which abounds on tropical shores in both hemispheres. Characterized by its numerous roots which arch out from its trunk and descend from its branches, mangroves form thick, dense growths along the tidal muds, reaching lengths hundreds of miles long.

manioc: The cassava plant or its product. Manioc is a very important food-staple in tropical America.

maquis: Scrubby, thick underbrush found along the coast of the Mediterranean Sea.

marginal land: Land that could produce an economic profit, but is so poor that it is only used when better land is no longer available.

marine life: The life that exists in, or is formed by the sea.

maritime climate: The climate and weather conditions typical of areas bordering the sea.

maritime rights: The rights that protect navigation and shipping.

market access: Market access refers to the openness of a national market to foreign products. Market access reflects a government's willingness to permit imports to compete relatively unimpeded with similar domestically produced goods.

market economy: A form of society which runs by the law of supply and demand. Goods are produced by firms to be sold to consumers, who determine the demand for them. Price levels vary according to the demand for certain goods and how much of them is produced.

market price: The price a commodity will bring when sold on the open market. The price is determined by the amount of demand for the commodity by buyers.

Marshall Plan: Formally known as the European Recovery Program, a joint project between the United States and most Western European nations under which $12.5 billion in U.S. loans and grants was expended to aid European recovery after World War II.

Marxism *see* Marxist-Leninist principles.

Marxist: A follower of Karl Marx, a German socialist and revolutionary leader of the late 1800s, who contributed to Marxist-Leninist principles.

Marxist-Leninist principles: The doctrines of Karl Marx, built upon by Nikolai Lenin, on which communism was founded. They predicted the fall of capitalism, due to its own internal faults and the resulting oppression of workers.

massif: A central mountain-mass or the dominant part of a range of mountains.

matrilineal (descent): Descending from, or tracing descent through, the maternal, or mother's, family line.

Mayan language family: The languages of the Central American Indians, further divided into two subgroups: the Maya and the Huastek.

mean temperature: The air temperature unit measured by the National Weather Service by adding the maximum and minimum daily temperatures together and diving the sum by 2.

Mecca (Mekkah): A city in Saudi Arabia; a destination of pilgrims in the Islamic world.

Mediterranean climate: A wet-winter, dry-summer climate with a moderate annual temperature range.

mestizo: The offspring of a person of mixed blood; especially, a person of mixed Spanish and American Indian parentage.

migratory birds: Those birds whose instincts prompt them to move from one place to another at the regularly recurring changes of season.

migratory workers: Usually agricultural workers who move from place to place for employment depending on the growing and harvesting seasons of various crops.

military coup: A sudden, violent overthrow of a government by military forces.

military junta: The small military group in power in a country, especially after a coup.

military regime: Government conducted by a military force.

military takeover: The seizure of control of a government by the military forces.

militia: The group of citizens of a country who are either serving in the reserve military forces or are eligible to be called up in time of emergency.

millet: A cereal grass whose small grain is used for food in Europe and Asia.

minority party: The political group that comprises the smaller part of the large overall group it belongs to; the party that is not in control.

missionary: A person sent by authority of a church or religious organization to spread his religious faith in a community where his church has no self-supporting organization.

monarchy: Government by a sovereign, such as a king or queen.

money economy: A system or stage of economic development in which money replaces barter in the exchange of goods and services.

Mongol: One of an Asiatic race chiefly resident in Mongolia, a region north of China proper and south of Siberia.

Mongoloid: Having physical characteristics like those of the typical Mongols (Chinese, Japanese, Turks, Eskimos, etc.).

Moors: One of the Arab tribes that conquered Spain in the eighth century.

Moslem: A frequently used variation of the spelling of Muslim; a follower of Muhammad in the religion of Islam.

mosque: An Islam place of worship and the organization with which it is connected.

mouflon: A type of wild sheep characterized by curling horns.

Muhammad (or Muhammed or Mahomet): An Arabian prophet, known as the "Prophet of Allah" who founded the religion of Islam in 622, and wrote *The Koran,* the scripture of Islam. Also commonly spelled Mohammed.

mujahideen (mujahedin or mujahedeen): Rebel fighters in Islamic countries, especially those supporting the cause of Islam.

mulatto: One who is the offspring of parents one of whom is white and the other is black.

municipality: A district such as a city or town having its own incorporated government.

Muslim: A follower of the prophet Muhammad, the founder of the religion of Islam.

Muslim New Year: A Muslim holiday. Although in some countries 1 Muharram, which is the first month of the Islamic year, is observed as a holiday, in other places the new year is observed on Sha'ban, the eighth month of the year. This practice apparently stems from pagan Arab times. Shab-i-Bharat, a national holiday in Bangladesh on this day, is held by many to be the occasion when God ordains all actions in the coming year.

NAFTA (North American Free Trade Agreement): NAFTA, which entered into force in January 1994, is a free trade agreement between Canada, the United States, and Mexico. The agreement progressively eliminates almost all U.S.-Mexico tariffs over a 10–15 year period.

nationalism: National spirit or aspirations; desire for national unity, independence, or prosperity.

nationalization: To transfer the control or ownership of land or industries to the nation from private owners.

native tongue: One's natural language. The language that is indigenous to an area.

NATO *see* North Atlantic Treaty Organization

natural gas: A combustible gas formed naturally in the earth and generally obtained by boring a well. The chemical makeup of natural gas is principally methane, hydrogen, ethylene compounds, and nitrogen.

natural harbor: A protected portion of a sea or lake along the shore resulting from the natural formations of the land.

naturalize: To confer the rights and privileges of a native-born subject or citizen upon someone who lives in the country by choice.

nature preserve: An area where one or more species of plant and/or animal are protected from harm, injury, or destruction.

neutrality: The policy of not taking sides with any countries during a war or dispute among them.

Newly Independent States: The NIS is a collective reference to 12 republics of the former Soviet Union: Russia, Ukraine, Belarus (formerly Byelorussia), Moldova (formerly Moldavia), Armenia, Azerbaijan, Uzbekistan, Turkmenistan, Tajikistan, Kazakhstan, and Kirgizstan (formerly Kirghiziya), and Georgia. Following dissolution of the Soviet Union, the distinction between the NIS and the Commonwealth of Independent States (CIS) was that Georgia was not a member of the CIS. That distinction dissolved when Georgia joined the CIS in November 1993.

news censorship *see* censorship

Nonaligned Movement: The NAM is an alliance of third world states that aims to promote the political and economic interests of developing countries. NAM interests have included ending colonialism/ neo-colonialism, supporting the integrity of independent countries, and seeking a new international economic order.

Nordic Council: The Nordic Council, established in 1952, is directed toward supporting cooperation among Nordic countries. Members include Denmark, Finland, Iceland, Norway, and Sweden. Headquarters are in Stockholm, Sweden.

North Atlantic Treaty Organization (NATO): A mutual defense organization. Members include Belgium, Canada, Denmark, France (which has only partial membership), Greece, Iceland, Italy, Luxembourg, Netherlands, Norway, Portugal, Spain, Turkey, United Kingdom, United States, and Germany.

nuclear power plant: A factory that produces electrical power through the application of the nuclear reaction known as nuclear fission.

nuclear reactor: A device used to control the rate of nuclear fission in uranium. Used in commercial applications, nuclear reactors can maintain temperatures high enough to generate sufficient quantities of steam which can then be used to produce electricity.

OAPEC (Organization of Arab Petroleum Exporting countries): OAPEC was created in 1968; members include: Algeria, Bahrain, Egypt, Iraq, Kuwait, Libya, Qatar, Saudi Arabia, Syria, and the United Arab Emirates. Headquarters are in Cairo, Egypt.

OAS (Organization of American States): The OAS (Spanish: Organizaciûn de los Estados Americanos,

OEA), or the Pan American Union, is a regional organization which promotes Latin American economic and social development. Members include the United States, Mexico, and most Central American, South American, and Caribbean nations.

oasis: Originally, a fertile spot in the Libyan desert where there is a natural spring or well and vegetation; now refers to any fertile tract in the midst of a wasteland.

occupied territory: A territory that has an enemy's military forces present.

official language: The language in which the business of a country and its government is conducted.

oligarchy: A form of government in which a few people possess the power to rule as opposed to a monarchy which is ruled by one.

OPEC *see* OAPEC

open economy: An economy that imports and exports goods.

open market: Open market operations are the actions of the central bank to influence or control the money supply by buying or selling government bonds.

opposition party: A minority political party that is opposed to the party in power.

Organization of Arab Petroleum Exporting Countries *see* OAPEC

organized labor: The body of workers who belong to labor unions.

Ottoman Empire: A Turkish empire founded by Osman I in about 1603, that variously controlled large areas of land around the Mediterranean, Black, and Caspian Seas until it was dissolved in 1918.

overfishing: To deplete the quantity of fish in an area by removing more fish than can be naturally replaced.

overgrazing: Allowing animals to graze in an area to the point that the ground vegetation is damaged or destroyed.

overseas dependencies: A distant and physically separate territory that belongs to another country and is subject to its laws and government.

Pacific Rim: The Pacific Rim, referring to countries and economies bordering the Pacific Ocean.

pact: An international agreement.

Paleolithic: The early period of the Stone Age, when rough, chipped stone implements were used.

panhandle: A long narrow strip of land projecting like the handle of a frying pan.

papyrus: The paper-reed or -rush which grows on marshy river banks in the southeastern area of the Mediterranean, but more notably in the Nile valley.

paramilitary group: A supplementary organization to the military.

parasitic diseases: A group of diseases caused by parasitic organisms which feed off the host organism.

parliamentary republic: A system of government in which a president and prime minister, plus other ministers of departments, constitute the executive branch of the government and the parliament constitutes the legislative branch.

parliamentary rule: Government by a legislative body similar to that of Great Britain, which is composed of two houses—one elected and one hereditary.

parochial: Refers to matters of a church parish or something within narrow limits.

partisan politics: Rigid, unquestioning following of a specific party's or leader's goals.

patriarchal system: A social system in which the head of the family or tribe is the father or oldest male. Kinship is determined and traced through the male members of the tribe.

patrilineal (descent): Descending from, or tracing descent through, the paternal or father's line.

pellagra: A disease marked by skin, intestinal, and central nervous system disorders, caused by a diet deficient in niacin, one of the B vitamins.

per capita: Literally, per person; for each person counted.

perestroika: The reorganization of the political and economic structures of the Soviet Union by president Mikhail Gorbachev.

periodical: A publication whose issues appear at regular intervals, such as weekly, monthly, or yearly.

petrochemical: A chemical derived from petroleum or from natural gas.

pharmaceutical plants: Any plant that is used in the preparation of medicinal drugs.

plantain: The name of a common weed that has often been used for medicinal purposes, as a folk remedy and in modern medicine. *Plaintain* is also the name of a tropical plant producing a type of banana.

polar climate: Also called tundra climate. A humid, severely cold climate controlled by arctic air masses, with no warm or summer season.

political climate: The prevailing political attitude of a particular time or place.

political refugee: A person forced to flee his or her native country for political reasons.

potable water: Water that is safe for drinking.

pound sterling: The monetary unit of Great Britain, otherwise known as the pound.

prefect: An administrative official; in France, the head of a particular department.

prefecture: The territory over which a prefect has authority.

prime meridian: Zero degrees in longitude that runs through Greenwich, England, site of the Royal Observatory. All other longitudes are measured from this point.

prime minister: The premier or chief administrative official in certain countries.

private sector: The division of an economy in which production of goods and services is privately owned.

privatization: To change from public to private control or ownership.

protectorate: A state or territory controlled by a stronger state, or the relationship of the stronger country toward the lesser one it protects.

Protestant: A member or an adherent of one of those Christian bodies which descended from the Reformation of the sixteenth century. Originally applied to those who opposed or protested the Roman Catholic Church.

Protestant Reformation: In 1529, a Christian religious movement begun in Germany to deny the universal authority of the pope, and to establish the Bible as the only source of truth. (*Also see* Protestant)

proved reserves: The quantity of a recoverable mineral resource (such as oil or natural gas) that is still in the ground.

province: An administrative territory of a country.

provisional government: A temporary government set up during time of unrest or transition in a country.

pulses: Beans, peas, or lentils.

purge: The act of ridding a society of "undesirable" or unloyal persons by banishment or murder.

Rastafarian: A member of a Jamaican cult begun in 1930 as a semi-religious, semi-political movement.

rate of literacy: The percentage of people in a society who can read and write.

recession. A period of reduced economic activity in a country or region.

referendum: The practice of submitting legislation directly to the people for a popular vote.

reforestation: Systematically replacing forest trees lost due to fire or logging.

Reformation *see* Protestant Reformation.

refugee: One who flees to a refuge or shelter or place of safety. One who in times of persecution or political commotion flees to a foreign country for safety.

revolution: A complete change in a government or society, such as in an overthrow of the government by the people.

right-wing party: The more conservative political party.

Roman alphabet: The alphabet of the ancient Romans from which the alphabets of most modern western European languages, including English, are derived.

Roman Catholic Church: The designation of the church of which the pope or Bishop of Rome is the head, and that holds him as the successor of St. Peter and heir of his spiritual authority, privileges, and gifts.

romance language: The group of languages derived from Latin: French, Spanish, Italian, Portuguese, and other related languages.

roundwood: Timber used as poles or in similar ways without being sawn or shaped.

runoff election: A deciding election put to the voters in case of a tie between candidates.

Russian Orthodox: The arm of the Orthodox Eastern Church that was the official church of Russia under the czars.

sack: To strip of valuables, especially after capture.

Sahelian zone: Eight countries make up this dry desert zone in Africa: Burkina Faso, Chad, Gambia, Mali, Mauritania, Niger, Senegal, and the Cape Verde Islands. *Also see* Club du Sahel.

salinization: An accumulation of soluble salts in soil. This condition is common in desert climates, where water evaporates quickly in poorly drained soil due to high temperatures.

Samaritans: A native or an inhabitant of Samaria; specifically, one of a race settled in the cities of Samaria by the king of Assyria after the removal of the Israelites from the country.

savanna: A treeless or near treeless plain of a tropical or subtropical region dominated by drought-resistant grasses.

schistosomiasis: A tropical disease that is chronic and characterized by disorders of the liver, urinary bladder, lungs, or central nervous system.

secession: The act of withdrawal, such as a state withdrawing from the Union in the Civil War in the United States.

sect: A religious denomination or group, often a dissenting one with extreme views.

segregation: The enforced separation of a racial or religious group from other groups, compelling them to live and go to school separately from the rest of society.

seismic activity: Relating to or connected with an earthquake or earthquakes in general.

self-sufficient: Able to function alone without help.

separation of power: The division of power in the government among the executive, legislative, and judicial branches and the checks and balances employed to keep them separate and independent of each other.

separatism: The policy of dissenters withdrawing from a larger political or religious group.

serfdom: In the feudal system of the Middle Ages, the condition of being attached to the land owned by a lord and being transferable to a new owner.

Seventh-day Adventist: One who believes in the second coming of Christ to establish a personal reign upon the earth.

shamanism: A religion of some Asians and Amerindians in which shamans, who are priests or medicine men, are believed to influence good and evil spirits.

shantytown: An urban settlement of people in flimsy, inadequate houses.

Shia Muslims: Members of one of two great sects of Islam. Shia Muslims believe that Ali and the Imams are the rightful successors of Muhammad (also commonly spelled Mohammed). They also believe that the last recognized Imam will return as a messiah. Also known as Shiites. (*Also see* Sunni Muslims.)

Shiites *see* Shia Muslims.

Shintoism: The system of nature- and hero-worship which forms the indigenous religion of Japan.

shoal: A place where the water of a stream, lake, or sea is of little depth. Especially, a sand-bank which shows at low water.

sierra: A chain of hills or mountains.

Sikh: A member of a politico-religious community of India, founded as a sect around 1500 and based on the principles of monotheism (belief in one god) and human brotherhood.

Sino-Tibetan language family: The family of languages spoken in eastern Asia, including China, Thailand, Tibet, and Burma.

slash-and-burn agriculture: A hasty and sometimes temporary way of clearing land to make it available for agriculture by cutting down trees and burning them.

slave trade: The transportation of black Africans beginning in the 1700s to other countries to be sold as slaves—people owned as property and compelled to work for their owners at no pay.

Slavic languages: A major subgroup of the Indo-European language family. It is further subdivided into West Slavic (including Polish, Czech, Slovak and Serbian), South Slavic (including Bulgarian, Serbo-Croatian, Slovene, and Old Church Slavonic), and East Slavic (including Russian Ukrainian and Byelorussian).

social insurance: A government plan to protect low-income people, such as health and accident insurance, pension plans, etc.

social security: A form of social insurance, including life, disability, and old-age pension for workers. It is paid for by employers, employees, and the government.

socialism: An economic system in which ownership of land and other property is distributed among the community as a whole, and every member of the community shares in the work and products of the work.

socialist: A person who advocates socialism.

softwoods: The coniferous trees, whose wood density as a whole is relatively softer than the wood of those trees referred to as hardwoods.

sorghum (also known as Syrian Grass): Plant grown in various parts of the world for its valuable uses, such as for grain, syrup, or fodder.

Southeast Asia: The region in Asia that consists of the Malay Archipelago, the Malay Peninsula, and Indochina.

staple crop: A crop that is the chief commodity or product of a place, and which has widespread and constant use or value.

state: The politically organized body of people living under one government or one of the territorial units that make up a federal government, such as in the United States.

steppe: A level tract of land more or less devoid of trees, in certain parts of European and Asiatic Russia.

student demonstration: A public gathering of students to express strong feelings about a certain situation, usually taking place near the location of the people in power to change the situation.

subarctic climate: A high latitude climate of two types: *continental subarctic*, which has very cold winters, short, cool summers, light precipitation and moist air; and *marine subarctic*, a coastal and island climate with polar air masses causing large precipitation and extreme cold.

subcontinent: A land mass of great size, but smaller than any of the continents; a large subdivision of a continent.

subsistence economy: The part of a national economy in which money plays little or no role, trade is by barter, and living standards are minimal.

subsistence farming: Farming that provides the minimum food goods necessary for the continuation of the farm family.

subtropical climate: A middle latitude climate dominated by humid, warm temperatures and heavy rainfall in summer, with cool winters and frequent cyclonic storms.

Sudanic language group: A related group of languages spoken in various areas of northern Africa, including Yoruba, Mandingo, and Tshi.

suffrage: The right to vote.

Sufi: A Muslim mystic who believes that God alone exists, there can be no real difference between good and evil, that the soul exists within the body as in a cage, so death should be the chief object of desire, and sufism is the only true philosophy.

sultan: A king of a Muslim state.

Sunni Muslims: Members of one of two major sects of the religion of Islam. Sunni Muslims adhere to strict orthodox traditions, and believe that the four caliphs are the rightful successors to Mohammed, founder of Islam. (Mohammed is commonly spelled Muhammad, especially by Islamic people.) (*Also see* Shia Muslims.)

Taoism: The doctrine of Lao-Tzu, an ancient Chinese philosopher (about 500 B.C.) as laid down by him in the *Tao-te-ching.*

tariff: A tax assessed by a government on goods as they enter (or leave) a country. May be imposed to protect domestic industries from imported goods and/or to generate revenue.

temperate zone: The parts of the earth lying between the tropics and the polar circles. The *northern temperate zone* is the area between the tropic of Cancer and the Arctic Circle. The *southern temperate zone* is the area between the tropic of Capricorn and the Antarctic Circle.

terracing: A form of agriculture that involves cultivating crops in raised banks of earth.

terrorism: Systematic acts of violence designed to frighten or intimidate.

thermal power plant: A facility that produces electric energy from heat energy released by combustion of fuel or nuclear reactions.

Third World: A term used to describe less developed countries; as of the mid-1990s, it is being replaced by the United Nations designation Less Developed Countries, or LDC.

topography: The physical or natural features of the land.

torrid zone: The part of the earth's surface that lies between the tropics, so named for the character of its climate.

totalitarian party: The single political party in complete authoritarian control of a government or state.

trachoma: A contagious bacterial disease that affects the eye.

trade unionism: Labor union activity for workers who practice a specific trade, such as carpentry.

treaty: A negotiated agreement between two governments.

tribal system: A social community in which people are organized into groups or clans descended from common ancestors and sharing customs and languages.

tropical monsoon climate: One of the tropical rainy climates; it is sufficiently warm and rainy to produce tropical rainforest vegetation, but also has a winter dry season.

tsetse fly: Any of the several African insects which can transmit a variety of parasitic organisms through its bite. Some of these organisms can prove fatal to both human and animal victims.

tundra: A nearly level treeless area whose climate and vegetation are characteristically arctic due to its northern position; the subsoil is permanently frozen.

undeveloped countries *see* least developed countries.

unemployment rate: The overall unemployment rate is the percentage of the work force (both employed and unemployed) who claim to be unemployed.

UNICEF: An international fund set-up for children's emergency relief: United Nations Children's Fund (formerly United Nations International Children's Emergency Fund).

universal adult suffrage: The policy of giving every adult in a nation the right to vote.

untouchables: In India, members of the lowest caste in the caste system, a hereditary social class system. They were considered unworthy to touch members of higher castes.

urban guerrilla: A rebel fighter operating in an urban area.

urbanization: The process of changing from country to city.

veldt: In South Africa, an unforested or thinly forested tract of land or region, a grassland.

Warsaw Pact: Agreement made 14 May 1955 (and dissolved 1 July 1991) to promote mutual defense between Albania, Bulgaria, Czechoslovakia, East Germany, Hungary, Poland, Romania, and the USSR.

Western nations: Blanket term used to describe mostly democratic, capitalist countries, including the United States, Canada, and western European countries.

wildlife sanctuary: An area of land set aside for the protection and preservation of animals and plants.

workers' compensation: A series of regular payments by an employer to a person injured on the job.

World Bank: The World Bank is a group of international institutions which provides financial and technical assistance to developing countries.

world oil crisis: The severe shortage of oil in the 1970s precipitated by the Arab oil embargo.

yaws: A tropical disease caused by a bacteria which produces raspberry-like sores on the skin.

yellow fever: A tropical viral disease caused by the bite of an infected mosquito, characterized by jaundice.

Zoroastrianism: The system of religious doctrine taught by Zoroaster and his followers in the Avesta; the religion prevalent in Persia until its overthrow by the Muslims in the seventh century.

INDEX

This index contains terms from all nine volumes of this encyclopedia. The number of the volume in enclosed in brackets. The volume number is followed by the page number. For example, the reference [8]73 means that the indexed term can be found in volume 8 on page 73.

A

Aare River [8]83
Abadan, Iran [4]93
Abdali, Ahmad Shah [1]12
Abidjan, Côte d'Ivoire [2]211
Aboriginals, Australia [1]94
Aborigines see Orang Asli [5]126
Abu Dhabi, United Arab Emirates [9]23
Abuja, Nigeria [6]87
Abyssina see Ethiopia
Acajutla [3]71
Acapulco, Mexico [5]208
Accra, Ghana [3]205
Achaemenid Empire [4]94
Acropolis [3]230
Adams, Sir Grantley [1]164
Addis Ababa, Ethiopia [3]17, [3]105
Addis Ababa University [3]115
Adenauer, Konrad [3]196
Aegean Sea [3]219, [8]205
Afars [3]16
Afghanistan [1]1
Agora [3]230
Agra, India [4]53
Aguán River [4]13
Agusan River [6]200
Ahidjo, Ahmadou [2]60
Akaev, Askar [4]276, [4]278
Akaishi Mountains [4]173
Akan, Japan [3]206
Akayev, Askar A. [4]281
Aksumite Empire [3]108
Åland Islands [3]125, [3]127
Alaska [9]58
Albania [1]13
al-Bashir, Omar Hassam [8]38
Aleichem, Sholom [9]22

Alexander II [7]27
Alexander the Great [1]4, [1]139, [3]58, [3]231, [4]94, [4]109, [5]93, [6]131, [8]100, [9]109
Algeria [1]23
Al-Kuwayt see Kuwait [4]263
Alps [1]105, [3]139, [3]140, [3]189, [4]147, [8]83
al-Qadhafi, Mu'ammar [5]58
al-Qadhafi, Mu'ammar Muhammad [5]64
Al-Qahira see Cairo [3]53
al-Sadat, Anwar [3]60, [4]138
Altai Mountains [4]207
Amazon Basin [3]43
Amazon rainforest [6]183
Amazon River [1]249, [6]183
Amber Palace, Jaipur [4]69
Amerindian [3]71
Amerindians [2]202, [3]44, [3]242, [3]273
Amhara-Tigray [3]107
Amin, Idi [5]58
Amsterdam, the Netherlands [6]29
Amundsen, Roald [6]118
Anatolia see Turkey [8]208
Andaman Island [4]49
Andes Mountains [1]65, [2]111, [2]149, [3]41, [6]183, [9]131
Andorra [1]39
Andorra la Vella, Andorra [1]39
Andrés, Domincan Republic [3]34
Angel Falls [9]131, [9]146
Angola [1]47
Ankara, Turkey [8]205
Ankobra River [3]205
Annam Cordillera [9]147
Antall, Jozsef [4]30
Antananarivo, Madagascar [5]101

·

Uganda

Ukraine

United Arab Emirates

Uzbekistan

Vanuatu

The Vatican

Yemen Republic

Yugoslavia

Zambia